Wimbledon

A Personal History

Also by Sue Barker

Calling the Shots

Wimbledon

A Personal History

The players, the place, the magic

Sue Barker

with Sarah Edworthy

EBURY
SPOTLIGHT

2

Ebury Spotlight, an imprint of Ebury Publishing
20 Vauxhall Bridge Road
London SW1V 2SA

Ebury Spotlight is part of the Penguin Random House group of companies
whose addresses can be found at global.penguinrandomhouse.com

Copyright © The Final Set LLP 2024

Sue Barker has asserted her right to be identified as the author of this Work
in accordance with the Copyright, Designs and Patents Act 1988

First published by Ebury Spotlight in 2024

www.penguin.co.uk

A CIP catalogue record for this book is available from the British Library

ISBN 9781529927399

Printed and bound in Great Britain by Clays Ltd, Elcograf S.p.A.

The authorised representative in the EEA is Penguin Random House
Ireland, Morrison Chambers, 32 Nassau Street, Dublin D02 YH68.

Penguin Random House is committed to a sustainable future for
our business, our readers and our planet. This book is made
from Forest Stewardship Council® certified paper.

CONTENTS

PREFACE

Wimbledon has been the cornerstone of my summer for more than 50 years, but in the months before the 2023 Championships, the build-up left me feeling weirdly out of my comfort zone. My credentials as a broadcaster and as the host of the BBC's live Wimbledon coverage were rooted in the fact that I had been a former top player, and I'm immensely proud of being one of very few former athletes who have gone on to present multisports programmes on a high-profile channel. Now that I had retired, I was also a former TV presenter. Where did that leave me? A player-turned-broadcaster-turned ... what? Well, a happy and carefree fan, for starters. Suddenly I was watching the traditional Wimbledon warm-up tournaments for fun, without having to make copious notes that might be useful to refer to during the fortnight of Grand Slam action down at the All England Club. I went to Queen's Club and just sat and watched tennis – entire matches from the warm-up to the final handshake at the net – without talkback in my ear. Bliss!

But what about Wimbledon? The Sunday before the first round of play has always been my favourite day. During my 30-year stint in the BBC host's chair, I made sure I had a bit of 'me time' before the glorious craziness of the tournament started to unfold each year. I'd go up to the turfed rooftop garden on the top of the Broadcast Centre and look out over the pristine courts and the colourful array of blooms that frame the show courts and walkways. The perfect stage awaiting sporting drama in a timeless landscape. It always moved me as I tapped back into my own childhood dreams of glory, and began to consider what stories would evolve that year and wonder which new stars might emerge.

Had I tried to do that last year, I would have been robustly refused entry. The first shock of my Wimbledon retirement was learning that I would be prevented from entering the grounds if I turned up to make my annual pilgrimage to the roof. No one, not even All England Club members, is allowed in on the Sunday before the tournament starts; only people with accreditation to work at the tournament are permitted. No longer eligible for an Access All Areas pass, I wouldn't have got past the security on the gates! That was when I started to worry about how these two weeks would be for me. Would I feel like an outsider in a place I had come to regard as home? Would I regret my decision to retire and find this experience too painful? Would I miss 'the job' that I had loved for 30 years? I had hung up my racket in 1984, and now I had left behind a wonderful team and the studio with my personalised coat hook – H.R.W.H., Her Royal Wimbledon Highness (a humorous practicality organised by my indispensable floor manager Liz Thorburn). Where did I belong?

Like a brave new world, the expansive grounds of the All England Club stretched before me ready to be explored. The

Wimbledon I had known for the last three decades was basically a rabbit run from my studio to the broadcast positions on Centre and No.1 Court and back again. And I was always running. My producer, Sally Richardson, used to call it the 'Sue Barker dash', when we – me, my floor manager, camera and sound – had 90 seconds between introducing action on No.1 Court and then having to be back in the studio to manage a break as a match came to an end on Centre. I would whip off my heels, slip into some flats and sprint back to the Broadcast Centre. The team in the studio would look out for 'the Sue-nami' – our team were all blonde and easy to spot as we charged back together as a huddle.

Now, I was braced to discover what Wimbledon could be like to explore at large, and at leisure, without professional commitments or working to an intense schedule. And it was an oddly scary prospect. I knew I would miss the banter on and off air, the adrenaline rush of live television, the emergency doses of chocolate, but I wouldn't miss the long, long hours and the constant searching through my notes. I had old friends from my playing days to meet up with, an invitation to the Royal Box, thank you very much, and that perennially magical fortnight of sporting drama to watch 'live'.

And I needn't have worried. Over the next 14 days I saw Wimbledon in a new light – the people, the place, the magic. I felt the warm embrace of the extended Wimbledon family. Those two weeks in 2023 delivered yet another memorable experience for me. They were different, very different, but I loved every second.

INTRODUCTION
Wimbledon 2023

A Magical Experience

Wimbledon is a star-making factory, and that's the draw for players and tennis fans alike. That familiar geometry of immaculate emerald-green grass courts is a production line that, each year, serves up champions the tennis world remembers and treasures forever. No player becomes a superstar of the sport without enjoying success on the historic stage of Centre Court, with the time-old traditions that go with it – the presentation of trophies beneath the Royal Box, the new champion's name inscribed in gilt letters on the honours board within minutes of victory, the automatic membership to the most prestigious tennis club in the world. That annually replayed champion-crowning scenario has whet my appetite each year, both as a player (oh, how I dreamt I was thrashing Billie Jean King with every ball I struck against the garage wall at home) and as a broadcaster, primed to tell the story of each year's Championships as they unfolded to an audience of millions. Whose long-held dreams will become a fairy tale shared around the world? Who is going to break records? Is a stunning breakthrough on the cards or an against-all-odds comeback? And with that comes the drama of the near-wins, the gut-wrenching disappointments, the 'you cannot be serious' outbursts: all the talking points that add up to another chapter in the epic Wimbledon story.

For five decades, The Fortnight – capital letters compulsory – has been the focal point of my year. Like a back-to-school feeling a lot of people recognise at the end of the summer, I have always had butterflies in my stomach for those magical back-to-Wimbledon weeks in late June and early July. As a schoolgirl competitor, a Grand Slam champion and world No.3, and as a broadcaster hosting the BBC coverage, I thought I had seen pretty much every way a victory could be earned and become an enduring memory. Joining the women's tour in 1973, my career coincided with the blossoming of Billie Jean's mission to empower female players to earn a living from competing around the world. It also dovetailed with the consolidation of the men's professional tour, following the advent of the Open Era in 1967. Whether hearing the gossip in the dressing rooms (where Mrs Twynam, whose husband was the groundsman, ran baths for the ladies) or leading the output from the host broadcaster's television studio, I have been lucky enough to witness so many of the standout moments that people chat excitedly about today when they recall their first pilgrimage to the All England Club in south London or their earliest recollections of watching it, enthralled, on the TV. Björn Borg's consecutive run of five victories in the late 1970s and the 'Borg mania' that caused court invasions of screaming fans, the era-defining rivalry between polar opposites Chrissie Evert and Martina Navratilova, John McEnroe's superbrat years, the eccentric wild-card entrant Goran Ivanišević beating Pat Rafter in 2001 on People's Monday, Venus Williams's first win – itself ushering in an era of sibling dominance in the women's game – and of course the sublime Roger Federer and his rivalry with Andy Murray, Rafa Nadal and Novak Djokovic in what became a 20-year domination of the roll of honour … More of all this later.

But the last day of Wimbledon 2023, on Sunday, 16 July, brought a different kind of magic. It is a day I can only call an utterly captivating experience. I suspect everyone will remember where they were when they watched Carlos Alcaraz topple the great, immovable champion Novak Djokovic 1–6, 7–6, 6–1, 3–6, 6–4 to win his first Wimbledon title on that final day. Watching the young Spaniard learn, literally point by point, how to deal with the best returner of all time, on grass, in his first final on Centre Court, was utterly spellbinding. Alcaraz described himself as 'a boy of 20 years old' that day, but the way he never gave up, never dropped his head during four hours and 43 minutes of battle, and then served out the match with a nerveless game that featured a brazen drop shot and a lunging volley winner, signalled a mature talent who had just caused a shift in the tennis hierarchy. I was among those lucky enough to be sitting courtside and feel the significance of the moment reverberating around the stands.

To add to the thrill, this was the first ever Wimbledon men's final I watched at leisure as a spectator. And as it happened, the stars aligned for me to watch it from a seat next to the actor Sir Ian McKellen, the revered Gandalf from the *Lord of the Rings* trilogy. His excitement was contagious, adding a very theatrical dimension to the proceedings. I had actually started off the match sitting in the Members' seats alongside friends. When Alcaraz lost the first set so quickly, we were thinking, *Crikey, this looks like it's going to be over in an hour and a half,* because, over the years, we have certainly seen some first-time finalists overwhelmed by the occasion. My husband Lance was sitting elsewhere on Centre and after the first set I saw that his friend had not turned up, so I went to join him. On my other side, I found Sir Ian. He didn't introduce himself, and he gave no indication of recognising me. Over the next four hours, and four mesmerising sets, I learnt exactly why he is one of the nation's greatest actors. He was empathising with every swing of the racket, every ball that went in or out, every emotional twist and turn in the match. With each point played, it seemed the contest became tighter, and tenser, until it was almost unbearable.

During every rally he grabbed me and the lady sitting on the other side of him by the arm and we were jumping up and going nuts, just so caught up in the action. I turned into a Spanish superfan, calling out *Vamos Carlitos!* We were two tennis fans bonded by the spectacle in front of us. And that is what made such a huge impression on me, the incredible experience of being carried along by a crowd so invested in the outcome of a match. That collective emotion, its dynamism, is so powerful. There, on that day, I was swept up in the support for the underdog – even though I really admire Djokovic. I think he deserves the record for holding the most Slams. It seems extraordinary, given my lifelong connection to Wimbledon, that this was the first men's singles final where I was exposed to the raw emotions of sitting in the crowd in that intimate arena, with no filter and no professional distractions. The collective 'oohs' and 'aahs', the random shout-outs for each player, the sound of the ball being steered with magnificent skill through the air around the court by these two incredible players, and the tension in the air between points: it was magic. Until I hung up my microphone after the 2022 Championships, I had been on site for the last 30 Wimbledon final weekends, witnessing the action from one stage removed – through the pixels of a television screen with the accompaniment of production talkback in my ears, under the bright lights of our soundproofed on-site studio. I interviewed Mac (John McEnroe), Tim (Henman), Chrissie and Tracy (Austin) and co for previews of the finals from the side of the court and I performed the post-match interviews during the trophy presentation, but I had never seen or heard a ball struck in play. And this Alcaraz–Djokovic encounter was the most intense of gladiatorial battles, with Novak smashing his racket on the net post when he lost his serve in the final set, setting up young Alcaraz with a chance for a dream win. Could Novak's first loss on Centre Court in ten years really be happening before my eyes, when so much was at stake? The Serb had looked unequivocally on track to equal Margaret Court's record of 24 Grand Slam titles by claiming an eighth Wimbledon victory, his fifth in a row.

To have seen Alcaraz's triumph as my first men's final, well I don't know whether I'll ever do better than that. As the

New York Times writer Matthew Futterman put it, 'there is no longer any question; Alcaraz has pushed tennis permanently into its future.' While Mac said, 'He has taken the game to a different place. He does things no one thought was possible.' To sit alongside Sir Ian, who was so invested in the unfolding of the drama that saw Alcaraz join Borg and Boris Becker as the three youngest ever men's champions, was out of this world. Much as I admire Djokovic, this felt like one of the most exciting breakthroughs in tennis. And I've seen a few! Alcaraz doesn't just want to win, he wants to win in style, with unexpected drop shots followed by topspin lobs, a dazzling, dynamic all-court game executed with devastating changes of pace. He's a showman. And such a lovely guy. In his interview on Centre Court with Annabel Croft, he came across as a humble, well-mannered youngster from a lovely family, not spoiled in any way, a lot like Rafa when he burst onto the scene. I thought, *wow*, what a great role model he is. Even simply with the way he holds himself.

I was a young up-and-coming player in the mid-1970s, when tennis first became a box office sensation thanks to Björn Borg and Chrissie Evert bringing rock-star glamour to the top levels of our sport. And here I was, in retirement, whooping along with a distinguished actor and knight of the realm! Fifty years on, I saw that Wimbledon's blockbuster allure remains undentable. It was a very special final flourish to my first visit to Wimbledon as a regular spectator, free to soak up every point and deep breath of tension as a gripping sporting and psychological drama unfolded.

A Different Kind of Championships

I have loved every minute of my life in tennis but, on top of that passion for the game, nervous tension and professional self-discipline are the emotions I carried through the gates into Wimbledon every year in half a century as a player and a broadcaster. I felt fear as a competitor, bubbling with dreams of one day being crowned champion while facing the challenge of outwitting every opponent, each one different from the last, that the draw threw my way; I required focus as the host of the BBC's live tournament coverage, bringing all the action from the courts to viewers, across two channels, as it unfolded. It is a matter of pride that during my broadcasting career I never used autocue. So I imagined I would feel nothing but excitement for 2023, my first tournament unburdened of responsibilities, footloose and fancy-free of any official involvement – but I arrived in utter trepidation. Wimbledon as a fan – this was something I had never trained for!

Nerves, I was used to. I was always petrified before a match. I don't think I slept for an entire week before my first match in the main draw of the ladies' singles in 1973. It wasn't so much the place – I had played many times at Wimbledon as a schoolgirl and in the junior events – as the occasion. I was up against Lita Liem of Indonesia. I had no idea what she looked like or how she played, so in my training and in the lead-up to the match I was unable to visualise her across the net. Back then, there was no television coverage of international tennis, no Google to search for information on the internet, no social media. Pictures of the stars were in magazines, but I only got to know the regular players' names from the results sections I studied obsessively in the newspapers; players such as Jane 'Peaches' Bartkowicz, who was one of the most successful juniors of all time, and Kristy Pigeon, both of whom are still ingrained in my memory. Lita Liem was one of those names in tiny print. One thrill of that first Wimbledon in 1973, when I was just 17 and had also entered in the girls' singles, was that I could go from court to court, matching players with the names on the scoreboards. Even then, I had to check the name of the server against the person actually tossing the ball in the air and starting each point to work out who was who.

That Wimbledon was also the only one that my coach Arthur Roberts came to watch. We stayed in Earl's Court and he said he'd do some digging to find out about Lita Liem's playing style. Just before the match, he told me she was a leftie, but assured me everything would be fine if I just hit the ball to her backhand. I walked onto the court a bundle of nerves, and as soon as we started trading balls in the warm-up, I could see she wasn't a leftie at all, she was ambidextrous! The idea of hitting to her backhand was ridiculous. I looked over at Mr Roberts in the stands, shrugging my shoulders in consternation, and saw he was sitting there with his pipe, convulsed with laughter. It was so clever of him. He knew I would have a giggle and relax. I beat Lita Liem 6–0, 6–4.

As the 2023 Championships approached, I knew that I wouldn't have a first-round match or first day of coverage to host. With nothing to focus on, I had no idea what to expect.

My trepidation was a fear of the unknown. I had no doubt that my retirement from the BBC at the end of Wimbledon 2022 was the right time to go. With Roger announcing his retirement later that year, Rafa revealing he might be saying his farewells in 2024, and the women's draw opening up in the absence of recent champions Serena Williams, Ash Barty and Simona Halep – all for very different reasons – 2023 looked set to be a transitional year. I wouldn't see my former broadcast colleagues rushing down to interview Roger or Rafa or Serena. I wouldn't be struck by the fear of missing out. But how would I feel without that sense of involvement? I had never been free to indulge in the national pastime of simply watching tennis for these two weeks. I was worried about how I would feel without the sense of purpose that came with arriving each day with a backpack bulging with media notes. I was used to organising my Wimbledon stints with military precision – and that habit proves hard to break. Almost on autopilot, I rented the same flat for the Championships that I have done in recent years, within walking distance of the All England Club, and began to get excited about planning this very different fortnight for myself, intent on seeing as many different aspects of the Wimbledon experience as I could, as a typical fan might do.

First, I had to learn some basics. The week before the tournament started, I dropped into the club. It felt so special to be back. It always does, even in the winter when the courts are just rectangles of grass under cultivation without their Championships stands and screens. As I stepped through the gates, my mind flitted back to my first visit as a schoolgirl playing for my Marist

Convent team in the national schools competition, the Aberdare Cup. In those days, we played on red shale courts at the southern end of the grounds – where the new show courts 3 and 12 are today. That first visit when I was 13 made a huge impact on me. I can find the exact spot where I stood in 1969 and looked back towards the creeper-clad Clubhouse, hardly believing I was playing at Wimbledon, the place I had dreamt about so much. The roof has gone up in height with the new retractable system, but the club otherwise still has that same stately facade that was so intimidating for a young kid coming up from Devon.

On this visit, I particularly wanted to take time to say a fond farewell to my old studio. At the end of a 14-day run, you are so exhausted, you just pack up and go, and I had pretty much scarpered at the end of my last Wimbledon for the BBC. So, while the warm-up event at Queen's Club was garnering all the attention up the road in Barons Court, I made the most of the empty grounds. I wandered along the deserted lino corridors of the Broadcast Centre and climbed the stairs to the roof to look out over the beautiful site, watching workers busy with last-minute primping and painting and sweeping and gardening, all that incredible attention to detail. I just wanted to breathe it in, feel the magic of the place with the smell of freshly mown grass in the air. As I mentioned earlier, this was always my ritual when I was there to work long, long hours in the high-pressure environment of live TV: to stand in that spot for a good 30 minutes and gaze over the familiar landscape – Centre Court and the competitors' balcony to the right with the steeple of St Mary's Church in the distance, No.1 Court and Henman Hill to the left,

Courts 14, 15, 16 and 17 ahead of me. I used to crave that private moment in the evening before the tournament started. It was invigorating, a reminder of how much I loved my job. I would sense the anticipation in the air and recognise the calm before the storm of what would surely ensue in the forthcoming days of sporting combat. And then I would go down to meet my editor Ali and plan Day One of our coverage.

I followed my familiar route up to the Broadcast Centre roof but I couldn't get inside, as it was closed, to see the swanky new media theatre and interviewing facilities that had been completed in time for 2023 – ever evolving, my old stomping ground had already moved on without me! From there, I wandered round the back of Court 18 to the top of Henman Hill for a different perspective across the grounds. This area, which includes the practice-court complex, is still called Aorangi from the days when it was rented from the All England Club by the London New Zealand Rugby Club. Originally, however, the land belonged to a department store called Barkers of Kensington. I used to say to Tim Henman, 'You've got your hill, but I've got all those courts!' Very fitting, as I played my best tennis in practice!

Then, homage to the old workplace ticked off, I set off to do a full recce and work out where the Members' seats are situated on courts around the grounds. I have long been a member of the All England Club, but until 2023 I had never been able to use the Members' seats on Courts 2 or 3, 12, 18 or whatever during Wimbledon, and I had no idea how to access them. If I didn't arm myself with that information, I was in danger of cutting a poignant figure, the former BBC's Face of Wimbledon having to ask stewards for directions around the place. I needed to get my bearings before I joined the 10am stampede, which I had so often witnessed, when the Voice of Wimbledon announces over a tannoy that the gates are about to open and the fans run to their favourite viewing spots. The courts were dressed for the tournament and I discovered each court has a notice by a particular entry point indicating the seats designated for 'Members, International Box, Players' Stand, Press and Ticket Holders'.

With my surveillance mission accomplished, I was set to leave, primed for the day when I would officially return as a fan. As I was about to walk out onto Somerset Road, I glimpsed a friendly figure in Jamie Delgado up in the competitors' restaurant.

'Hello, Sue!' he shouted from the balcony.

'Are you on your way to Queen's?' I called back, as I knew Grigor Dimitrov, who Jamie is coaching these days, was playing later that day.

'Not yet,' he said. 'We popped in to have a coffee. Come and join us!'

So I sat outside on the balcony and had a coffee and a croissant with Jamie and Dani Vallverdu, both of whom used to be in Andy Murray's training setup, and Ross Hutchins, the former GB player who is now chief tour officer with the Association of Tennis Professionals (ATP). I suddenly realised, in the time spent with these three, how fabulous it is to be a member of the All England Club. You know, there I was, with a nice latte and a croissant, which I could put on my members' account, having a lovely catch-up with Jamie, who I used to help coach when he was a young boy and part of the Slater Squad alongside Tim

Henman. (We go back a long way, back to the time when, after training, I was often asked to drop the boys back at their school in Cobham, and I used to dole out naughty treats like chocolate and hamburgers – I felt so sorry for them on their strict nutrition-led diet!) Sitting chatting to the boys in the sunshine was another key moment of discovering 'how to do Wimbledon'. I promised myself I would be sure to enjoy my membership more in the future.

Billie Jean Back on Centre Court

Long before I ever stepped foot inside Wimbledon, there was one match that I played in my imagination hundreds, if not thousands of times, and the result was always the same – it was me, heroically beating Billie Jean King on Centre Court with a series of last-gasp winners in a tight final set. That was the dream that motivated me in practice, but unfortunately when I did get to play Billie Jean on Centre – not until 1978, in my sixth Wimbledon – it didn't quite turn out how I had hoped. It was a fourth-round match. I was seeded 14; she was the No.5 seed, and she beat me 6–2, 6–2. My forehand was my big weapon – it was regularly voted the best forehand on the women's tour – but on the occasion I actually got to play my hero on Centre Court, the wily Billie Jean didn't allow me to get into a rhythm. She kept slicing the ball on both sides to keep my forehand at bay. Perfect tactics – on the very fast grass back then, everything that came off my racket went flying up into the Royal Box!

And at Wimbledon 2023, this whole scenario came flooding back. I had wandered back into the club again on the Saturday before the tournament started. I popped in because I knew Saturday is traditionally a day of dress rehearsals on the show court for the umpires, Hawk-Eye, the microphone system, the ball kids and so on, and they let new members play against long-standing members in mixed-double pairings to provide some action for this final practice. I was on my way up to the Members' restaurant to get a bite to eat when I bumped into my friend Denise Parnell, who, having been named as the Championships referee for 2024, becomes the first female Grand Slam referee. 'You'd better hurry up,' she said. 'We're off to watch Billie Jean on Centre Court!'

Billie was in London as a special guest at Wimbledon to mark the 50th anniversary of the formation of the Women's Tennis Association. I knew this already because I had been asked to host a dinner celebrating that famous meeting on 21 June 1973 in the Gloucester Hotel, just off the Cromwell Road in South Kensington, in which she urged a group of players to agree to form what became known as the WTA – and where she had the imposing figure of Dutch player Betty Stove on the door as a bouncer making sure no one left without agreeing to join the cause. (When Billie Jean asked me why I wasn't there at that 1973 gathering, I have to remind her I was only 17 years old and couldn't afford to stay at that hotel. I was down the road in Earl's Court digs arranged by my coach Mr Roberts.)

Debbie Jevans, the incoming chair of the All England Club, had asked Billie Jean if there was anything she would like to do while she was back in London for the 50th anniversary. Billie replied that she would love to hit a few balls on Centre Court again. Debbie made it happen for her, and so I grabbed a sandwich and joined Denise and a few others, sitting in the third row back behind the umpire's chair, and watched the pair of them take to the court.

People talk about the timelessness of Centre Court – on that day, it was honestly like stepping into a time capsule. It really brought back memories. There was Billie Jean in her tracksuit, pounding out her ground strokes then standing at the net for some volleys, all the time commentating on herself with her familiar chastisements: 'Take it earlier!' '*See* the ball.' Denise and I started heckling – at Debbie, not Billie Jean, we wouldn't dare! And Billie Jean was calling over to me, 'How did you hit your forehand, Sue?' She was always fascinated by my forehand. We used to say if I had her backhand and she had my forehand, we would both have a better package. But now she was remembering that day in 1978. 'Clear the first few rows of the Royal Box!' she cried. 'Do you remember? We needed to clear the rows when you were teeing off!'

She must have been on court for about 30 minutes, loving every second of it. Billie Jean may now be 80, but she and her partner Ilana still play a few times a week. They had booked the club's indoor courts at Wimbledon to keep that routine up during their visit. I could see how chuffed Debbie was too. To be on the opposite side of the net from Billie Jean King on Centre Court – not many people can say they've done that. We all had photos taken afterwards with the officials, and Billie Jean was asking all the ball kids their names and questioning them about their training. It was really relaxed, and a lovely start to the Wimbledon fortnight. Always the trailblazer for women, Billie

Jean must have loved seeing Debbie as the new chair of her beloved All England Club, with Denise coming in this year as the first female referee, alongside chief executive Sally Bolton in the leadership group.

That was a highlight, but on Sunday I felt aimless. I had the saddest day just watching telly in the rented flat – even though it is a lovely private enclave and had always been the perfect retreat after a long day in the studio. I recovered when Lance, my husband, arrived to join me, and we started plotting how we would enjoy experiencing the magic of Wimbledon the next day, when 256 of the best male and female tennis players in the world would arrive with hopes and dreams and heavy racket bags to start their Championship campaign.

Roger and Out

I decided coming into the 2023 Championships that I would do no media. I wanted to speak to people that I know and like – and trust – but I thought how could I then turn other people down? And where then would I stop? My decision was also out of respect for the new team at the helm of the BBC coverage, Isa Guha and Clare Balding. I knew their routine. I used to get into the studio at half seven, eight o'clock in the morning. I would pick up the newspapers and read through the tennis stories just to make sure I was aware of every strand of interest in the tournament that I might need to refer to or bring into our own coverage. If I were Isa or Clare, the last thing I would need is to see Sue in the Royal Box, Sue watching the tennis, Sue's views on x, y and z. So I said absolutely no to everything. I was invited on every programme going and I just thought, *No, I'm not doing it.*

One offer, though, was irresistible. Paul Davies, the boss of Wimbledon coverage for the All England Club, contacted me about ten days before the start of Wimbledon to ask if I would do a little interview with Roger Federer. I thought, *What a way to go out! After that, I don't think I'll ever want to interview anyone again!* The interview was to be filmed in a garden setting. When the time came, Roger was so relaxed, such easy company and a joy to spend time with. Once we were set up with microphones, the cameras rolled and – of course – it soon started to rain. I hadn't even got to my questions about his future plans when it began pelting it down. We scuttled into the house at the back and he and I just sat there chatting about all sorts of different things while watching the rain tip down, hoping it was a passing shower. In the end, his agent said they would have to move on because they had an engagement with ESPN up next. So I never finished the interview, but it was a lovely experience. I've often had the chance to speak to Roger as a professional interviewee, but I'd never had the chance to chat freely with him for 20 minutes – unscripted, if you like. He is such a genuinely nice guy. He quizzed me about my life and what I was going to do now. We talked about our memories of the previous year, 2022, when his entrance was the grand finale to the celebrations to mark 100 years of Centre Court. Typically, he deflected that back and said it was so nice to see the applause and ovation I received when John McEnroe, the rogue, went off script and paid a generous farewell tribute to me live on television at my last ever Wimbledon with the BBC. That's the measure of Roger, a great champion and a great person.

We agreed he had come a long way from his start in The Championships as a junior. Roger tells a funny story about his first match on the Wimbledon grass, when he was so nervous he couldn't hit a ball over the net – so much so that he went to the umpire and asked him to please check the net height. 'I have a feeling that the net's way too high because I can't get a serve in, and the whole thing feels super-odd,' he said to the official in the chair. It is so funny to picture the scene: the young Roger, with his boyish haircut and baggy fresh white shirt, totally convinced that the net height is wrong, and the umpire politely pointing out that he had already checked it. 'Mr Federer, I've already measured the net before the match. We always do that here at Wimbledon, and it's absolutely fine.' Roger then implored the umpire: 'Please, please check it again. It's definitely too high.' The umpire clambered down from his chair and re-measured the net, with all the spectators whispering in their seats as he announced triumphantly, 'Mr Federer, the net is the right height' – and Roger said he felt like he wanted to die.

In my interview with Roger I had also planned to go through highlights of his memorable finals, particularly one shot in the 2009 final against Andy Roddick. He was a set down and the second set had gone to a tie-break, in which Roger was 6–2 down. So, four set points to Roddick. I'd mentioned it earlier to Paul Davies, who had been the producer 'on the buttons' of that match, and said I needed to ask Roger about that point – and that little half-volley backhand cross-court. I remembered it so clearly, Paul too. But Roger? When I reminded him of it, he didn't recall it at all. I guess he struck so many sublime winners in his career.

'How do you not remember?!' I remonstrated. 'That was one of the greatest shots *ever* on Centre Court? Roddick hit this massive forehand down the line, almost behind him, and your response was a little flick half-volley. It was amazing.' Paul joined in, 'You must remember it, Roger. It was incredible.' Roger thought it was hilarious. 'I can't believe I can't remember,' he said. 'I'm going to Google it.' Imagine having to Google your own genius!

It's a Fan's Life

So, on the first day of the 2023 Championships, I walked down the hill with my husband. I was wearing sunglasses and a baseball cap, jeans and a T-shirt – no telegenic bright jacket, no backpack stuffed with notes – and we set off incognito, like two ordinary fans looking forward to a day out at the tennis. It was so much fun. I particularly wanted to sit on the outside courts in the first week to watch the wild cards, qualifiers and lower-ranked players. In my mind, Wimbledon is about trying to earn your airfare home. I remember the feeling of having to win matches to get enough money to afford the journey home. Today's prize money means that's no longer an issue; nevertheless, players enjoy their successes so much more when they remember the struggle to become an established player on the tour. We saw the young Czech player Markéta Vondroušová at close quarters from the benches alongside Court 7 and marvelled at all her tattoos. She has quite a collection, including her lucky number 13, an inking of the Olympic rings (she won a silver medal at the Tokyo Games) and one above her right elbow that reads, 'No rain, No flowers', meaning that success only comes after a struggle. I had last seen her beat Jo Konta in the semi-finals at Roland-Garros in 2019 so I knew how crafty she is as a player, but as we watched her defeat Peyton Stearns of the United States I certainly didn't foresee her becoming the 2023 Wimbledon ladies' singles champion 12 days down the line.

Lance and I queued up for a hot dog. A day at Wimbledon demands certain rituals, headlined by a punnet of good old-fashioned strawberries and cream, of course. (Back in the day when the All England Clubhouse menus were written in French, raspberries were served at lunch to Royal Box guests as a Wimbledon speciality. Strawberries were sold to the public, because they were in season and were farmed locally, but raspberries were considered a more exclusive fruit.) Sausages became another staple from 1963, when the Oscar hot dog was particularly popular. A contributor to the book *The People's Wimbledon*, a collection of memories shared by fans of their visits to The Championships through the years, recalls the moment he bumped into Chris Evert with his star-struck teenage friend. They had both just bought their hot dogs and his friend impulsively offered Chrissie a bite of his Oscar. She politely declined. I can just picture that encounter! There was also 'the Dutchee' – about 60,000 of this spicy sausage were sold each year. There was even a brief phase of hamburgers, but that fried burger-and-onion smell was so bad, they were quickly off the menu. Anyway, we had a very nice hot dog and then went and sat on Court 17, tucked into seats in the corner, where we watched a fabulous match between Magda Linette, the No.23 seed from Poland, and Jil Teichmann, a Swiss player ranked outside the top 100. Gosh, it was ferociously competitive. I loved observing the players' respective camps sitting so close to each other. So often the matches on the big show courts in the early rounds can be very one-sided, but we found ourselves caught up in a great atmosphere for a match-up between two players who are hardly household names. It was a fantastic experience just to go to a court, find a seat and see players giving their all, because these are the competitors scrambling for their survival in the ruthless world of the modern tours.

Sitting on Court 17 – at the furthest end of the run of courts I used to look over from my BBC studio – I realised this is what Wimbledon offers: the opportunity to see the strength and depth in the game often overshadowed by the likes of Djokovic and Alcaraz, Świątek and Gauff. And with that came the understanding of how skilled you have to be to dominate a Grand Slam event – because the players are just so good further down the ranks.

The standard of play on the outside courts is amazing. For years, in my television role, I had been focused on the show courts, particularly Centre and No.1 courts – where the top players of course are scheduled throughout the competition – and I only really ever saw these lower-ranked players when, courtesy of the draw, they came through and played a big name on the biggest stages.

On the second day, Lance and I went to No.1 Court and watched Alcaraz's first match of the tournament, against Jérémy Chardy of France, which was tremendous. This kid was the newly crowned US Open champion, but I had never seen him play live anywhere in the world. I always want to support home players, and we stayed on No.1 that day to watch Cameron Norrie overcome Czech player Tomáš Macháč. We spent the third day on Centre to see Jodie Burrage, the British wild card, up against the 11th seed Daria Kasatkina. You just never know how a young Brit is going to respond to the massive pressure of playing on Centre. It can be so overwhelming and yet we have those incredible memories of brilliant upsets or near shocks. Who can forget Heather Watson's third-round match in 2015, when she served for the match at 5–4 in the decider against Serena Williams, then a five-time Wimbledon champion, only for the American to recover and win 6–2, 4–6, 7–5? And at The Championships in 2023 Liam Broady had the Centre Court crowd on their feet thanks to his five-set victory over the Roland-Garros finalist Casper Ruud. He described coming out onto that stage as both terrifying and exhilarating, but he was cranking out winners galore and cracking jokes at the end.

His mum had been too nervous to watch, he told the Centre Court crowd in his post-match interview, but he had told her, 'Look, I've already won 80 grand this week, so you can chill out!'

I was enjoying the freedom of choosing where to go and who to watch, as well as the fabulous atmosphere, nicely summed up when one of the umpires had to issue the warning, 'Ladies and gentlemen, if you are opening a bottle of champagne, don't do it as the players are about to serve.'

On the second Monday I watched Madison Keys against Mirra Andreeva on Court 2. The 16-year-old Russian was being talked about as the next superstar in the women's game. I watched her on TV at the qualifying. She was very impressive, but the big talking point was the Netflix crew following her every move. During the match, I sat just behind the players' guests: on one side of the aisle Madison had five supporters in her team, on the other, Andreeva's spanned four rows! That's the lure of being the next 'big thing'. Everyone wants a part of you. However, with that comes immense pressure, which for one so young is difficult to cope with. The controversial end to her match will have made the Netflix producers very happy, even if it wasn't the perfect ending. I found myself witnessing the sort of incident I used to have to comment on, live on air, during our 30-second clips from around the grounds. At 2–5 in the third set, Andreeva slipped and fell, her racket hitting the ground as it flew from her hand. As she'd already had a warning earlier in the second set for throwing her racket, the umpire gave her a point penalty. That gave Madison match point, a decision which seemed a bit harsh, but the umpire, I think, must have missed seeing Andreeva slip before the racket left her hand. The teenager protested and then refused to shake the umpire's hand. It was an awful way to end a three-set fourth-round match, and the crowd were vociferous in showing their support for Andreeva. Awful, but fabulous for me to see it all unfold from the stands and feel part of 'a Wimbledon moment' – a talking point that will no doubt be recalled for years. She is an exciting, talented player, so I hope the pressure doesn't overwhelm her. We will see.

I had a great time milling around during the day before joining the more mellow crowds mesmerised by entertaining doubles matches in the late evenings. Despite my baseball cap and sunglasses, I wasn't as incognito as I imagined. I must have been asked 35 times in an hour what it was like, to not be working. And it was amusing to see people in the seats in front of us take 'selfies' to send to friends and say, 'Guess who's sitting behind us!' I was careful not to say anything controversial!

Fellow spectators were just so lovely. I had the nicest chats and messages. People said the most heartwarming things – I had never realised just what you become to people as a familiar face and personality on the television when you present an event that is such an important feature in their lives. Wimbledon is not just a tennis tournament. For many people, it *is* summer. I met people who said they take two weeks off work each year to watch every hour of coverage. A few admitted they don't actually know how to score, but they love the drama of it. Some women admitted their families don't expect cooked food for the Championships fortnight as they can't drag themselves away from the screen. Some people come not for the sport but for a day out, while others pop down after work, queue and luckily get a Centre or No.1 court ticket through the re-sale system. I heard wonderful reminiscences from people who made me proud of what I had achieved on television. I honestly hadn't fully understood how much these two weeks matter to people until I was out there as one of them.

The Last 8 Club

It was glorious spending time in the Members' areas of the All England Club, where I could mill around with my old muckers from junior days, players who I practised with or competed against in county tennis. We all still remember those all-important U-14 matches and reminisced about the golden days. I hadn't seen some of these old tennis friends for decades, and it was fantastic to catch up with them. Again, socialising wasn't something I ever had the chance to do while I was hosting the BBC coverage.

One thing Wimbledon does so well is The Last 8 Club, a sort of club within the Club that welcomes all players who have ever reached the singles quarter-finals, the doubles semi-finals or the mixed-doubles final. Run as a drop-in hospitality space by John Feaver, who I grew up with in the juniors, it is an example of how the Club cares for its extended family. Tucked away by Gate 5, it was established in 1986 when it came to the then-chairman's attention that a couple of older players were queuing with the public to try to get tickets, and he set about giving access to former players who he felt, quite rightly, had contributed so much to the show when they were competitors. John oversees a daily allocation of tickets to the show courts, and conducts a ballot for the big matches while wearing a hard hat, in jest, to escape the protestations of those who miss out. There are refreshments available all day, a six o'clock happy hour and an annual dinner, which I discovered attracts about 70 former players each year. It was my first appearance here, and I joined Billie Jean, Rosie Casals, Christine Janes, Tracy Austin and the 1974 finalist Olga Morozova, as well as Mark Woodforde, Jan Kodeš, Peter Fleming, Fred Stolle and Chris Lewis, the finalist from 1983. To me, almost everyone represented a memory from my career. Chris Lewis, for instance, now lives in Newport Beach, where I was based when I left for California aged 17 to turn pro, and I was quizzing him about all my old haunts. I learnt that, not surprisingly, it has changed a lot since the 1970s, but my favourite restaurant is still there!

We had such a laugh at dinner. John Lloyd and I both gave speeches, as did Chris. I told stories from my memoir, *Calling the Shots*, and Lloydy, who is a great raconteur, told the tale of how he nearly died in the men's locker room at Wimbledon after one cruel defeat. He had lost a four-hour, first-round, five-set match to Phil Dent – a nightmare result for a Brit fancied to do well at Wimbledon, as he was in 1976 – and then done the exhaustive rounds of media that a home player used to have to endure (these days there are time limits and players can take a shower and have a massage before facing the press). It was 9pm when he got to the locker room and found it empty. As he tells the story, he ran a deep, steaming hot bath and wallowed in it, going over in his mind all the crucial points of his match, angry that he had lost it. When he reached for the soap, his hand cramped, and soon he had seized up all over with an excruciatingly painful full-body cramp. 'I was sliding down into the water. I was sinking, I was going to bloody well drown in the Wimbledon bath,' he recalled. And then he had us in stitches. 'It's funny what goes through your mind at such moments,' he said. 'My life should have been passing before my eyes, but my ego took over and I started to imagine the headlines in the newspapers the next day: "British player commits suicide in bath after devastating loss".' Luckily for Lloydy, a former player had dashed into the locker room bursting for a pee after a Wimbledon cocktail party – and the urinals were close to the bath. His distress was noted and he was safely hauled out of the water, and lived to tell the tale.

Wimbledon remains a draw for its former stars, no matter what their age or circumstances. At 89, the Australian Neale Fraser, a former number one amateur, was probably the oldest visitor I met in the Last 8 Club in 2023. He was happily reminiscing about winning Wimbledon in 1960, and the adventures his feat involved. This was back in the day when only the top-ranked amateur players competed for the Gentlemen's Singles Trophy and a £10 voucher for the sports retailer Lillywhites. Neale duly set off to Piccadilly Circus, primed to buy some sportswear at the central London department store. Alas, he found that it was closed. What really sums up the spirit of prize money in those days was the fact that the cost of Neale's return taxi journey amounted to £17, leaving him out of pocket for winning the world's most prestigious tennis title. When you think young Alcaraz won £2.35 million for lifting the trophy …

When I was hosting the BBC's Wimbledon coverage, I used to get a bit jealous when Billie Jean came to the studio for a chat and then said she was off to meet Rosie Casals for lunch, or when other guests let slip that they were meeting up with other friends from the tour. I had FOMO, or a fear of missing out, before the term was even invented! Now it was my turn to meet up with the old gang at Wimbledon. I was thrilled to hear from Rosie that my old doubles partner Ann Kiyomura was over from the States for Wimbledon so we arranged to meet, and it was lovely seeing old 'Sword' again – her nickname still sticks years after she earned it for being lethal at the net. We had first met in the girls' singles competition in 1973, so that's 50 years of special friendship. The way memories work, though, is bizarre. She didn't remember half the things that I told her about and yet she was telling me things that I had zero recall of! I am still trying to get her to reveal the meaning of the Japanese words she coached me to say to the public after we won a tournament in Tokyo back in the day. I had asked her to teach me something I could say to the crowd in their own language. The two sentences I announced on Ann's instruction had the crowd burst out laughing, so I don't think I was thanking them for their support. That memory has haunted me all my life, but here she was saying she doesn't remember it at all! I reminded her about how in awe I was of the way she could chill out before a match. She could sit in a chair, anywhere, and have a power nap; meanwhile I would be pacing up and down the room, getting nervous. She has no memory of ever taking a nap. But she did it every day.

We had so much fun reminiscing about all the madness we would get up to when rooming together to save money. We wondered whether, in 40 years' time, the players of today will be in the Last 8 Club, having a giggle over their experiences together. I don't think they will, because today's players don't have the same rapport with each other. Back then, we didn't travel with entourages of coaches and physios so we became close-knit as friends, even though we were all sporting rivals. Off-court, we were each other's company and confidantes. During this reunion, I also met up with Paula Smith, who I reached the US Clay Court Championships doubles finals with in Indianapolis in 1981, and we had a photo taken of us. We hadn't seen each other for years, but I told her that I had a framed picture of the two of us on my wall at home. She couldn't believe it. Luckily, Lance had it on his phone to show Paula. The picture shows us celebrating at the end of our semi-final – we had edged out a victory over the top seeds Andrea Jaeger and Anne Smith 8–6 in the decider. It had been a testy match. All four of us were quite fiery competitors and Paula had won the event with Anne the previous year, so Paula and I were absolutely jubilant. We only played one tournament together, and the fact that we reached the final of this prestigious event was amazing. We played the semi as if it were the final … but then lost quite meekly to JoAnne Russell and Virginia Ruzici.

But the most surprising reunion of all on that day in 2023 came when I was walking out of the official transport office and bumped into the American Mona Guerrant, a doubles special-ist who was known as Mona Schallau in our playing days. She held up the Last 8 Club lanyard that was around her neck and said, 'Hey, I have you to thank for this!' – and she gave me a massive hug.

'What are you talking about?' I said.

'I got in the Last 8 Club because of you,' she exclaimed.

I'm thinking, *Why? Did she beat me in the last 16?*

Hmmm. 'I don't remember playing you here,' I said.

'No! We played *together*. In the doubles in 1978 ... and we made the semi-finals. You must remember our quarter-final match?'

I didn't.

She then reminded me that we beat Billie Jean King and Martina Navratilova 6–4 in the deciding set. To have beaten Billie Jean and Martina at Wimbledon, I thought I would have remembered that! But I had absolutely no recall. We got on our mobile phones and searched the match and there it was: 6–4 in the final set!

'You've got to be joking!' I said. 'That's unbelievable.'

She went through the ball-by-ball details of our amazing victory and I made her tell Lance and some friends in the Last 8 Club. 'You've got to tell the story again,' I urged Mona, 'because people won't believe it!' So she described how we had match point on Martina's serve: 'We were mid-rally and I hit a half-decent volley to Martina, who decided she wanted to lob you, Sue, because you were near the net and I could see that it was a really good lob so I started scampering back. I thought it was over your head, and Martina came charging into the net, and you leapt up like a salmon and hit this ball for a winner down the tramlines.'

We had beaten them!

Mona did then qualify our big moment by saying that day was freezing cold, the court was in shocking shape and the home crowd was going so ballistic supporting me that it upset the opposition. But I can't believe I could beat those two icons of women's tennis and not remember it. Unbelievable.

A Royal Guest

After years of announcing the guests in the Royal Box on the middle Saturday of the tournament – when stars from the world of sport traditionally receive an ovation – it was an honour and a treat to be invited there myself. Champions and legends from tennis, football, cricket, rugby union, wheelchair rugby league, gymnastics, hockey, track and field, horse racing and rowing filled the seats at the invitation of Ian Hewitt, then chairman of the All England Club. For many years I would have spent the morning finessing my script to introduce guests to the crowd from the court below, with the production team making regular calls to the chairman's office to check that all the guests had arrived. I could hardly invite someone to stand up and receive the crowd's ovation if they were stuck in traffic on the A3!

Having handed the baton to Clare Balding, I was free to enjoy Super Saturday, as it's called, a day that's a touchstone of emotion as Wimbledon looks back at remarkable sporting feats of the past (for those representing anniversaries of their achievements) and of British sporting heroics from the past year. First, it was wonderful to be in the Royal Box alongside Billie Jean and see our tour founder and mentor get the credit she deserved on the 50th anniversary of the formation of the WTA. She was introduced along with Judy Dalton and Rosie Casals – fellow members of the Original Nine, whose actions led to the formation of the women's tour – and the spectators showed their appreciation as only the knowledgeable and appreciative Centre Court crowd can. My name was announced with the other tennis invitees, as well as Jan Kodeš – in acknowledgement of the 50th anniversary of his singles title – and two-time Wimbledon champion Stefan Edberg. To stand up in the Royal Box and receive a rapturous ovation … well, words can't describe my emotions. It was just amazing and very moving. I don't know where they found the video footage of me winning the 1976 French Open and becoming a Grand Slam winner at the age of 20, and I don't think people in the crowd clicked that the young winner holding the trophy aloft was me until the montage moved on to the images of me in my blue trouser suit presenting with Mac the previous year. I was caught up in the emotions and then, hilariously, I heard Clare acknowledging my role as Wimbledon host on the BBC for 50 years! I was very impressed – the last 20 years have really flown by!

The presence of so many stars from other sports adds a frisson of extra excitement to the day's play. I remember one year when Tuffers – Phil Tufnell, one of my team captains on *A Question of Sport* – was a guest and his cricketing credentials were called into action when a ball whacked by Roger Federer was heading towards a distinguished dame sitting close to him. He leapt up to catch the ball – and dropped it, needless to say, much to the amusement of the crowd.

I had met many of my fellow Royal Box guests before, often in the green room of *A Question of Sport* during the 24 years I hosted the quiz – former rugby players Sir Gareth Edwards and J.P.R. Williams (who sadly died in January 2024), the Olympic rower Steve Redgrave and jockey Tony McCoy. My old BBC colleague Gary Lineker was there and we had an incredibly fun gossip. I was particularly pleased to meet some Lionesses – Leah Williamson, Beth Mead and Fran Kirby, who sadly were all dealing with injuries and had been unable to travel to Australia that summer for the World Cup, and the now-retired Jill Scott. I was so impressed with Leah because she immediately started talking about the importance of the Lionesses' legacy for the next generation. I nodded my head and said, 'Leah, I've got to introduce you to Billie Jean King. She's going to love you,' and it goes without saying that they were soon immersed in a long conversation. Often today, many athletes just think about themselves, especially now that they're able to earn good money, and it was so refreshing to hear Leah's concern for the future of the game.

This glorious day of sporting fellowship started with lunch in the inner sanctum of the All England Clubhouse, in the same dining room that members use throughout the year for lunch and dinner, so I was familiar with the space. It's a long, beautiful mirrored room. Other guests that day included eleven members of the 1st Battalion, Grenadier Guards, who carried out the pallbearing duties at Queen Elizabeth II's funeral in September 2022. Most of them seemed to come over to me with their mums, and one who didn't have his mum with him came over with his telephone, saying, 'I've got my mum on the phone to talk to you!' It was sweet. 'You must be very proud of him,' I said.

To my delight, I was invited back to the Royal Box for the ladies' final. In between those two Saturdays I had spent a morning with Billie Jean at the flat she rents in Wimbledon, chatting about all sorts of things. I've always loved our conversations. She was asking me about my childhood coach, Arthur Roberts, and quizzing me about what sort of comments he used to make. We talked about the players of today, and what Billie Jean herself had sacrificed in personal ambitions in order to push the women's game as a whole forward. The conversation went all over the place, as they tend to do with Billie. I value her views highly. She has always been the most amazing friend and mentor to me, ever since I met her as an excited, lonely but determined 17-year-old English girl setting out as a pro. It was extraordinary how quickly my hero turned into such a valued friend. Throughout my life she has always been there to offer advice – and it was lovely to sit with her then, uninterrupted, knowing I wouldn't have to run off in half an hour to go live on air. Incredibly, that morning in Billie's flat was the first time we had really indulged in a long chat together about the old days, with neither of us needing to rush off to fulfil a professional commitment.

We discussed our families and the sacrifices they had made, and wondered how selfish we were as kids driven only by our goals. I was saying how I never really thanked Mr Roberts – or my parents – as much as I should have done. When you're a teenager, you just think the world is all about you. Billie Jean was recalling the money that people in her local community, the Long Beach Tennis Patrons, the Century Club and an individual called Harold Guiver, raised in order to send her to London, to play at Wimbledon, for the first time in 1961, where she, aged 17, and Karen Hantze, who was 18, became the youngest doubles partnership to win the Wimbledon ladies' doubles title.

Billie was particularly keen to meet Lance because she had heard so much about him. On the day of the ladies' final, she insisted we all have tea together, the four of us. In the end, Ilana and I just left them to it, because Billie loves crime stories and Lance is a former detective, so she was grilling him, soaking up his answers like a sponge, just rat-tat-tatting questions at him! During tea, someone came over to Billie with a message – some of her friends were here and wanted to say hello. The friends were Katherine Jenkins, the Welsh mezzo-soprano, and her husband, Andrew Levitas, who socialised with Billie Jean in New York City. Without so much as a hello, Katherine pointed me out to her husband like she was identifying a criminal in a police lineup and blurted out, 'SHE broke the rules on Centre Court.' I knew exactly the moment she was referring to: the official opening ceremony for the Centre Court roof, which she was going to sing at.

That day, we had Andre Agassi and Steffi Graf and Tim Henman and Kim Clijsters on court. After I had interviewed the star players, Katherine was going to sing 'Amazing Grace' with fellow soprano Faryl Smith as the roof opened theatrically – and then give a solo rendition of her hit '(Everything I Do) I Do It for You', a ballad written by Bryan Adams for the film *Robin Hood: Prince of Thieves* (1991) that she dedicated to the service stewards. Following that, I was going to have a chat with her for the crowd. She was wearing a pink lace strapless dress and lovely sparkly little flip-flops, and I walked towards her with my microphone, in heels. She just looked me up and down and exclaimed, live on air, 'But I was told I couldn't wear heels!' So the first part of our interview was me trying to pretend that I wasn't really in heels (you know, because *obviously* the rules are you're not allowed to wear heels on the Centre Court grass). It was hugely embarrassing! That was 2009 – nearly 15 years ago – and her first association on seeing me again was to recall my illegal high heels! But we had a lovely chat, another really special time just relaxing with someone rather than the fleeting catch-ups I had when I was relentlessly working.

Lunch with the Royal Box guests on ladies' final day was incredibly special. I was sitting next to the chairman, who was to present me with an award for distinguished service, which is given for 'outstanding contribution' to The Championships. It comes on a ribbon and looks like an Olympic gold medal, so I like to think, and it was presented in a smart box with 'Distinguished Service Award' engraved on the back with my name. It was fabulous because Billie was there, as were Martina and other Wimbledon ladies' champions and finalists: Conchita Martinez, Marion Bartoli, Angela Mortimer, Christine Janes, Ann Jones and Judy Dalton. The chairman said it was up to me to say a few words if I wanted to. I stood up and said how honoured I was to be given this award, though sadly not as a champion, and how much I just love this place ... I became very emotional and started talking about when I stood outside the Club for the very first time and what it meant to me just to be on the threshold of those gates and then to walk through them, having earned the right to compete there, and to be here now, all these years later, receiving this incredible accolade from the All England Club. It was overwhelming because my journey through the Club ran from playing there with my school in the national schools tournament on the old shale courts to returning as a player on the women's tour, and then ultimately as a broadcaster. I have had the most incredible journey over the past five decades and it meant so much to be recognised for my time at Wimbledon and in the world of tennis. I was awash with emotions, but I'm sure most of the foreign guests might have thought, *Who the hell is she?!*

And then, I got rumbled for stealing chocolates. On our side plates at lunch we each had a white box emblazoned with the Wimbledon logo – two crossed rackets and a ball – which contained four little chocolates to eat with our coffee. The actual chocolates had cross rackets on them as well! They looked almost too good to eat straightaway, so I thought I should save mine for later. But I couldn't squeeze them in my small handbag, so had to tote them around with me wherever I went in case they were cleared away. I even took them into the ladies' toilet and accidentally left them behind. Someone came running out after me when I was chatting to the chairman and said, 'I think you left these in the loo!' So embarrassing.

I've still got the box, though the chocolates have gone (they were delicious), but, honestly, trust me to get rumbled in front of the chairman! Memo to self: always take a handbag big enough to put freebie chocolates in.

On-court Interviews

A few days before the finals, I had a meeting with Annabel Croft, who wanted advice on how to conduct the now traditional on-court interviews with the new champions and runners-up. I understood her anxiety. If I'm honest, I never enjoyed the interviews. The feeling beforehand was worse than nerves, it was dread. However wonderful it is to congratulate a new Wimbledon champion, you have to first put a microphone under the chin of someone who is still dazed from defeat. I hated that. I know myself how painful that moment is, how the defeat takes time to sink in and accept. The last thing a runner-up is ready to do is banter with a TV presenter and make crowd-pleasing remarks. And my feelings were not helped by the first one I did in 2000, when I emerged from the cocoon of the studio to stride onto Centre Court to talk to new champion Pete Sampras and the runner-up, Pat Rafter, with our BBC producer Martin Hopkins's words in my ears: 'Sue Barker, at Wimbledon, just the 500 million people watching you right now. Good luck!'

The technical challenge is that you have to conduct that natural chat to the jubilant winner and the deflated runner-up in front of 500 million television viewers and the Centre Court crowd while hearing a lot of talkback in your ear. I was speaking on a PA mike as well as to the television cameras. I had to wait to hear my television cue above the noise while hearing myself on the stadium speaker. But Annabel is an absolute pro. I told her how I prepared and suggested she watch some of the stories that the BBC typically compiles before the finals to gather a bit more insight into each finalist's path to this potentially life-changing day. It was sweet of her to ask my advice but she does these interviews at tennis tournaments all over the world and has loads of experience. She knows to keep it simple when you're throwing questions at athletes whose English may not be fluent. She didn't need my tips, though I do understand that the status of Wimbledon, with its global TV audience of millions, makes it more daunting. One way or another, she was going to have a first-time Wimbledon champion at the end of the ladies' singles final, which is lovely for the interviewer, because it's obviously so special for the player to win their first title and fantastic to be part of that experience with them. Whether it was Ons Jabeur or Markéta Vondroušová, it was going to be an exceptionally happy occasion for them. So that's a nice interview. Trying to engage the player who's lost out is never easy, but you can talk about what a great tournament they've had, and how the spectators have taken to them, and so on. The crowd always helps out on these occasions. In the 2023 men's final, there would either be a first-time Wimbledon champion in Alcaraz or Djokovic would be making history, equalling Margaret Court's record and in fact equalling Federer's eight titles at Wimbledon. So, stories either way.

It was really touching because, after the ladies' final, Annabel did her lovely interviews and walked off to stand courtside. As she went, she looked up at me in the Royal Box and I gave her a thumbs up. 'Oh thank you,' she mouthed. I found that moving that she looked up to me at that moment, it was like we'd handed over the baton, and now she was off and running. Once you've got the first year out of the way, you know what to expect. She did a fabulous job. I left that role in safe hands. She did say it was very nerve-wracking … but I don't think it could have been as daunting as doing *Strictly*. She's braver than me.

1

ROD LAVER

I may have spent hours imagining myself tactically outwitting Billie Jean King in a Wimbledon final as I peppered balls against our garage wall at home in Paignton, but the first tennis super-star I shared a court with was Rod Laver. I even joined him in his trademark victory hurdle over the net – there's a picture of us both with fellow Australian Ken Rosewall to prove it. Me and the Rocket, no less, as Laver was known, and without whom Wimbledon as we know it would not exist.

They say that no champion is bigger than the sport, but there is one player alone who is responsible for Wimbledon becoming the magical fortnight of history-creating tennis that we all know and love today – and that is Rod Laver. Tennis would have become a professional sport eventually, but Rod speeded up the process – and it was perfect timing for me and my career. Despite the record-breaking achievements of Roger, Rafa and Novak, the cheery, red-haired dynamo who mesmerised the Wimbledon faithful in the 1960s is still regarded as the GOAT, the Greatest of All Time. Only five foot eight, the nimble Australian was a left-handed genius, whose repertoire of shot-making brilliance was out of this world. I remember seeing him play and marvelling at his natural talent and the power he created on his ground strokes with his unusual wrist strength. 'Most of it is timing the ball, rather than brute force,' he later told me. 'Just at the last minute you're flicking the ball and it's a surprise that the ball takes off so quick!' In person, he had a lopsided look; his left wrist was an inch bigger than his right, and his left forearm similarly overdeveloped compared to his right. Rod remembers Howard Cosell, the combative American sports broadcaster, telling him he thought his left arm was bigger than Rocky Marciano's, the world heavyweight champion. 'I said, "Get out of here!" But he said no, I just measured it. And yes it was a little bit bigger!'

So Rod was the star attraction of the day, and yet, from 1963 to 1967, he was absent from proceedings, banned from amateur competitions, having joined the professional circuit in order to make a living. Today it may seem ridiculous that the world's most electrifying player was denied court time on the greatest courts of the world, but this was the era of amateur sports – a hangover from the age when tennis was a sport of kings and a recreation for the wealthy, and people played without any form of remuneration. Tennis was not alone in having to re-address its status as an amateur sport. But Rod's star appeal was so sorely missed that the All England Club found a way to welcome him and his professional peers back. I'll go into the story in full later, but suffice to say it was announced that from 1968 The Championships would no longer be restricted to amateurs. Wimbledon would be open to all players (hence the term 'the Open Era') – and Rod 'The Rocket' Laver could once again thrill the Wimbledon faithful by blazing his explosive trail of magical shots and never-say-die heroics against all-comers.

It was at the height of this elation when Rod was back winning the majors in front of adoring crowds that I was lucky enough to experience some of that stardust in person. At the age of 13 I was invited by BP, the oil company, which sponsored a lot of tennis tournaments, to attend a junior international coaching clinic in Maida Vale, in north London, with Rod and Rosewall. This was 1969, the year Rod achieved his second calendar-year Grand Slam, meaning he had won all four majors – the Australian, French and US Opens, and Wimbledon – twice over, as both an amateur and a professional. He remains the only player, male or female, to pull off that clean sweep. He was the god of tennis, technically perfect, and an absolute hero to me. So much so that when Mr Roberts offered me the pick of the new rackets in his silver-steel lock-up kit cupboard as a reward for doing well in a junior tournament, I picked the model used by Rod. If it seemed bizarre for a skinny little girl to play with the same size racket and chunky grip as the top men's player in the world, I didn't care. It worked for me. I kept with it right the way through my career. The bigger grip boosted my forehand; and when I signed a deal with Dunlop on turning pro, I was asked which racket I wanted: 'A replica of this, please,' I answered.

I was so proud to bounce up to Rod that day in London and tell him I had the same racket and same grip as him even though my hands were half the size of his. He was great with us all: his enjoyment of the game, even with a bunch of kids, was contagious. Much to the annoyance of the other juniors attending the clinic that day, I was singled out by Rod as a future star. To mark the moment, a photograph was taken of me jumping the net alongside him in his trademark victory celebration. I've treasured that photo for decades. The smile on my face could not have been broader. I look at it and see my passion for the game at that age and the thrill I felt for the path that lay ahead. Little did I know then that 50 years later I would travel to meet Rod at his home in California for my BBC documentary *Our Wimbledon* – a film to celebrate the great legends who have graced the famous grass courts of SW19. It's the one I'm most proud of. Towards the end of filming, I delved into my handbag and brought out my precious photo to show him. I wanted to thank him on behalf of everyone in tennis for making a career in the sport possible and for taking tennis to where it is today. I wanted future generations to know that Rod was the catalyst for the sport turning professional.

Throughout my career, Rod has been ever present. It was an honour to sit with my idol on the porch of his house in San Diego for our interview. He was as friendly and welcoming as ever, and he even showed me his vegetable patch. When, as a naive 17-year-old, I had signed with IMG and moved to California to pursue a career in tennis, I was living alone in a townhouse in a resort-style development on Newport Beach, with two private courts in the middle. It turned out that Rod lived in the same enclave of housing, and one day he asked me to hit with him. Can you imagine? I rang home as soon as we finished on court – even though it was about 3am in Devon. I had to tell my mum!

Roll on a few decades, and I was visiting him to hear how he felt his life had been changed by The Championships. As we chatted, it struck me that behind the story of his success are three factors I've learnt are common to all the great players wherever they hail from: an absolute love of the game, a supportive and selfless family and an eagle-eyed coach who demands a never-say-die fighting spirit. Rod, the icon of our sport, grew up in Rockhampton in the outback of Queensland, Australia, with all three of these boxes ticked. His skills were honed on a back-yard court rolled out on his family's cattle farm almost 10,000 miles and a nine-hour time difference from the genteel lawns of Wimbledon. The Laver family court was made from 'ant-bed', crushed termite mounds that were rolled to create a playable surface, and watered every day to prevent it cracking in the heat or being washed or blown away by floods and storms. Rod and his brothers were responsible for its intensive upkeep, and they must have been mad about tennis given that heavy-duty daily chore. Their father, Roy, was a rancher, and their mother, Melba, was an accomplished local tennis player; the pair had met at a tournament in the local town of Dingo. Rod, the third of four children, was keen to keep up with his older siblings. As the youngest child in my sporty family, I can identify with that.

His father certainly didn't have a small-town mindset: he instilled in all of his boys the idea that they could take the tennis world by storm and that one of them would certainly play at Wimbledon one day. A tough-talking man called Charlie Hollis was called in to coach Rod's brothers. 'The first time Charlie laid eyes on me, I was 10 and he was putting Bob and Trevor through their paces,' Rod recalled in detail in his 2013 autobiography *Rod Laver: A Memoir*.

> I crept out of bed to watch and was peeping through the chicken wire fence of our court when he spied me. Before I could run away, Charlie said to Dad: 'Aw, let the little bugger have a hit. I can see he's as keen as mustard.' And there, barefoot and in my pyjamas, Charlie and I had a knock, and I got that ball back over the net more times than I didn't.

At first Hollis thought Rod was the least likely of the Laver brothers to progress. 'I was, after all, a skinny runt, and a left-handed runt at that,' Rod wrote in his recollections. 'Then, after a bit, he saw something in me and changed his mind. "Rod will be the best of the boys," he told Dad. "I'll coach him for nothing, even if he is a midget in need of a good feed. He's got the eye of a hawk."'

And that was the start of it, a full-on family effort to steer Rod as far as his talent and his exceptional hand–eye coordination would take him. 'When I turned 11, they drove me to junior tournaments all over Queensland,' he wrote.

> We'd be out of bed at 2 or 3am, with Mum preparing sandwiches and thermoses of tea before Dad drove us

from Rockhampton to Bundaberg, Brisbane or wherever we had to go, hundreds of kilometres – and this was in the days when dirt tracks, not asphalt roads, linked the towns. Those treks could take seven or eight hours. Not that Dad watched my every match. He liked to drop me off and say: 'See you at 5', and you'd find him in a congenial pub enjoying a rum and milk and reading his newspaper.

As a youngster, Rod was introduced to the legendary Australian Davis Cup team captain Harry Hopman at a tennis camp that was sponsored by the local newspaper. Rod is immortalised in the tennis world by his nickname, 'The Rocket', but he was dubbed that ironically. 'I was a slow little kid, the slowest in Hopman's class,' he told me. 'I was lackadaisical before I grew physically stronger. That's why he called me "Rocket". Of course Harry added Rockhampton to it, so I was "the Rockhampton Rocket" and that made it easy to take.'

I look back at the junior coaching clinic in London where I met Rod and Ken and see that Rod was keen to inspire youngsters in the way that he had experienced support himself. There he was at the top of the sport in 1969, the undisputed best player in the world, giving his time to a gaggle of promising 13-year-olds in north London! The Hopman coaching camp that had made such an impression on him in his youth included a roll-call of the top Australian players of the time; Rod was just a few years younger, still a junior, still physically small. As he recalled,

That was some programme. Roy Emerson came by to work with us, Mal Anderson, Rosewall, Ashley Cooper. They were only a few years older than me, but when you get the chance to hit a few balls with a group of great players, that makes a difference. You're watching and learning, you're keen to impress, and then you realise how much you've got to learn. You play with them at the age of 14, 15 or 16, and they're not hitting the ball hard, but they're powerful. I remember playing with Lew Hoad on one occasion and he said, 'Don't rush anything. Just play your game. Don't go for winners all the time.'

It was great advice, and that is what amazes people today: in such a competitive sport, the players hailed as the legends of the game all helped and encouraged each other to improve – as fellow players, not as rivals. 'Everybody became such good friends,' Rod told me.

There'd be maybe six on a touring team, we'd all be together – Emerson, Anderson, Cooper and that group – practising, travelling and then they'd face each other in competitions. If someone was having a problem with their serve, Anderson would pop up and say you're not throwing the ball high enough. They'd help each other. That was the unique camaraderie we had back in those years. It's outlawed these days. Now it's a case of, don't tell your opponents your problems!

The Juniors of Today

I had a wonderful life as a junior, competing for my school and county and as an individual all around Britain, making friends that have lasted a lifetime. I really looked forward to seeing the boys' and girls' singles competitors in action in the second week of Wimbledon 2023 – again, an aspect of the tournament I never had time to immerse myself in when I was hosting the BBC coverage. Those matches are where you see the hunger and the raw talent, and where you can spot the potential stars of the future – the kids who have the drive and the skill but who also deal well with knockbacks, such as ambitious shots that don't quite land. You still see that youthful, unbridled showmanship in Alcaraz, even though he's 20 years old and a two-time Grand Slam champion. These youngsters are driven to win, but also to impress. Those qualities are what make junior tennis fun to watch. I love observing the players' on-court mannerisms, and working out who their heroes are. The clenched fists, the tension-releasing screams, the admonishing thigh slaps, the anguished glances towards their coach or parent: all of the theatrics of the young imitating their seasoned professional role models. I well remember once venting my frustration in tune, I thought, with Billie Jean's brand of competitive self-admonishment – and it did not go down well with the crusty colonel who was referee at that particular junior event!

Watching juniors takes me right back down memory lane. I entered the junior girls' singles at Wimbledon in 1973 and 1974. The thrill of arriving at the gates as a bona fide competitor – with matches scheduled in the same order of play as the second week of the main draw competitions – was a jolt of confidence in itself. At my first attempt, I was beaten by my future doubles partner Ann Kiyomura in the quarter-finals – that's where we met and became friends – and she went on to beat a certain Martina Navratilova in the final. In the following year, I was knocked out at the semi-final stage by Mima Jaušovec, whose name went up on the honours board after she beat Mariana Simionescu in the 1974 girls' singles final (Mariana, famously, was Björn Borg's girlfriend and would marry him in 1980). Entering the girls' singles in 1973 was a continuation of my path: I'd first travelled to the All England Club as a 13-year-old playing in the Marist Convent team in the national schools event, competing for the Aberdare Cup. Our little school in Devon won it for four consecutive years from 1969 to 1972, cheered on by our very own barmy army of nuns in black habits and swinging rosary beads. I also competed as an individual in the junior national championships. Both these grass-roots competitions were staged on the long-gone red shale courts in the south of the grounds – close to the new Southern Village spectator area, which now gets dressed up for Wimbledon with striped deck chairs, a large TV screen and a food stall selling prosciutto, artichoke and pimento pepper pizza. And I was grateful for those opportunities to familiarise myself with playing tennis in the most prestigious club of them all, and to take confidence from that. I thought to myself, if I'm good enough to play at Wimbledon, I'm good enough to have a shot of making a career of it.

The game is so established now that there can be a big future for the best young players out there, but there are so many of them coming up through the ranks from all over the world – all amazing athletes with technically sound games. But do they all have the hunger to make the breakthrough, and then maintain it? You see very, very few late bloomers. As Australian player Lleyton Hewitt once said, 'If you stay on the Challenger circuit more than three years, you'll never get out.' Ultimately, it's about the mental side of the game. The players who break through the ranks have a mental strength that does not allow self-doubt. I didn't have the same intensity of mental strength as Billie Jean, Chrissie and Martina; the belief to keep going, chasing major titles year after year, without negativity creeping in. All the greatest champions have that psychological resilience – Roger, Rafa, Novak, Andy Murray, Venus, Serena. It will be interesting to observe Coco Gauff now that she finally has a Grand Slam title under her belt, four years after she burst into the reckoning at Wimbledon in 2019 – her win in 2023 at the US Open makes her the 19th different winner of the women's singles in the last 32 Grand Slams. She didn't get further than the quarter-finals in the Wimbledon girls' singles on her debut in 2018, but followed up a year later by becoming the youngest player to reach the main draw via the qualifiers, and then reached the fourth round, upsetting her role model Venus Williams on the way.

On the first court of juniors I walked past in 2023, I saw two man-mountains! These kids of 16 years old are six foot four inches and look like they should be in the main draw. I was visualising the scrawny junior I had been, but you'd be pushed to find a difference between this current crop of young-sters and the 20-year-olds on the tour. This certainly wasn't the case in my day. I watched two 14-year-old British girls playing their third-round matches on adjacent courts: Hannah Klugman against Sayaka Ishii of Japan, and Mingge Xu against Nikola Bartunkova, yet another talent from the Czech Republic. Both Hannah and Mingge Xu sadly lost. In the boys', Henry Searle's feat had the home crowd cheering as he became the first British boys' singles champion at Wimbledon since Stanley Matthews, son of the England footballer, in 1962. John Lloyd said Henry was serving as hard as the pros.

I always have to temper my enthusiasm for British junior achievements on grass with the fact that juniors from other nations have little, if any, experience of playing on the surface. But there are certainly some promising talents in the ranks. Hannah, Mingge Xu and co can take encouragement from the fact that winning the junior singles title at Wimbledon has never been a reliable indicator of being crowned a future senior cham-pion on Centre Court. I joined the tour in 1973 and saw only Pat Cash, Stefan Edberg and Roger Federer do the double (though Borg had won the boys' singles in 1972). On the girls' side, only Martina Hingis, Amélie Mauresmo and Ash Barty consoli-dated their junior success by holding up the Venus Rosewater Dish. But there are plenty of other notable junior Wimbledon champions who went on to become champions of other Grand Slams – notably Ivan Lendl, Tracy Austin, Jeļena Ostapenko and Caroline Wozniacki – or enjoy lucrative careers as Top 10 pros, such as Grigor Dimitrov, Gaël Monfils and Denis Shapovalov.

Nevertheless, they will all claim their taste of early success on the Wimbledon grass as a career highlight.

Evonne

It seems extraordinary that even in an era before cheap air travel, Wimbledon – a pocket of grass courts in a leafy corner of affluent southwest London – was known and revered as the best tennis tournament in the world, the place where champions are made and history created, the place in the sights of every young player with ambition. Past Wimbledon champions include not only Rod Laver, but his compatriot Evonne Goolagong, the daughter of a sheep farmer, and one of eight children in the only Indigenous family in a small town called Barellan in New South Wales. I played against Evonne in 1971 at the age of 15, when Mr Roberts, my coach, organised the Dewar Cup competition at the Palace Hotel in Torquay, and fixed the draw to blood his young charges with experience against the best. Even though we were playing on my home courts, I was overawed by Evonne's aura, and won just one game. She had turned up in Devon in a glamorous fur coat, every inch the reigning Wimbledon champion, and we were all wowed by her star presence.

Yet Evonne's journey started when she read about a magical tennis court in a princess magazine. When she learnt that this fantasy venue called Wimbledon actually existed, it fired her passion to play there. She honed her skills, hitting balls against the wall, a water tank, an apple crate board. Opportunities were scarce for Indigenous people in rural Australia in the 1960s, but everyone could see Evonne's natural talent, her fluidity with the racket, and her standout skill inspired the local community to nurture her. She was sent to Sydney to receive coaching, arriving there with a dress made by her mother from bed-sheets and equipment funded by locals in her home town. By the time she arrived at Wimbledon in 1970, she was heralded as 'La Belle Evonne', a special talent who was put straight on to the show courts. To complete the fairy tale, a year later she was back, wearing a bespoke Ted Tinling scallop-edged dress, and won her first Wimbledon singles title by beating defending champion Margaret Court in straight sets. And perhaps bought a fur coat with her prize money!

Similarly, Rod was 17 when he first walked through the gates at Wimbledon, on a trip funded by the Australian Association. 'I was in awe of the place,' he said, and he must have had a tremendous sense of arrival after a journey from Australia to Europe on a Super Constellation plane that took three days and two nights. 'There was an eight-hour ride to Singapore, where we'd stop at the Raffles Hotel, because the pilots had to rest. From there, we'd fly to Karachi, in Pakistan, again to rest the pilots, and the next day continue on to Europe,' Rod said. 'There'd be maybe 50 of us on the plane; we all knew each other. It was an adventure. We were just excited to be staying at Raffles, and getting to Rome and planning trips to see the Colosseum. And on to London for Wimbledon. The thrill of the journey itself was always there.'

On the last stop of that round-the-tennis-world trip, Rod competed in the Pacific Southwest Championships in California on his way back to Australia. It was clear he had been noted as an up-and-coming star of the future. Billie Jean King told me that she attended the same event at the Los Angeles Tennis Club that year, when she was only 12 years old. 'I asked everyone, "Who should I see?",' she said. 'They all directed me to a faraway side court. That's the first time I saw Rod Laver, then only 17.' I love that picture of two young players, one future great of the game clocking another, both with dreams of Centre Court glory...

The Rocket at Wimbledon

In 1959, at the age of 21, Rod reached all three finals at Wimbledon, winning the mixed doubles title with American player Darlene Hard. As an unseeded player, he lost the singles final to Peruvian Alex Olmedo; playing with Bob Mark, he lost to Roy Emerson and Neale Fraser, 8–6, 6–3, 14–16, 9–7 (a score that screeches entertainment). His first Wimbledon singles title came in 1961, when he beat Chuck McKinley, an American college sophomore from St Louis, Missouri, who had the habit of screaming, 'Oh Charley, you missed that one,' after every bad shot!

Having been in the men's final two years previously (losing to Olmedo and then his compatriot Fraser in 1960), it was third time lucky for Rod. 'It was a walloping!' he said. 'Three sets, 55 minutes, Fred Perry was timing it at the side of the court and it was one of the quickest finals Wimbledon had ever seen.' Rod said he found it hard to absorb the importance of winning his first title, but mostly he remembers

the thrill of being able to go out in front of a packed audience and feel like you can play the game, and not be so nervous that you think, *God, how am I going to do this?* I had a few butterflies getting onto the court, but as soon as I got there my concentration level increased, my nerves went away and I played some of my best tennis. That was the best thing that happened to me – to play my game without my nerves being a factor and enjoy the thrill of winning my first Wimbledon. And the next time I played, I thought 'I'm a better player … I got there.'

His butterflies returned as soon as he left the court. The prospect of the Wimbledon Ball loomed. Unlike the other Grand Slams, Wimbledon had traditions and formality: the Royal Box, which required bowing and curtsying protocol; bouquets of flowers brought on court for the ladies' singles finalists; and the end-of-tournament ball held at the Grosvenor House Hotel in Park Lane. It was customary for the men's and women's champions to start the dancing, and the prospect of this floored Rod. He had never stepped in a ballroom in his life. He could quickstep his way around a tennis court, but he couldn't put on a tuxedo and morph into Fred Astaire on a dancefloor.

Angela Mortimer – a fellow Devonian, 24 years my senior, who was also trained at the Palace Hotel in Torquay by Arthur Roberts – once told me about being 'pounced upon' by Rod that year. As the newly crowned ladies' champion, she would be Rod's dance partner. She had had a whirlwind change out of her tennis kit and into her black-tie outfit and had been hoping for a quiet moment to check her dress and make-up when she got to Grosvenor House. Instead, she was confronted by a distressed Rod.

'Mort – thank goodness you're here,' he exclaimed. 'Mort, I can't dance. We have to start off the ball, and I can't dance a step. What can we do?'

As Angela tells the story in her book, *My Waiting Game*, she suggested they could request a waltz, on the grounds that it's an easy dance and surely he could do a waltz. 'I *can't* do a waltz. And I can't begin learning now. Mort, whatever are we going to do?'

Angela sent him across to the band, hoping they would come up with something to reassure him. He came charging back towards her, with a cheeky grin. 'Okay, Mort, there's no need to worry. It's all settled. We're beginning with a quickstep. They tell me that is just walking round the floor – and I think I can manage that...'

But the ordeal wasn't over yet. 'At last the first chords of the evening's music struck up and I felt Rod's hand gripping me tensely,' Angela recalled.

I was relieved once we were underway and dancing slowly round the ballroom. At least, now we had begun, I felt sure Rod must have his nerves under control. I was quite enjoying myself until I heard him whisper despairingly in my ear: 'This is rather a long floor, isn't it?' Steadily we plodded on, while Rod went through an ordeal which to him seemed a hundred times worse than his Wimbledon final.

Rod went on to win four men's singles titles – 1961, 1962, 1968 and 1969. In 1962, his second Wimbledon title helped earn him the first of his two Grand Slams – claiming all four majors in one calendar year. 'I almost burst with pride when I beat Martin Mulligan to win my second Wimbledon singles title and was presented with the trophy by Queen Elizabeth II,' he recalled in his autobiography. 'By now a Wimbledon veteran, I had perfected my bow and was no longer a bundle of nerves.' And by 1969, he had mastered the ceremonial dance at the Wimbledon Ball, doing a relaxed foxtrot to 'Fly Me to the Moon' with Ann Haydon-Jones at the Grosvenor House. 'I wasn't too worried, I just didn't want to stand on Ann's toes,' he told me with a grin.

A Shared Bond

The aforementioned quickstepping Angela Mortimer and her wonderful husband John Barrett, a former player and distinguished commentator, are two of my favourite people in tennis. They're both now in their early nineties and it's always a joy to see them every year at Wimbledon. John Barrett helped me so much with my broadcasting career, I first worked with him for Channel 7 in Australia in the late 1980s, then with BSkyB and the BBC. He is one of the most thoughtful, generous broadcasters and is hugely respected for his commentaries, which were always firm but fair.

I obviously didn't get to see Angela win her Wimbledon title because I was only five years old when she beat fellow Brit Christine Truman and our family didn't have a television. I didn't ever get the chance to watch her play, because she was a generation older than me, but Mr Roberts always used her as an example of a determined fighter on court, someone who simply refused to lose. He said that (a bit like me) she wasn't the most talented player, but her strengths elsewhere made her exceptional; to have her become crowned a Wimbledon champion I know made him so proud. I wish I'd been able to do the same.

At Wimbledon in 2023, there was an old video feature going around on social media of me at 15 years old playing Evonne Goolagong in the Dewar Cup at the Palace Hotel in Torquay. The footage included me being interviewed by Angela Rippon, who also spoke to Mr Roberts. When I watched it, I was in floods of tears, as it was the first time I'd heard his voice since the mid-1980s, just before he died. I have no videos of him so I had forgotten what he sounded like. When I saw Angela Mortimer at The Championships this year in the Members' Lounge I went up to her and, as always, gave her a big hug. As pupils of Mr Roberts, we have a special bond. I got out my phone to show her the interview with Arthur. As I was trying to find it, I told her I hadn't heard his voice for 40 years and she said it was more like 50 or 60 years for her. We both became very emotional and smiled at some of the things he was saying about dedication, what he expected from his students and one of his favourite subjects … keeping boys away from us so we wouldn't be distracted. I emailed the video to Angela and she and John watched it that night on their computer in the peace and quiet of their home. It was even more emotional for her. I'm sure, like me, she has watched it many times since.

The Story behind Wimbledon as We Know It

Rod Laver's 1962 Grand Slam feat came on top of winning the Italian and German titles and, back in Brisbane, helping Australia win the Davis Cup, defeating Mexico 5–0, by winning both his singles matches and the doubles with Roy Emerson. He achieved all this as a globe-trotting amateur, trying to make ends meet and cover his expenses as he travelled from tournament to tournament. Amateur rules meant competitors could earn only US$300 per tournament, and, from that, had to pay their accommodation, meals and travel expenses. It could never add up to a sustainable way to earn a living. There was no financial reward, only the bonus of being able to see the world and the sporting satisfaction of beating your rivals. 'I won Wimbledon in 1961 and 1962 and got a £10 voucher and a firm handshake,' he told me.

> I wasn't allowed to cash in the voucher, otherwise I would have turned pro, so I went to Lillywhites and got a shirt, I think. The prize money got you from A to B, and then the next tournament would get you from B to C. If you came home with anything more in your pocket, you were doing well. Not that you were doing well. But you'd survive.

At the end of his remarkable year in 1962, Rod turned professional. He was 24. In doing so, he disqualified himself from the Grand Slam tournaments, which were played under amateur regulations. For five seasons, while in his prime, he played exhibition matches on the fledgling professional tennis circuit promoted by Jack Kramer. 'I just wanted the chance to play against the best players in the world, and that's why I turned pro, plus the financial remunerations were an important part of tennis back in those days,' he said. 'I signed for US$110,000 for three years. To me, that seemed like a good contract.' Having accepted Kramer's offer, he spent those years showcasing his skills on portable canvas courts rolled out in sports stadiums, concert halls, even bullrings and ice rinks, while the amateurs continued to play on the hallowed courts of Roland-Garros, Wimbledon and Forest Hills.

Despite the financial soft-cushioning, it can't have been an easy decision to forgo playing at Wimbledon, the event he described as 'my most favourite tournament. Ever.' When I spoke to Rod about this phase of his career, he was philosophical. 'I had to tell myself I had moved on from amateur tennis. That life was gone, I was now a professional. I had to realise that was the end of the line when it came to Wimbledon,' he said.

> I told myself I'd had a great time in the amateur world but now I'm a pro, and I have a good chance of a secure future by playing with Lew Hoad, Ken Rosewall, Pancho Gonzales and Frank Sedgman, who had already been wooed away. It was a risky decision but I was prepared to do whatever it took. Life changes – you've got to think about your future and your responsibilities. Back in those days, tournament organisers seemed to think the players could just travel around and not

ever have any need for money. It doesn't work that way. I decided that I had no option. If I wanted to carry on playing tennis, I had to turn professional.

When I spoke to Rod for the documentary *Our Wimbledon*, I was curious to find out how he had coped during that period. It seems to everyone that these were five lost years – five years when crowds missed out on watching him, and he missed out on collecting more Grand Slam titles. Was it really so enjoyable on the fledgling pro circuit? Rod confessed to mixed feelings:

I did miss being able to go to Wimbledon and to play at the Australian, but at the same time it was a chance to become a better player and make some dollars. I look back at it and think, I was just an ordinary player when it came to working out how I was going to beat Hoad and Rosewall [who had signed up for Kramer's pro tour five years earlier, in 1957]. They volleyed deeper and faster, they didn't miss a first serve. I learnt a lot from the way they conducted their game. All of a sudden, I'm having to think [more tactically]. But I was lucky. I had a great amateur career, and turning professional enabled me to keep competing. My best years were still ahead of me. And when I came back to the amateur/Open world in 1968, I was a different player. Emerson said, 'I used to be able to knock that second serve of yours around, you're nearly serving aces with it now.' I had to grow up pretty quick on the professional circuit.

To all the tennis fans who flocked to Centre Court, Rod's star quality was sorely missed. In 1962 the dazzling dominance of Rod and Billie Jean King and Margaret Court attracted attendances of more than 275,000 over the course of the fortnight. Each day's action was broadcast live on the BBC; tennis players were household names. To this day, people reminisce about their memories of Rod's distinctive style and mannerisms, the ferocious backhand topspin drives he'd direct down the line or cross-court, his forehand on the run, the occasional self-admonishing slap on his thigh after an error. His continued absence eventually prompted the then chairman of the All England Club, Herman David, to organise a one-off televised professional event after the 1967 Championships – the year of the BBC's first colour broadcasts from Wimbledon. 'We [the pros] used to play a big tournament at Wembley Empire Pool,' Rod recalled.

We were out there for years, playing tournaments. Herman came out to watch in 1966 and said, 'Why do I have to come to the Wembley Empire to watch Laver play?' He came to the decision – next year, he said, he wanted to organise a pro Wimbledon, two months after the amateur Wimbledon. He said, 'You guys get your best eight grass-court players and we'll play on the Wimbledon Centre Court,' and that was the beginning of it ... The place was packed out for the last three days. I played Rosewall in the final. Afterwards Herman said, 'You're invited to play in next year's Wimbledon.'

Herman David's experimental pro event was so successful that the club announced that in future the annual fortnight would be open to all players. Everyone could compete. The 1968 Championships was the first to offer prize money: a total of £26,150 – the winner of the men's title earned £2,000 while the women's singles champion earned £750. 'That's the short story; Herman David got the ball rolling,' Rod said.

> I know the Australian, French and US Grand Slam organisers weren't too amused but they came to a point when they all said, 'Why don't we have Open tennis?' I was just thrilled that in 1968 I'd be able to get back to Wimbledon, along with Rosewall and the players that were in that top group: Gonzales, Hoad, Rosewall, Fred Stolle, Dennis Ralston, myself, and Butch Buchholz.

It was Rod who made Wimbledon as we know it possible. His star appeal was the catalyst. That small cohort of professionals were the trailblazers, but Rod also emphasised the brave stance taken by Herman David in his role at the helm of the All England Club. David, a former British Davis Cup player who famously served with his left hand and played with his right hand, was tennis through and through, and had always advocated open tennis. 'Wimbledon, they created Open Tennis,' Rod stated. 'The idea was vetoed two or three times earlier by the ITF [International Tennis Federation], but for Herman David to go at it alone and make it happen, it's been the greatest thing. And then, being at Wimbledon in 1968 was a great feeling.'

Billie Jean told a story in her recent book, *All In* (2021), that illustrates the emotional impact of the 1968 Championships, when all former champions had their membership reinstated. 'Laver was playing Wimbledon for the first time since he'd been suspended six years earlier for turning pro on one of Kramer's tours,' she wrote.

> Though Rod won his third Wimbledon title by beating Tony Roche the day after I beat Judy [Tegart], he said he actually felt the proudest on the opening day of the tournament ... Rod said when he captured his first Wimbledon title in 1961 he received an All England Club tie, the same as all the men's winners did then. When he turned pro two years later, he received a stern letter from the All England Club ordering him never to wear the tie again. He'd been banished ... 'I took enormous satisfaction from dragging out my old purple and green Wimbledon tie that had been ceremoniously yanked from my neck, and putting it on,' Laver said after he won the 1968 title, adding that he wasn't the only former champion who felt that way. Thirteen former winners in the men's field had returned to Wimbledon now that it was open to all.

Thanks to Roger and Rafa and Novak and their incredible accumulation of major titles, there is an emphasis now on record numbers of Grand Slam wins and a debate about who is the Greatest of All Time. When I spoke to Rod, I wondered if there was a part of him that muses on 'what could have been' if he hadn't missed those five years – potentially 20 more Grand Slam titles. He was sanguine and typically self-deprecating: 'Once you accept a position, as I did, there's no going back. People say you might have won a couple more but you're thinking about who's in the draw with you – you've got them all. What could have been, what if, it doesn't register too much.'

Heroes Are Fans Too

Rod Laver regularly returns to Wimbledon, even now in his mid-eighties. The camera picks him out – this tiny, elderly, cheery man in the Royal Box – and as a broadcaster I always wanted to introduce him to new fans of tennis and remind people of his remarkable influence on Wimbledon. He was a guest of honour to mark the opening of the new No.1 Court in 1997 and at various champions' parades. As the applause he received from fellow players and the crowd at the Centre Court Centenary celebrations in 2022 showed, he is revered by every champion and player, past and present. Three years into the Open Era, he became the first player to earn more than US$1 million in prize money, showing players that they could earn a good living as entertainers in the sport they loved. He's treasured not just for his magical shotmaking and preeminence as a two-time winner of a calendar Grand Slam. And it's worth repeating that this is a feat that has never been equalled once, even by Novak Djokovic (who has held all four titles in 2015 to 2016, but not in a calendar year, and has four times won three out of four in a year – in 2011, 2015, 2021 and 2023 – but never quite clinched it in a single season). The Rocket is loved by the tennis world for his humility, his sportsmanlike example and his heartfelt encouragement of juniors – as I was lucky enough to experience myself – and of the game's leading players.

Everyone looks up to him: John McEnroe leads a cohort of fellow lefties; Sampras and Agassi cite him as their inspiration; Federer cried on his shoulder when Rod presented him with the trophy for winning the 2006 Australian Open. That hero-fan cycle is so important. Rod himself idolised Frank Sedgman, Lew Hoad, Ashley Cooper and Mal Anderson – 'you look at the past champions, they were the ones that I idolised and wanted to compete with,' he says.

It's a dynamic that Wimbledon showcases so well by inviting back its former champions. All the greats remember being fans too. Björn Borg told me how, in 1972, he rushed from winning his Wimbledon junior final to watch Ilie Năstase take on Stan Smith in the men's final. 'I beat Buster Mottram in the final,' Borg said.

And the funny thing was that, that same morning, Ilie had asked me if I could practise with him. I was so nervous because he wanted to hit before he's going to play the Wimbledon final. Buster and I were playing on Court 2 and we finished in three sets, and all the time we were playing, I was looking at the giant score-board to see the score between Ilie and Stan Smith. The minute we finished the junior final I just ran to Centre

Court. Lucky enough, it was 1–1 in the fifth set between Smith and Năstase so I could see the decider. That was an amazing final, awesome, amazing fun.

Roger Federer has talked about the 'surreal' experience of making his Centre Court debut in 2001 against Pete Sampras, his absolute hero, then a record seven-time Wimbledon champion aiming to be the first man ever to win eight titles. Roger was 19; he wore his hair in a ponytail with a bandana and sported a wooden-bead necklace when he took on 'Mr Invincible' on grass. The balls were rolled out to signal the start of the warm-up, and when Sampras hit the first ball back to him, Roger started chuckling. He just couldn't believe he was on Centre Court with his hero. It was a fourth-round match but Roger showed no sign of nerves – he quashed his role model's dreams, winning 7–6, 5–7, 6–4, 6–7, 7–5 in an epic match. A newcomer on Centre Court, overcome with emotion, he needed a prompt from his hero, the defeated Sampras, to bow to the Royal Box when they made their exit. Remarkably, Federer would break Sampras's record by claiming an eighth Wimbledon title in 2017. And eight years earlier, when he was poised to surpass Sampras's then record of 14 Grand Slam titles, the American returned to Wimbledon in 2009 to witness the triumph that got Federer to 15. 'I want to be there when Federer breaks my record. I want to see it, I want to feel it,' Sampras said in the spirit of respect between great champions. When I had my private chat with Roger during our rain-stopped interview last summer, I said that I wished Pete would come back to Wimbledon again. Roger then revealed that he had personally asked him to come over in 2009, and he suggested maybe I should ask him again. What a fabulous idea, and how cool it would be to see them sitting together watching tennis. (I'd love to bag the seat next door but I think I'm a long way down the queue for that treat!) Roger said he was going to make it happen, so let's watch this space...

Billie Jean, ever the historian, likes to say, 'Wimbledon is a continuum, to cherish and honour.' Time will tell how Coco Gauff's similar experience in beating her role model will pan out. At Wimbledon 2019, she beat Venus Williams – 24 years and five singles titles her senior – but has never made it further on the grass than the fourth round, though she is a Roland-Garros finalist and the 2023 US Open champion.

But the hero-fan cycle is evident on court at every Wimbledon. There is so much respect for the great players of the past. Ash Barty opened her 2021 campaign wearing a distinctive scallop-hemmed 'Trailblazer' dress that was designed to commemorate the 50th anniversary of Evonne Goolagong's first Wimbledon singles title in 1971, when the carefree 19-year-old emphatically beat defending champion Margaret Court in straight sets. Ted Tinling dressed Evonne and his creations for her often featured scallop edging. Like Evonne, who is Wiradjuri, Barty describes herself as 'a proud Ngarigo woman', and she often talked about her shared heritage with her seven-time-Grand-Slam-winner role model, and their mutual support for Indigenous communities across Australia. Wearing a dress modelled on that of her all-time hero, Barty pulled off her own fairy tale, defeating Karolína Plíšková to become the first Australian woman to win the title since Evonne's second Wimbledon victory in 1980. After her triumph, Barty said: 'For me to be able to wear an outfit inspired by her iconic scallop dress, an image that inspired me and our generation of Indigenous youth, is amazing. I hope that my version of it, my outfit, can do the same for the next generation of Indigenous youth coming forward.'

Stars and Tennis

Rod Laver's star allure also helped to take tennis beyond the sport. In that very first trip to California, when he was clocked by the 12-year-old Billie Jean, he was also watched by film stars such as John Wayne. The star of the Westerns that were so popular in the 1940s, '50s and '60s was a keen tennis player; he founded the John Wayne Tennis Club (now the Palisades Tennis Club) in Newport Beach, California, where I trained when I moved there on turning pro in 1973. Other screen luminaries such as the singer and actress Dinah Shore and leading men Charlton Heston, Burt Lancaster and Kirk Douglas all played tennis and mingled with the top players based in sunny Southern California. As Rod said, 'It was such a great time back in those years, knowing those people, getting to know Frank Sinatra. It was a golden era for all of us back then, tennis and entertainment.'

Friendships between the leading men of the silver screen and sport were genuine. As tension mounted before the US Open in 1969, when Rod had won the Australian and French Opens as well as Wimbledon, and was on track for his second Grand Slam, Charlton Heston invited him to stay in his luxurious penthouse at the top of a skyscraper on Manhattan's East Side. 'Charlton had a big place in New York. He said, "Take it; use it, that's your headquarters."' So Rod happily settled into the film star's Tudor City apartment, taking refuge from the frenzy of the tennis world, which was descending upon Forest Hills to see if he could pull off a remarkable second Grand Slam. With a fridge stocked with steak, eggs, fresh orange juice and beer, he was well set up. In Rod's autobiography, he reveals that during the tournament he and his Kiwi friend John McDonald would have friends over for dinner and drinks, 'or just hang out watching TV or listening to Aretha Franklin, Dave Brubeck and José Feliciano records while I wound and unwound the grips on my racquets, the closest thing I had to a nervous tic'. Naturally, there was a big champagne party in the penthouse after he had won. Rod paid tribute to Heston's role in his accomplishment: 'Chuck was renowned for his heroic roles as Ben Hur, Moses and General Charles Gordon, and his generosity in '69 made him a hero to me.'

In fact, the link with Hollywood stretches back to Wimbledon's own three-time champion Fred Perry, the benchmark for British men until Andy Murray took on that mantle in 2013. Perry was raised in Stockport, in the north of England, but after turning professional in 1936 he travelled around the United States in a head-to-head touring contest against Ellsworth Vines. 'Perry was a handsome man with a superb physique, and in America he had Hollywood starlets falling at his feet,' writes Richard Jones in *The People's Wimbledon* (2021). 'He married one – Helen Vinson – and in 1937 he and

Vines invested some of their profits from their tour by buying the Beverly Hills Tennis Club. The link between tennis and Hollywood was thus firmly cemented.'

The two worlds have been inextricably linked ever since Perry's playing days – I remember playing Chrissie Evert in the 1977 Virginia Slims Championships final in front of a crowd of 11,651 in Madison Square Garden and she had Burt Reynolds sitting courtside in her camp of supporters. And just look at the celebrities today who flock to Wimbledon each year: recently we've seen Hugh Grant, Emma Watson, Benedict Cumberbatch, Idris Elba, Lin-Manuel Miranda, Bradley Cooper, Gerard Butler and, of course, Sir Ian McKellen, to name a few. They were very useful to us in the BBC studio during the long rain delays, when it was a struggle to fill airtime with something fresh, rather than resorting to re-runs of classic matches. My producer would be running all over the grounds asking celebrities to come and join me in the studio for a chat.

Sometimes the production team got desperate. On one very wet Wimbledon we were discussing how we might close BBC One at six o'clock when one bright spark in the office suggested we play Morecambe and Wise's closing song 'Bring Me Sunshine' and that Mac and I could then skip off Centre Court in true Eric and Ernie style. I must have been tired after a tough day as I agreed to do it. Down I went to Centre Court to interview Mac to close BBC One. While we aired the highlights of the day – very short, thanks to the weather – I asked Mac if he'd ever seen Eric and Ernie's show or knew how they closed it. To my surprise, he said yes, and he was well up for doing the dance.

Mac is always up for anything like that, he likes having fun. So to the delight of the patient, rain-soaked Centre Court crowd, Mac and I sang a couple of lines of 'Bring Me Sunshine' and then skipped off Centre Court. It made the papers, needless to say!

Most memorably, there was the year I took 007 hostage. Pierce Brosnan, who played James Bond from 1995 to 2002 in *GoldenEye*, *Tomorrow Never Dies*, *The World Is Not Enough* and *Die Another Day*, had been spotted suited and booted as a guest in the Royal Box. Unfortunately, it was a day of incessant rain – always a challenge for the BBC team to fill that length of a live-coverage schedule with studio chitchat. By 3pm, we'd run out of pundits to invite in for a chat. Someone suggested Pierce. *Brilliant*, I thought. That would end the day's BBC One coverage on a high. Somehow we managed to get a message to a Club member in the Royal Box, who asked Pierce if he could help us out, and he gamely agreed. Almost like a scene from a Bond film, he ran from the Royal Box, out of the Clubhouse doors, round the corner and up the steps alongside the Press Centre to reach the Broadcast Centre, and then up more flights of stairs to our BBC studio. We quickly got him miked up and sat him under the lights ready to go. He was fantastic, but his tennis knowledge was not extensive enough to fill the half an hour or so. And the studio was hot. While I was faffing about asking him questions about his visit to London, his life in California, his spell on the hit TV show *Remington Steele*, he started to sweat profusely. When we went to a quick VT (video clip), one of the team would dash over and dab his face with tissues, but then bits of tissue would get stuck on his face. After

20 minutes he said he needed to go – he couldn't bear the heat a minute longer.

'I'm sorry, Pierce,' I said. 'I can't let you go. We have another 10 minutes to fill. You can't leave me. I've got no one else to talk to.' He was a trooper and stayed. He got 10 out of 10 for bailing me out. Talk about Die Another Day.

The Rocket's Review

The Rocket has often returned to Wimbledon since he played his last competitive match on Centre Court in 1977, and what's so inspiring is that his feelings for the place have not dimmed. 'The Centre Court at Wimbledon, there's only one,' he reminisced with me.

> The atmosphere when you're watching a match, when the action is so close to the 14,000 seats around the court. The knowledge of the spectators is so much more accurate than at other places. They know who's playing, the history behind it, they applaud at the right times. Sometimes back in '69, the linesmen and umpires were a little older than they are now so their eyes didn't help them, but all of Wimbledon is a history book. It's grown in size, it's got the roof, but when you walk onto the court, or just watch a match from a seat, it's still exactly the same. It's still the best tournament. Ever.

2

BILLIE JEAN KING

Still Trailblazing

Like Rod Laver, Billie Jean King's Wimbledon story is a tale of two worlds. As a feisty competitor, she won an incredible 20 Wimbledon titles between 1961 and 1979 – aged 17 through to 35 – six in singles, ten in women's doubles and four in mixed doubles. As a redoubtable campaigner, she helped create the women's tour and fought for equal prize money. I've always admired the fact that she fought for equality right through the ranks, even lobbying the All England Club to allow girls to have the opportunity to be ball girls. Wimbledon introduced ball girls in 1977 and mixed teams in 1980. In 1986 ball girls were finally deployed on Centre Court for the first time. She never gave up.

Billie Jean grew up playing on the free courts in Southern California; her father was a firefighter, her mother a homemaker, and they didn't own a television. All she knew about

Wimbledon, she learnt from books. By her bed, she had books about Althea Gibson – the dignified African American player who won five titles at Wimbledon, two singles (1957, 1958) and three doubles (1956, 1957 and 1958). She devoured *Tennis with Hart*, by Doris Hart, who in the 1940s and '50s reached 67 Grand Slam finals and won 35 titles, and was notable for the rare feat of winning at least one title in singles, doubles and mixed doubles at all four Grand Slam events. She read *Use Your Head in Tennis* by Bob Harman. As she told me when I chatted to her for the documentary, 'I read everything. I loved the history. I knew every champion in singles, doubles and mixed from 1877 or whenever the Wimbledon Championships started. I always wanted to be somebody.'

She hadn't actually heard of tennis, let alone Wimbledon, until Susan Williams, a girl in her fifth-grade class, asked her if she played, and she replied, 'What's tennis?' She knew about professional team sports (her younger brother Randy Moffitt went on to have a career in baseball, as a pitcher for the San Francisco Giants, among other teams). Once introduced to tennis, though, she told me she knew it was her destiny.

> When I embrace something, that's it. When I was 12, I had an epiphany that I wanted to fight for equality for the rest of my life and I knew tennis was the platform. At university, I'd take a tennis ball and go to the library and just stare at it, just envisioning what I wanted the future of our sport to look like. Not only our sport, but the world.

The Long Beach tennis community wanted to send her to Wimbledon when she was 15, but she said no. She thought she wasn't good enough. 'I didn't feel I'd developed well enough and earned the opportunity,' she explained. When she was 17, the offer was there again. That was 1961, when Karen Hantze Susman asked her to partner her in doubles. 'I thought I'd gone to heaven because Karen was just head and shoulders above me, just amazing.' On arrival at the All England Club, Gerry Williams, a tennis writer with the *Daily Mail*, took Billie Jean to Centre Court. 'He had me close my eyes,' she remembers.

> He takes me up a ramp and then he says, 'Now you can open your eyes.' I open my eyes and see the clock with Roman numerals diagonally across. I loved that old clock. I loved the intimacy. I loved the symmetry. This was the place I'd been dreaming about for at least seven years of my 17-year-old life and I immediately fell in love with it. The way Gerry introduced me to it, I'll never forget. That was special.

Billie's first singles match against fifth seed Yola Ramírez from Mexico was played over two days on Centre Court. Only Billie Jean would find a silver lining in an overnight rain delay on a Wimbledon debut!

> We got out, and we split sets, and then it rained, surprise, surprise. Yola didn't know how to play me because we'd never met before, but that night she talked to people

and she killed me the next day. But I look back and I had two days of singles on that Centre Court! I think that's extraordinary – my first experience ever on a court at Wimbledon.

Her reminiscence reminded me of my first match on Centre in 1976, against Maria Bueno – a scheduling I learnt mid-mouthful at breakfast in the Mottram family's Wimbledon home. (I couldn't afford the Gloucester Hotel that most of the players stayed at, so I lodged with my friends and fellow junior players Linda and Buster, whom Björn Borg beat in the 1972 Wimbledon boys' singles final). Billie used to think of the great champions who had played there before and the champions of the future, she relished the history of the place; I just wanted to get off court without embarrassing myself! When I first heard I was playing on Centre Court I immediately felt a little sick. I guess I didn't want to play badly. I didn't want to let the crowd down, or Mr Roberts, or myself. This was the dream we had been working towards: testing myself against a champion at Wimbledon. Why was I being so negative? Mr Roberts gave me a good talking-to and assured me that my nerves would disappear after a few games. He said I must be positive (easier said than done) and then I did start to get excited … until I thought of the curtsy we had to do to acknowledge the Royal Box. The fear of messing that up caused more anxiety. Never mind my tennis! Being British, I thought I really couldn't mess that up. I practised the curtsy for hours. The last hour before the match felt like five hours, and as the clock ticked down, agonisingly slowly, my nerves ramped up. I was playing against one of the greats. Maria Bueno. She was not only experienced, talented and very familiar with Centre Court, she was much loved by the tennis cognoscenti. I was so nervous walking out alongside her to the cheers of the crowd. When it came to the curtsy, every limb was shaking. I thought I was going to crumple in a heap. I stayed down so low because I couldn't get back up again. It was terrifying, but at least I stayed upright!

I remember feeling that the court suddenly seemed so small as there was so much run-back space behind the baselines. It took me a moment to get my bearings on a court that I had mostly only seen on television. Also there is no getting away from the layers of history that are wrapped around the place. It truly is like no other court – it's special and such an intimate arena. Mr Roberts was right about the nerves. The first few games were dominated by Maria because I was rushing my shots and making silly mistakes. But the butterflies started to ease as I told myself I had earned my place here and I deserved to be playing in the match. My confidence suddenly kicked in. The home support was amazing as the spectators urged me on, applauding my winning strokes, and then I was in this dream zone, where it felt so good to be out there playing well. It was far better than I had ever imagined. It was magical. I will never forget it.

After losing the first set, I began to dominate the match and I was flying! Everything about my game was working, and my love affair with this place was complete as I sealed match point. To beat a legend of the game in my first match out there, well, it doesn't get better than that. Your first match out on Centre

Court can have a lasting effect, particularly if you are British and under the spotlight. The intense scrutiny the home players are under can be overwhelming and hard to deal with. Having been through it myself, I feel for the players of today, but you have to find your own way to deal with all the distractions because you may not get another chance. When you get the opportunity to play in front of the home crowd at Wimbledon, on Centre Court, you have to take your moment and you want to have a success story to remember.

Billie's first match was in the era when players did not sit down at the change of ends. It was only in 1974 that chairs were provided for the changeovers at Wimbledon. Before then we just grabbed a drink from our bags while standing. The older players thought sitting down between games was ridiculous. I remember playing with Ann Haydon-Jones in an exhibition match at Crystal Palace against Virginia Wade and Michelle Tyler. When I went to sit down, Ann said, 'What are you doing?! I don't want to sit down, we've only just started!' I explained that it had been brought in because of ad breaks on American TV, but she still didn't sit. Billie Jean wasn't keen on sitting down either; she never wanted to stop, famously always entering singles, doubles and mixed matches. 'I just love to hit the ball. I love the way it feels, the pure joy of hitting the ball, so if I get three opportunities in three events to hit the ball more often, I have more fun,' she says. 'I also love to collaborate so I preferred doubles over singles. I loved mixed first, then women's doubles, then singles. I took my doubles even more seriously because there's another person involved.'

Ask Billie Jean to nominate a favourite moment at Wimbledon and quick as a flash she says 'the first time winning with Karen'. In that first visit in 1961, she gained international recognition when she, aged 17, and Karen, just 18, both lodging like students with a local landlady, became the youngest pair to win the Wimbledon women's doubles title. With $3 each left from their budget, they couldn't afford to go to the Wimbledon Ball. The legendary tennis writer Bud Collins, then a young reporter from Boston, said he would take them out to toast their achievement. 'Karen and I went with him to a downstairs Italian place in Knightsbridge. I'm sure we had pasta. Bud goes, "Let's get some champagne and celebrate your victory," and Karen and I say, almost in unison, "We don't drink." And he says, "Well, that's great, you're the two cheapest dates I've ever had!"'

Big Collars and Gold Lamé

When I visualise Billie Jean at Wimbledon, I remember her cat-eye glasses and the button-through dresses with big collars, colourful embroidery and matching shorts. And of course the permed hair! The hairstyles we can put down to the prevailing fashions of the time, but the outfits Billie took a keen interest in. I don't remember her being much bothered by what she wore off court, but I know she spent a lot of time thinking about what she'd wear throughout a tournament. She used to sit us down throughout the 1970s and '80s to tell us about the importance of putting on a good show as the women's tour strived to estab-lish itself to potential sponsors to be as big a draw as the men's.

An important aspect of that was that we maintained our individuality in our style of play, but also in how we presented ourselves on court. We needed to think about what would look good on television. Billie actually used to call her opponents the night before a match to discuss what they would both wear – as if they were going to a wedding and didn't want to clash in the photos! She hated the mirror-image kit scenario you see so often today, when players with the same clothing sponsors walk onto court in the same look. For her, it was all about the spectacle. 'It's important to the audience, and the audience is everything,' she'd say. Funnily enough, decades later, she would call me before her appearances in the BBC studio to go through what she would be wearing and make sure we wouldn't clash or be too similar. Ever the professional!

In Ted Tinling, the flamboyant tennis-loving fashion designer, she had a key ally, especially at Wimbledon, where, from 1963, the competitor regulations had outlined a strict dress code. The conditions of entry stated that players must be dressed predominantly in white throughout (this was clarified in 1995 to mean 'almost entirely white'). Pre-1995, the rules gave licence for subtle and colourful decorative touches, especially for the top players who were dressed by Teddy. From Maureen 'Little Mo' Connolly and Doris Hart to Maria Bueno and Evonne Goolagong, his dresses throughout the 1950s, '60s and '70s were synonymous with Wimbledon champions right up to 1979, when Martina Navratilova wore a button-through design with a wide collar and embroidered peacock motifs – a fitting ensemble in which to strut in triumph after winning both the singles and doubles events. In 1983 Billie Jean wore her last Tinling outfit in a final – a white dress with pink embroidery – when she and Steve Denton reached the mixed doubles final. The last Tinling dress seen at Wimbledon was worn by Rosie Casals in 1984.

Being British, I had to wear Fred Perry, but I did get one memorable Tinling dress. Billie, too, started off wearing Fred Perry clothes. 'When Fred gave me four shirts and two skirts with my initials on, that was a big deal, I thought I'd gone to heaven,' she told me.

I knew he'd won three Wimbledons in a row: '34, '35, '36. I saw a bit of old footage. But Gladys Heldman kept telling me I needed to be with Ted. So we got together. Ted called me 'Madame Superstar' and I loved talking fashion with him. He had strong opinions about where tennis should go, its future. He liked innovation. He talked about the different experimental materials he used in his dresses. He always used the latest. We talked about collars or no collars! Margaret [Court]'s collars were the biggest. We always had fun. He was a total character. He loved to gossip. He loved everything. And he let you know it. In a very loud voice.

Having designed her dress for the groundbreaking Battle of the Sexes match in 1973 – in which Billie Jean trounced Bobby Riggs, a former Wimbledon champion, watched on television by 90 million households across the United States – Ted and Billie became close friends. It made sense: both were forward-thinking in their particular missions in tennis: Billie in creating and enhancing the women's tour and Ted in conjuring pretty dresses in cutting-edge new materials that enhanced athleticism. For the exhibition match, played at the Astrodrome in Houston, she wore a modest, pale mint green-and-blue polyester-knit dress with trademark wide collar. It was actually her back-up outfit, as she found the original dress 'too scratchy'. Those experimental fabrics! Typically, on the morning of the match, Ted sewed rhinestones around the neckline so that Billie would glitter under the lights. The match was central to her campaign to underline the skill and professionalism of female athletes. Riggs claimed women's tennis was far inferior to men's. In the run-up, he made a series of totally unacceptable comments in a TV interview, saying that he wanted 'to prove that women are lousy, they stink, and they don't belong on the same court as a man'.

Billie Jean called him out big time in that dress. 'It was the B dress,' she confirmed to me. 'But I loved it. And I had a green sweater to wear with it. Ted had different colours each year. One season we all had black dresses, the next year pink. In 1973, it was green. That was the colour that year.'

There was a clash at Wimbledon in 1975 when Tinling's creativity ran up against Billie Jean's superstitious nature.

Oh my God, he made me about seven dresses for Wimbledon. I'm playing everything – singles, doubles and mixed. I won my first match, and I just loved the dress I wore for that. It had blue embroidery and buttons. I called it "the teapot dress".

'Ted,' I said, and I know he's not going to be happy. 'I'm really superstitious about this dress. I'm going to have to wear it every round.' I was only thinking about the second round actually, because I never looked at the draw.

'What? I made seven different dresses for you!' he goes.

'Well, I promise, if the doubles goes well, I'll wear every one of them.'

'Oh my God, Madame Superstar, are you serious?'

I said, 'I am.'

I hated to tell him, because he spent so much time on each dress.

As kids, Billie Jean and I were both humiliated for wearing shorts rather than a pretty tennis dress or skirt. She was taking her place for a photo alongside fellow juniors on the front steps of the Los Angeles Tennis Club when the president of the Southern Californian Tennis Association pointed at her, 'You! Little girl! Out! You can't be in the picture wearing shorts. You need a skirt or dress.' I had an almost identical experience back home in Devon. My coach, Mr Roberts, insisted girls wore shorts and I knew nothing different until one junior tournament. The organisers were lining up a photograph of the winners and I was turfed out because I wasn't in 'a nice skirt'. I wonder if that was why we were both so drawn to Ted Tinling's creations. I longed to have elegant dresses like those Maria Bueno wore. Teddy only made me one dress. It was lovely of him because he said he really wanted to create something for me, and he was going to design a dress to reflect how he saw me. I was thinking this is going to be so cute. I'm going to emerge on court like a little English rose. But no. It was gold lamé with turquoise straps! I said to him, 'Are you expecting me to wear this?' I played Rosie in a Virginia Slims match in it. I walked out looking like a Christmas tree. Every time I served, tiny bits of gold fibres fluttered onto the ground. Rosie was going mad, saying, your dress is dropping gold all over this court! Dear old Ted. I said, 'What have you got against me?' He just thought it was hilarious. 'That's how I see you!'

My Tinling dress is now in the Wimbledon Lawn Tennis Museum, because it became such a talking point during the 2002 Championships, years after I wore it on court to bedazzle Rosie. In fact, it nearly had a second outing at Wimbledon … modelled by Pat Cash. Pat, the 1987 men's singles champion, was a regular studio guest. He was so dismissive of Tim Henman's chances of winning the men's singles title that year, he declared that if Tim ended the fortnight as champion, he would wear one of my tennis dresses. So of course I said, 'Well, I have a very nice gold lamé one that I can just see you in.' That became a running joke right through to the semi-finals, when Tim was beaten by Pat's fellow Aussie Lleyton Hewitt, who went on to lift the trophy himself. It would have been a double triumph to see Tim win Wimbledon *and* see Pat eat his words in my Tinling frock! After the tournament, I had a call from the Wimbledon Lawn Tennis Museum asking if I would like to donate the dress for their fashion showcase. So there it is to this day, glittering in all its glory.

After Ted's death in 1990, we were amazed to learn that he had been a spy for the British intelligence services during the

Rod Laver leaping over the net in victory after winning the men's single title at Wimbledon for the first time, 1961.

Rod Laver's triumphant return to Wimbledon in 1968. I wonder how many more titles he would have won in those lost years.

Recreating Rod's trademark victory celebration with him and Ken Rosewall in 1969 – a dream come true and a photo I will always treasure.

Billie Jean King wins the first of her 20 titles at the All England Club – her favourite Wimbledon memory. Little did we know then how she would change so many lives, breaking down barriers on and off court.

Chris Evert and Billie Jean King in 1973 waving from the dressing room and waiting for the rain to stop before the women's singles final.

In 1973, Borgmania arrived at Wimbledon and catapulted the 17-year-old Swede (and tennis) into superstardom, as police had to fend of hundreds of screaming girls to steer Björn around the grounds.

Another story dominated the
front pages in 1974 … Chrissie
and Jimmy were dubbed the 'love
double' as the newly engaged
tennis superstars claimed the
men's and women's singles titles.

The Centenary Championships and
the Queen's Silver Jubilee in 1977
saw a historic win for Virginia Wade.
It may have been my Wimbledon
horribillis but for 'Our Ginny' it
was a fairytale win in such a
memorable year.

Martina won nine Wimbledon singles
titles. Her playing career moulded the
legend but her multi-layered life story
delivers inspiration way beyond the
confines of a tennis court.

Chrissie was often given the best view of Martina's grass-court brilliance but got her revenge on the clay courts of Paris where she was all-conquering. I was so proud to play in this wonderful era.

As a teenager, Martina left her country and family behind to follow her dream of playing tennis. After the sadness of winning her first Wimbledon singles title without her family court side, her second in 1979 was shared with her proud Mum Jana.

One of the most talked-about rivalries in sport. Borg v McEnroe. Their 1980 final produced arguably the most talked about 20 minutes in tennis history with the tie-break to end all tie-breaks. Mac won the breaker but Borg won the match.

One of the fiercest rivalries in sport merged into one of the strongest friendships. The predominantly white rule wasn't as strict in the 80s!

Super Mac got his revenge a year later, beating Björn to claim his first Wimbledon crown.

Boom Boom Boris becoming the youngest man to win Wimbledon in 1985.

From overnight sensation in 1985, Becker's powerful game saw him clinch three Wimbledon singles titles, his last in 1989 against Stefan Edberg.

Pat Cash during the 1987 final and below pioneering The Climb to celebrate winning the title with his loved ones. His celebration has been imitated many times and is now affectionately known as 'Doing a Cashy'.

Second World War. Perhaps the peacock motif he created on Martina's 1979 dress was a coded message, an in-joke he could chuckle about to himself about his tendency to ruffle the feathers of the tennis establishment. Transparent fabrics, embellished knickers, hipster shorts, even furry poodles with sequin eyes – the embellishment on Maureen Connolly's favourite dress – his sartorial flair always caused a stir at Wimbledon. And his legacy is still evident, not just in the museum. Each year, much attention is paid to the women's outfits, with sections of the media poised to splash a fashion 'controversy'.

Remember the white catsuit worn by American player Anne White in 1985? It was more like a body stocking with white leg warmers. That was a tabloid sensation: *The Sun* published a picture of White accompanied by the headline, 'ANNE IS A BIT OF ALL WHITE!' Asked for his opinion, Tinling, then 75 and still promoting glamour with practicality for athletes, said, 'It's totally logical. I hope it sets the tone for the future.' Tournament referee Alan Mills did not agree and asked Anne not to wear it again.

At six foot six inches, Ted Tinling is the colossus in the Wimbledon fashion story of living memory, but it all started in 1919, when the brilliant French player Suzanne Lenglen abandoned her corset, cumbersome petticoats and heavy starched cotton for a low-neck, short-sleeved dress that bared her leg to the calf. *Quelle horreur!* Her attire scandalised the Wimbledon faithful, the controversy overshadowing her victory.

Another shocking 'first' came in 1934, when the English player Eileen Whittingstall, who won six Grand Slam doubles titles from 1927 to 1931, turned up on Centre Court in 1934 in shorts – technically, an above-the-knee form of divided skirt. Hot on the heels of these outrages, and seared into the collective memory of SW19, came the 'Gorgeous Gussie' saga of 1949. Gertrude 'Gussie' Moran was a glamorous American player. 'I'm strictly feminine and colour is the essence of my life,' she theatrically told Tinling when he confirmed he would look after her tennis togs for the Wimbledon season. Acknowledging the Club's stance against colour, he decided her dresses had to be all-white, but wanted some detailing 'to harmonise with Gussie's own sparkle' – and so the famous frilly lace panties were born.

'I thought a little lace trimming might look nice,' Ted said. 'It was nothing special. In fact it was nothing more than what my mother would have called kitchen lace.' Gussie wore them to play at the annual Wimbledon reception at the Hurlingham Club. As soon as she was in action, she was garnering feverish interest, culminating in a photographer from *Life* magazine requesting a special shoot with her. He made Gussie serve a ball time after time, and each time she tossed the ball in the air and stretched up to extend her racket arm, his camera went click, click, click, as any eyeful of the lace underwear was revealed. One lady approached Ted, hooting with laughter about the photographers in attendance that day. 'Gussie! There's tremendous excitement. They're all on their stomachs!'

The big question was, would Gussie wear them at Wimbledon? She teased the swarm. A journalist from the *Daily Mail* revealed that hourly bulletins were posted in the press room 'on her wearing of the panties'. Cannily, she didn't wear them on the first day. When she did appear in them, it prompted a mass media frenzy as photographers elbowed each other out of position to get the best low-angle shots of the tantalising knickers. Tinling was not unaccustomed to controversy, but he was taken aback by the response. Sir Louis Greig, the All England Club chairman, admonished him for 'having drawn attention to the sexual area' and, despite Ted's 22-year involvement at The Championships, he was not invited back the following year. He only returned 33 years later, in 1982, when I knew him as a player liaison official. The newspapers had a field day. While Wimbledon officials at the time accused Moran of 'putting sin and vulgarity into tennis', Gertrude herself was more popularly nicknamed 'Gorgeous Gussie'. As well as being overwhelmed by requests for personal appearances, she was voted the best-dressed sportswoman by the US Fashion Academy. It was a classic case of there being no such thing as bad publicity.

Locker-room Lore

In the days before the development of the competitors' facilities at Wimbledon – which today boast vast fitness studios, physio rooms, relaxation lounges, a coffee bar and restaurant, ice baths, an outdoor terrace, a crèche and a hairdresser – the locker room was our inner sanctum. I should say locker rooms, because there were three just for the female competitors and a hierarchy according to your ranking: top, middle and bottom. You had to earn your place in the top locker room. When Billie Jean came over at the age of 17, she was surprised to find herself allocated to the middle dressing room, not the bottom one.

Probably because I was playing with Karen [Hantze Susman, who was ranked in the world Top 10]. I was in the middle and Karen was in the top, but she didn't want to be up there. So she came down to the middle one with me. She said she preferred it, because we were blue-collar kids. Middle is comfortable for us. When we go to the Members' room, we're a little uptight, afraid we're going to do something wrong.

Over time Billie realised that the top locker room was fine, not least because she could indulge her love for the history of the game. 'All the past champions would come up: Maureen Connolly, Althea Gibson, Doris Hart, Shirley Fry, Darlene Hard, who had helped me in California, Margaret DuPont … I knew all of their history. I loved that.'

It was in these locker rooms that we got ready for matches, whiled away rain breaks, enjoyed the thrill of coming off court after a win, recovered from the heartbreak of losing a tough match and made plans to practise the next morning or go out in the evening together. The tour was a tough existence, travelling from city to city, from country to country, with your mood dependent on your form. Mrs Twynam and Mrs Frasier, who ran the ladies' locker rooms at Wimbledon, provided for and pampered us. As Billie Jean recalled, 'Mrs Twynam, whose husband was the groundskeeper, was always there. One time I came off the court four times in a match because of the rain. Each time she'd iron my dress and get it dry.'

The top locker room had baths, showers, a lounge area with sofas and chairs, and two windows with ledges big enough to sit on, so you could look out over the grounds. The bottom half of the windows were glazed. I would sit there with just a towel around me. There were mirrors for hair and make-up, and it was all done up in shades of pink, very boudoir-like! We had so much fun peering out of the window. It was the perfect spot to watch the VIPs and Royal Box guests being driven in. I remember sitting on the window ledge with Chrissie and looking down at the astonishing scenes as Björn Borg was mobbed while being escorted by policemen en route to the court: from above, we just saw his distinctive blond hair and red Fila-clothed shoulders moving slowly through the crowds. It gave us a fantastic bird's-eye view of the grounds and a sense of the mood of the crowd. In the top ladies' dressing room today, there is a picture of Chrissie and me in exactly that pose. We all loved sitting on the ledge. There is another well-known photo of Billie Jean and Chrissie sitting there during an interminable rain break. 'We had to wait an entire day to play,' Billie Jean recalls.

> Colette, Chrissie's mom, would come up and bring us
> bonbons. We wondered if they were ever going to make
> a decision about whether we'd get on court. They finally
> confirmed at half past seven that there would be no play.
> So we waited a whole day. It was tough. But we were
> there together.

Today the dressing room is a five-star enclave with showers, baths, a seating area with a big TV screen, further screens for scores and schedules, large dispensers of SPF sunscreen, central dressing tables with Chanel scent and beauty products, a sauna, treatment room, coffee-making facilities, spacious cubicles and lockers, and protein bars on the reception desk. In the early 1970s we didn't even have showers. There were only big, deep baths behind wood-panelled doors, and most of us had our favourite one. I was so naughty one year; it was probably when the old Virge and I were vying for the British No.1 position. Virginia's favourite bath was the one on the right. So I used to wait until she was finishing her match and then I'd get in and lock the door. I was like, no, you're not having your favourite bath. I used to stay in it for half an hour. She wasn't happy! Billie Jean had her favourite bath, too. 'I was superstitious about it,' she said. 'If someone else was in it, I would wait for it. When it was free, Mrs Twynam would go in and start running it for me. I'd go, "Mrs Twynam, please don't do that. We don't have servants at home. It's driving me crazy. I'll do it. You take care of my dresses."'

Mrs Twynam still persisted in running the baths. Billie Jean loved chatting to her and to Mr Twynam (though he was not in the locker room!). She wanted to know about the grass, what kind of grass seed he used, how he rolled the courts – 'I love learning about all aspects of the game. It adds so much to the experience.' I think Mrs Twynam saw more of Billie than any other player. She was the first player to arrive each day and the last one to leave. Each year she hired a car and drove herself to Wimbledon from the hotel in Gloucester Road. She remembers it like it was yesterday:

I had my rituals. Put the music on. I never wanted to leave at night because it meant another day had gone by.

One day less that I'm not going to be able to play here at Wimbledon. Mrs Twynam would see me each morning and go, 'You're here first again.' I'd go, 'Yeah, sorry.'

Doubles

The doubles competitions at Wimbledon have a uniquely popular status. With their quick-fire volleys and specialist partnerships, the matches are a particular type of entertainment. When you think of McEnroe and Fleming (or 'McEnroe and anyone', as Fleming modestly says), the Woodies (Mark Woodforde and Todd Woodbridge), the Bryan brothers, Martina and Pam Shriver, the Williams sisters, Jamie Murray and Jelena Janković, Billie Jean and Rosie Casals, Jana Novotná and Martina Hingis or the Czech pair Barbora Krejčíková and Kateřina Siniaková, you think of the ultimate in entertainment. Billie Jean is the biggest advocate for the doubles game. 'I love doubles because of the angles, the creativity, the variables, the position changes, the way players back each other up to go forward, to call out who's going to take the ball,' she says. 'I like the tactics, the communication, it's fascinating and I love having to think quickly.'

The events have also been a focus for the record-chasers, or for tennis observers keen on noting potential records, most memorably for both Martina and Billie Jean, as players themselves tend to play down attempts to make history. It was Martina's 2003 mixed doubles victory that took her to 20 Wimbledon titles, a tally she shares with BJK. She competed in a further three Championships, twice reaching the women's doubles semi-finals, but was adamant that her last Wimbledon wasn't about breaking records. 'People keep saying that, but it so wasn't. I just wanted to win one more title here, period,' she said at the time.

At the other end of the career trajectory, much-loved former players are welcomed back to pit their entertaining skills against each other in the Invitation Doubles events, which were introduced in 2007 in a round-robin format. These events immediately proved popular, pitting the old-school trickery of the likes of Mansour Bahrami and Goran Ivanišević against other retired top players, giving fans the opportunity to marvel again at the court craft of Kim Clijsters, Conchita Martinez, Martina Hingis, Agnieszka Radwańska and others – with occasional pantomime cameo roles played by members of the public. Who can forget The Man in the Skirt? Chris Quinn, captain of a tennis club in County Wicklow, was innocently spectating on Court 3 when he heard Kim Clijsters ask her doubles partner Rennae Stubbs what kind of serve she should go for next.

'Body serve!' he shouted from the stands.

Kim, quick off the mark, responded, 'Who said that?' and the next thing Quinn knew he was on the court, being hoicked into a short tennis skirt.

After inviting him on the court, Clijsters, the 2003 Wimbledon ladies' double champion, realised he was in violation of the Club's all-white clothing rules and grabbed a regulation white skirt from her bag for him to pull up over his shorts. The sight of this rather large fan – 'I used to play American football, I've big legs!' said Quinn after his star turn – was golden for fans and us in the BBC studio alike. One of the other players donated a white top and, properly dressed, Quinn tried his hand and managed to return the first serve. Cue, the entire stadium in fits of laughter. The video went viral. It's become one of Wimbledon's Top Five funniest moments ever.

For many fans, nothing encapsulates Wimbledon so much as sitting in a stand watching a fast-paced, skill-filled doubles match on a mellow summer evening. Or not so mellow.

In 1981 I was involved in a doubles match with Ann Kiyomura that turned into a mass pillow fight! Our intensely fought third-round battle against JoAnne Russell and Virginia Ruzici was halted at 9.35pm due to bad light, with the score poised at 5–5 in the final set. A rowdy crowd was really invested in the outcome – we'd been down 1–5 before getting back to 5–5, and with a British player poised for victory, the spectators were buzzing! Pantomime boos rang out when the referee suspended play. We were shocked when the booing continued and spectators started ripping their cushions off the seats and throwing them onto Centre Court. (There's a picture of the court strewn with them.) I think one padded cushion managed to tap my shoe and the next day the headlines were 'SUE BARKER HIT ON CENTRE COURT'. It was front-page news! Reporters came out the following day to monitor the end of the 'Rowdy Match', but it was back to a hushed garden-party atmosphere as we won 9–7 and went on to reach the quarter-finals (and then the semi-finals, where we lost over three sets to Martina and Pam).

Showing just how much the annual Wimbledon soap opera captivates the nation, our match prompted an article in the *Daily Mail* under the selling line 'THE TOP PAPER FOR TENNIS REVEALS THAT WIMBLEDON'S "RIOT" WAS NOT THE FIRST', illustrated with an astonishing picture of No.1 Court strewn with cushions, which it described as 'the aftermath of violent scenes' when a pre-war Davis Cup match between America and Germany was suddenly postponed. Here is the report, which I found in the meticulously collated leather-bound cuttings books kept in the Wimbledon Library (and reproduced here with kind permission from DMG Media). To me, it shows that the passionate fury evoked in fans when a captivating match has to be postponed through bad light is almost a Wimbledon tradition in itself. From the 1930s to my era in the late 1970s and early 80s and up to today, the calling-off of a match induces a collective groan (thankfully, rarely, with accompanying missiles):

> In the pre-war days when Wimbledon was a middle-class garden party, lady spectators wore their best hats and white gloves to the Centre Court and their men had stiff collars to match their stiff upper lips.
>
> It seems incredible then, that such people could have behaved as today's jean and anorak-clad crowd – by hurling abuse and cushions on to the Centre Court in an outburst of hooligan-like rage when a match was called off for bad light …
>
> … The crowd's anger was greater than that displayed at Wimbledon on Tuesday evening when the Sue Barker doubles match was stopped. Crowds booed the officials and pelted Centre Court with cushions … but nothing worse than cushions.
>
> In 1935, America was playing Germany in a Davis Cup match. It had been raining for much of the afternoon.

When the rain stopped, the covers came off Number 1 Court and the spectators settled down to watch Germany's Gottfried von Cramm play Wilmer Allison of America. Instead, officials decided that, with barely an hour left for play, the match should be postponed.

When the announcement was made by Mr D R Larcombe, the Secretary of the Club, the spectators rose and began booing. Suddenly, someone threw a cushion. Others followed, then came a barrage of cushions and worse. Beer bottles, coins, orange peel, glasses, hats, books, walking sticks, every conceivable missile to hand rained down on the horrified All England officials.

But that wasn't all. The crowd then stormed the Davis Cup office. Angry ladies clenched white-gloved hands and screamed that they had been cheated. Gentlemen in panama hats bawled and shouted that they wanted their money back. Officials locked the door and called the police, who moved in to disperse the crowd.

It has taken another 46 years for another cushion-throwing incident to mar the club's record.

And I would have to be at the centre of it!

The Little Waiting Room

There is a room to the left of the doors that lead out onto Centre Court that we used to call the 'Little Waiting Room'. It had a small, grass-green sofa and a little window that looked onto the back of the screen during the tournament; the walls were covered with photographs of former champions from all the different eras. It looked like a classic room in a sports clubhouse, but it could feel like a torture chamber, because you had to sit in there, alongside your opponent, before you were called to walk out to play. Matches are to be played in the spirit of the Kipling line that is inscribed above the entrance to Centre Court – 'If you can meet with Triumph and Disaster, and treat those two imposters just the same' – and it all started in that little room. For some rivals, the atmosphere was a bit like a dentist's waiting room, times ten. Even for the chattier, more philosophical among us, it was tense. 'That wait was tough, because you're in the zone by then,' Billie Jean recalls.

> But I had a bit of fun with Chrissie before our 1973 final. You know, I knew the history of all the champions on the walls. I knew she wanted to keep some distance from me, I mean, we're about to go out and try to beat each other. But we're pretty good friends, so I'd say, 'Do you know what that is or do you know who they are?' Chrissie pointed at a picture and asked, 'Who is that?' It was Maureen Connolly.'

Minutes before the start of a Wimbledon final, was this education or one-upmanship from BJK? I wonder.

'The fun part was when they open the doors, and you turn left and walk along the concrete facing a tiny section of the crowd,' Billie Jean said.

Then you turn right around the corner and that is just beautiful ... The whole stadium opens up. You see more and more of the crowd, the clock ahead of you, you're trying to look around and settle into the scene. The worst part was when we used to have to turn around at the service line and do the curtsy. That was the most difficult thing to do. Both players felt the same. We'd mutter to each other ... 'Okay, we're going to turn around now ...' We'd turn around, do the curtsy, and then whisper, 'I'm glad that's over.'

It's fair to say that most players' thoughts before a big match are focused on keeping calm and remembering their tactics. Not for Billie. She has this extraordinary sense of perspective, of visualising the bigger picture.

Whenever I went on Centre Court, I was thanking all the past champions who came before me. I still do. I think about people who never got to play on that court but played in the tournament; about players who tried to qualify, who just wanted to get to Wimbledon and never did. They're not very far off, they're trying to make it and they didn't. I feel sorry for them. I feel grateful for the players who got through qualifying and got the experience of playing on the Wimbledon grass just once. I think about the future. Which future champions are going to be here?

Personal Sacrifices

'Tennis is a perfect combination of violent action taking place in an atmosphere of total tranquillity.' This line, inevitably from Billie Jean, adorns a wall in Wimbledon's Broadcast Centre restaurant above the tea and coffee machines and the chiller cabinets that contain strawberries and cream. Billie is never short of a quote! 'Pressure is a privilege' is another. She has always been my mentor, and back in the mid-1970s it was forever fascinating to hear what she had to say when she used to sit us down and explain the importance for the women's tour of how we handle ourselves on court and off it. Today, she is keen to impart to the current competitors a sense of history and perspective, what they owe to players in the past and how they should be mindful for players of the future.

When she goes to a general WTA meeting, she asks players if they understand what being a professional tennis star means. She wants to draw attention to the fact that players today enjoy the privilege of being able to earn a living from a sport they love, and she teaches them about the history of how the Open Era came into being. 'To me, as a child growing up, pro meant you're the best. When I started, I found I was in a game that says I'm amateur. I'm like, really? We are the best, the best women playing,' she reminisced. Her off-court campaigning ensured a better future for young women who wanted to make a career of tennis. But she was fighting so hard off the court for women in general, I asked her if she thought it affected her performances? 'Oh sure. I didn't win as much,' she said.

I had this vision from a young age of how I wanted the game to look. I wanted men and women to be together, working hard together. That was always how I envisioned it. We're all in this world together. I believe in equality for all. So, if men were making less money right now than we did, I would be fighting for them. You want equality. The Original Nine of us, the women, I remember saying to them, if you want a lot of money, a lot of applause, don't sign up for this. I said, we're not going to make the big bucks. The big bucks will come in years ahead. Our dream, the nine of us, was that we wanted any girl in the world to have a place to play tennis and compete. We wanted girls to be appreciated for their accomplishments, not just their looks. And we wanted them to be able to make a living from what they love to do. That's what the WTA is all about. So when I talk to the players today, I say, 'You're living our dream. The nine of us. That was our dream before the WTA.'

In 1968, when Billie Jean won the Wimbledon title, she was shocked to discover her £750 prize money was less than half of what Rod Laver as men's champion earned. It wasn't until 2007 that the men's and women's singles champion took home the same amount from Wimbledon: £700,000. It took nearly 40 years to achieve parity and Billie Jean was fighting every month of the way. At Wimbledon, the prize money increases every year and remains equal, right up to 2023 when both champions earned £2,350,000 apiece. That's what the current generation owes to their trailblazer. 'We were the transition generation, from amateur to pro,' she says of the Original Nine.

> It's so important that the second generation is great and we got lucky with Chrissie and Martina. We spent an extraordinary amount of time mentoring them.
>
> They are exceptional – as players, as people. Here's how it goes in every sport. The first generation gives it up for the future. That's our job. We wanted to. In '73, we became an association, the WTA. That's why professional women's tennis is as it is today, because of us. When Serena got her $4 million cheques, that's why.
>
> When I look at the big prize money now, I love it. Any time a woman or a man can make money, it gives them mobility, opportunity and, more importantly, it gives them an opportunity to give back to others.

Wimbledon: Pure Heaven

When I asked Billie Jean to describe Wimbledon in three words, she was quick to flash back with, 'Just pure heaven.' And then, being Billie, she gave me more than three words. 'It's the gardens, the ivy, the surroundings, the people, the fans who stay up all night.' She particularly remembers talking to Roy Emerson, who won five titles at Wimbledon (two singles in 1964 and 1965, and three men's doubles in 1959, 1961 and 1971). 'I'll never forget Emmo saying to me, "Billie, what keeps me going is when I walk in at Wimbledon and see all those

people who've been up all night to see us. We are so lucky."
And he's right.'

Billie Jean hasn't missed a Wimbledon since 1961 – not
even during the COVID-19 pandemic, when she attended on
Zoom and we gave her a virtual tour – and the queue of fans has
become an institution in itself with its own culture and protocols, once meriting a special exhibition in the Wimbledon Lawn
Tennis Museum. 'I always think about Emmo pointing that out
to me,' she continues.

> He's right. The fans are there for the players. A lot
> of the young players think it's the other way around,
> that the players are there for the fans. They have their
> selfies and their social media; it's all about the self.
> I say to these players, Get out of yourself. Ask yourself
> not what you get out of life, but what can you give to
> life? You guys, you have an opportunity that very few
> human beings will ever have.

3

BJÖRN BORG

I couldn't have timed my career in tennis better. I was just 17 when I signed with Mark McCormack's agency, IMG, and embarked on life as a professional – just in time to ride the wave of surreal popularity that hit the sport of tennis thanks mainly to a man described in the recent documentary *Gods of Tennis* (2023) as a 'racket-wielding Adonis': Björn Borg. It was a dream come true for me to join IMG's roster of famous golf and tennis competitors. Arnold Palmer ... Björn Borg ... and Sue Barker! I discovered later that IMG signed a lot of promising juniors on the off-chance that one of them might actually hit the jackpot, so it wasn't that I was so special, but it gave me a lot of confidence and set me on my way. This was 1973, the year that Björn – also just 17 – had to be escorted by groups of uniformed policemen in bobby hats to and from the courts at Wimbledon. He had won the boys' singles title in the previous year and it wasn't just dedicated tennis followers who were abuzz about the athletic young bronzed Swede with the shaggy long blond hair and distinctive two-handed backhand. Teenyboppers arrived in hordes. 'I hope I was admired for my tennis,' Björn said to me rather forlornly many years later, but his supreme talent and good looks were a killer combination.

None of us were immune. 'Björn Borg was the biggest rock-star tennis has ever seen,' says Chrissie Evert, who knows a thing or two about being a popular icon. As America's Sweetheart, she herself had magazine-cover status from the age of 16, when she burst onto the scene, reaching the semi-finals of the 1971 US Open. 'He was a star before he ever won a match really,' says Martina. Everybody admired Björn. I always positioned myself in the players' restaurant so I got a good view of him playing. He really was godlike. It wasn't just that he looked great, it was his manner, and the way he played – with that unique double-handed backhand with heavy topspin, delivered from the back of the court. He was just so different. And he was enigmatic even among his fellow players; he'd give you a nod or a smile. When he did say a few words, it was without eye contact, almost as if he was speaking to a third person.

I was so in awe of him. I've dined out for years on the story of when I was his mixed doubles partner in an exhibition tourna-ment organised by IMG in Hilton Head Island, South Carolina – Borg and Barker against Năstase and Navratilova. To play doubles with him was a dream come true. If we won the tie, Björn would be guaranteed the top prize of £50,000. I was deter-mined to win our doubles to secure that for him. In the course of that match, he became my knight in shining armour, standing up to the volatile Năstase, who said something quite threatening to me when I had the audacity to pass him twice at the net. Björn came to my side and said to Ilie. 'If you have anything to say to her, say it to me first.' And I was like, 'Oh, he's my hero!' I was so happy that we won and he was guaranteed the top prize. It made my year.

But back to 1973. Overnight, Borgmania put tennis on the front pages. Wimbledon was no longer a polite Edwardian tea party but a box-office spectacle, with people queueing – and camping on the pavement in the queue – as far as the eye could see. There was no precedent for this kind of social phenomenon at the All England Lawn Tennis & Croquet Club in living memory (not since the 'Lenglan Queue' of fans who lined up to catch a glimpse of 'La Divine', Suzanne Lenglen, in the 1920s); you could feel the frisson of excitement in the air.

Some form of bush telegraph created the buzz, because this was an era long before social media and the Internet, when tennis news was limited to match reports and results in the sports pages. Round by round, the hysteria increased. When Björn reached the quarter-finals and played Roger Taylor, who had his own legion of admirers as the only British member of the so-called Handsome Eight, the Centre Court was overrun by hysteria and the screams of besotted girls squashed into the standing area. Roger won the five-set battle, but it was Björn who was mobbed by teenagers, rushing onto the hallowed grass to get to him as he packed up his racket bag, and by photographers keen to capture the moment. Poor Roger had got through to his third Wimbledon semi-final and was almost completely ignored.

Borgmania continued until his last appearance at Wimbledon in 1981. There were always 'a couple of hundred girls screaming outside, like it was the Beatles arriving in America', recalls McEnroe, who became his great friend and rival. Calm and fuss-free on court, Borg was quiet, courteous and camera-shy away from it, not a personality who courted attention. He was a young guy whose simple dream had always been to play well at Wimbledon and represent Sweden in the Davis Cup. His relationship with Wimbledon began, as it did for so many of us, imagining himself competing on Centre Court while drilling a ball against a wall. An only child, Borg's parents ran a grocery shop in a small town outside Stockholm. He started to play when he was eight years old. 'I loved it from the beginning,' he told me.

> In my club, in my home town, there were posters showing players in action at this special tournament in the world, Wimbledon. So it became my dream. I thought, maybe one day I will play there. When I played against that garage door outside our family apartment, I always dreamt I was competing on the Centre Court in Wimbledon.

Borg's first visit was in 1971. He lost in the first round of the boys' singles, but he wasn't too disappointed by the result. 'I just wanted to be there, to take a look at the buildings and the courts and the people. I really felt the magic inside the place,' he said.

> Walking up to those gates was like a dream. I couldn't believe it. I'm here at Wimbledon, at this amazing place.

I sneaked in to see Centre Court and wondered if I would ever play on it. I remember thinking of the number of players who compete at Wimbledon for years but never have the chance to play a match on Centre Court. I thought it would be a huge privilege. I never imagined what was going to happen in the years to come.

What did happen is legend: a record five consecutive titles between 1976 and 1980 (and Borg thinks it should have been six). He was the first player in the Open Era – ahead of Pete Sampras, Roger Federer and Novak Djokovic – to block-book the honours board with a series of back-to-back titles. Federer matched his record of five titles in a row, but no one has bettered it. No other champion dominated like he did; he owned Centre Court for more than half a decade. And what I think is remarkable is how he worked out how to adapt his game from the slow clay of Roland-Garros to the speedy grass surfaces in London in a matter of weeks between each event. He ended his career with a tally of six French Open titles and his five Wimbledon championships. Three times he achieved the double (in 1978, 1979 and 1980), a feat which Federer managed only once, and Nadal twice.

Sadly, Borg was also a victim of the sport's new aura of stardom. He was the first champion who struggled to deal with the consequences that come with global fame. Thrust into the limelight at an early age and in an era of unregulated tabloid-newspaper attention, his life became unbearable. 'The girls coming from the stands, running over Centre Court, that was fun in a way but still I wanted to focus on tennis,' he told me.

Something new was happening, a revolution. The sport had always been conservative and very strict, but here was something a little bit different. I think in general it was good for tennis and for me it was kind of a fun thing, but it was crazy. You know, I'd be staying in a hotel and I'd have to stay in my room because down in the reception, there were hundreds of girls just waiting.

When he arrived at Wimbledon, he had to have a police escort just to get to the practice courts – this was long before they built the tunnels underneath the ground. 'It was not a problem because I had the police,' he insisted when I spoke to him at length for our documentary.

I could handle it very well. It didn't bother me at all. I would get into my routine, then focus and concentrate on doing the things I'm supposed to do. That was never, ever a problem. I was aware that I was changing tennis a little bit, but no one is bigger than the sport itself. I was part of building up tennis in a way that meant more people looked at tennis and in a different light. And I'm very proud to be part of that.

But tennis, and winning at tennis with his almost supernatural calm demeanour, was his preoccupation. To keep his focus, he had plenty of superstitions.

On court, I wanted to have my special chair – the one on the left of the umpire. Sometimes you'd see two guys running up because they both wanted the same chair. It worked for me every time – I got my chair. So that was one thing. And then I had to have the same locker. I had to have the same room, in the same hotel. The courtesy car had to take the same route to Wimbledon every day. I didn't shave. I had a lot of things.

They worked. But not too many things. Some players had like 100 things but I just followed a few rituals, and it worked. They were all to do with my routine off the court. On court, you just get on with the job.

He certainly did that. 'Winning the last point in a Wimbledon final is the most beautiful thing that can happen to you as a tennis player,' he told me, recalling the moment in 1976 when he threw his racket in the air and pushed up his hair band to signal 'job done, dream fulfilled'. He had beaten Năstase in three sets.

It was the most beautiful feeling in my life. Even the week after my first championship title, I could not believe that I had won Wimbledon. People had always said I would find it very difficult to win. They said I was a good clay-court player but I would have problems on the fast grass. It took me a few years to work out how to play at Wimbledon. A lot of people remember me as playing from the back court all the time, but I didn't really do that. I played aggressively. Maybe I was the first one who played a lot more from the back court, but I had to find the balance: how to play my game, on the grass. It took me three or four years to feel comfortable on the grass, to serve and volley. I felt pretty comfortable doing that too. Even though I grew up on clay, grass became one of my favourite surfaces.

To win his five Wimbledon titles, Borg beat Năstase, Jimmy Connors (twice), Roscoe Tanner and John 'Superbrat' McEnroe. En route to his 1977 triumph, he was involved in a fabulous semi-final with his great friend Vitas Gerulaitis, which is regularly voted one of Wimbledon's most entertaining matches. But possibly Borg's most famous triumph was the 1980 final with McEnroe and *that* fourth-set tie-break – an electrifying 20 minutes described by the American sports columnist Bruce Jenkins as 'the most riveting episode in the sport's history'. To this day, people recall the moment in that fourth-set decider when Borg had championship point for a sixth time, only to be foiled when Mac hit a net cord, and the ball trickled over. The tension was off the scale. Borg's girlfriend Mariana Simionescu was filmed smoking in the player's box, looking pensive. John's father, John McEnroe Sr, who was also his agent, sat impassively in his favourite bucket hat. I've heard both Björn and Mac reminiscing about it and they both seem to remember every single point.

We've talked about that tie-break several times, me and John, and it's fun to remember the points. I missed five championship points in the tie-break ... Maybe we are hazy on a few points in the match, but in the tie-break we remember every single point with clarity. To play that kind of a tie-breaker with John was very special.

Björn's supremacy at Wimbledon quite simply made Mac strive to reach new heights. The fact that Björn looked unbeatable on Centre Court fired John's ambition to steal his crown, and the 1980 tie-break showcases that dynamic beautifully. When Wimbledon was impacted by the COVID-19 lockdowns in 2020, I got the chance to watch the entire tie-break again, which I hadn't seen in many years. I was stunned at the shot-making and the variety – but most of all the quality of the tennis. There wasn't a bad point in it. At 6–6 we thought they were at the pivotal point of the tie-break, but it was only the beginning. It stands as the most talked-about 20 minutes in tennis history. Truly stunning. John won the battle of the tie-breaker, but Borg won the war. I've sat and discussed that moment with Mac and he remembers thinking that winning the fourth set was the turning point for him.

I won the tie-break and I didn't want to show how elated I was. I sat at the change and thought, I've got him now. He can't not get super-negative about this, because he's blown multiple championship points. Much to my chagrin – I mean you can never tell what he's thinking – but he didn't seem all that down or negative about those missed chances. And that freaked me out! That he seemed perfectly fine. This was just another obstacle to deal with.

And there's no tie-breaker in the final set. I started to feel like, oh my God, I have to break this guy's serve and I just haven't been doing that. Mentally, it just caught up with me, and then next thing I know he's on his knees.

The 1980 final itself was described as 'the sport's single most compelling piece of court magic' by the *New York Times*. And the crowd's reaction was incredible. Björn has no recall of the broader picture. 'I was concentrating so much. I couldn't hear the spectators, I was so focused on the match. But I know we played so many unbelievable shots, me and John.' For his vanquished opponent, the occasion had deep ramifications, signalled by the BBC commentator who declared, 'McEnroe today didn't win the Championship but he won the respect of everyone around this Centre Court.' John himself recalls 'this incredible sense of satisfaction that I'd been part of something special but there was also incredible emptiness that after all that, I still hadn't won it'. Mary Carillo, the American sportscaster who grew up playing with Mac on the Douglaston Club tennis courts in the New York borough of Queens, travelled back on the same plane from London to the United States as the McEnroes. When I spoke to her for the 2019 BBC documentary *John McEnroe – Still Rockin' at 60*, she remembered the flight well:

John McEnroe Junior was out cold, and his dad had on his lap a pile of all those newspapers that for a couple of years had been excoriating John and they were full of magnificent tales about the greatest tennis match that had been played on the lawns of Wimbledon. Mr McEnroe turned around and there were tears coming down his cheeks.

That clocked up Björn's fifth consecutive win. In the following Wimbledon, in 1981, he and Mac played again in the final. There was a feeling around Centre Court that day that it was the end of an era. Björn's 41-match winning streak came to an end as Mac claimed his first Wimbledon title. I wondered if Björn looked back now and felt that was a match he should have won. 'Oh, sure. I should have won,' Björn admits readily.

I felt that, but after the match – and this had never happened to me before in my life – I thought okay, I lost that one. I'm not that disappointed. And that's not me. I hate to lose. It's the worst thing. I love to win and hate to lose. John played well, but after losing that match I felt something was wrong with me. I mean, if I don't care after losing a Wimbledon final, then it's time to really think about myself as a person and about my future. Maybe if I had been more focused, I should have had a very, very good chance to win that match.

Björn's malaise was the cumulative effect of the tabloid-fuelled obsession with the top players. Wimbledon coverage wasn't just about the sport; Björn had become front-page news, far more than any other player. He found the attention amusing at the start – and what teenage boy wouldn't? Mac recalls being 12 or

13 and seeing images of Borg and a couple of hundred screaming girls and thinking 'now this would be nice, to get a little bit
of that attention'. I asked Björn how the relentlessness of media
intrusion took its toll over the years. Was it the reason why he
stepped away from the game a month or so after he lost to Mac
at Wimbledon, and again at the US Open final? 'You're exactly
right,' he admitted.

> I am sure that I would have continued to play for many
> more years but because of things that were happening
> to me outside the court I could not go anywhere. I could
> not do anything. I was going crazy. I said I cannot live
> this kind of life. I'm fed up. I didn't hate tennis. I hated
> the life I was forced to live. Being on the tour involved a
> lot of travelling and at every airport, it was like a herd of
> cows, so many people. It was a tough life, not like today
> when players use private jets, so they feel secure about
> their safety and they can relax in private.

He didn't care about what the newspapers were writing about
him, he just didn't like being hounded.

> I wanted to go out and enjoy myself. I was so young.
> I was 25 years old. But if you don't have privacy to
> do that, then you don't enjoy going out. I was playing
> tennis. I was doing really well in tennis, getting to the
> finals of Wimbledon and the US Open. If life is peaceful
> with nothing harmful to stress you, you feel good about

yourself outside tennis. But it wasn't and that's the reason I stepped away. I could never say I hate tennis. And, looking back, yes, maybe it would have been nice to play another three or five years and who knows?

This makes me so sad that this great player and super-nice guy was hounded out of the game. How lucky the players are today to have the protection they have. I wonder how they would feel if they had to walk in Björn's shoes around Wimbledon for just one day. The only other players who were to suffer the same kind of intrusion were Andre, Boris and Mac, particularly during his time with Tatum O'Neal. John missed Wimbledon in 1986 because of the obsession with his private life. Every Wimbledon there was a tabloid frenzy about everyone's off-court relationships – something the full-time tennis writers despised, as it hurt their relationship with the players. That hasn't gone away completely in the papers today. But now there is the added problem of trolling on social media, which causes players and their families so much concern. The players are protected physically but not emotionally. Sadly, I don't see that changing any time soon.

Physically, Björn was always super-fit and could play six hours straight. He hardly seemed to sweat. Another of his legacies to the game was his attitude towards conditioning for stamina and endurance. 'I was one of the first players to start to really take care of my health and fitness, to work hard on that outside the tennis court,' he says.

I saw it was important to build up your body in different ways, not only to play tennis, but to be strong because that's good for the mental side of the game. If you feel you are strong in body, then you are mentally strong too. Even when I stepped away from the game I was physically really, really strong, but mentally I was somewhere else in this world. If I didn't care, I couldn't play. That's not me. I'm a 100 per cent committed person. I grew up like that. I don't feel good about myself if I cannot do a perfect job. I always want to do my best, 100 per cent. That's the person I am. And if I cannot do that, that's a big problem.

And so, nine or ten weeks later, the great Björn Borg did what no one expected him to do: the man who had made Centre Court his own walked away from the game at the age of 25. He and Mac had met again in the US Open final – a match Björn desperately wanted to win to avenge his defeat of the previous year. As John celebrated with his family and friends, Borg left the court before the trophy ceremony got under way, scooting in and out of the dressing room. He just couldn't get out of New York quickly enough. The thought of receiving the runners-up trophy, and the prospect of the media's questions, was just too much for the quiet, proud Swede. Tennis lost the man who had changed the game with his unique style – the game, the hair, the headband. He retreated from the game he loved because the attention everywhere he went proved too much. If you've ever met Björn, you can understand the mobbing and the mania that surrounded him! But what a loss.

Mac says Björn's absence hurt him personally. Not only had he lost his nemesis, he had also lost his friend in the locker room. They had just reached a tantalising balance in a rivalry based on an intriguing contrast of opposite qualities, setting up the prospect of many more great matches, but none would materialise. 'It was a damn shame is what it was,' said Mac with rare understatement.

Borg didn't come back to Wimbledon for almost 20 years. His enigmatic presence on court became an enigmatic absence from the game. In the early 1990s there was a half-hearted comeback phase, but he didn't win a single match. But he did at last return for the Parade of Champions on Centre Court during Wimbledon in 2000. I remember watching him walk out modestly in the procession behind Chrissie and ahead of Virginia Wade, Mac, then Boris. And the crowd's cheers went up several notches as Borg rounded the corner in his grey suit and pale grey tie, fidgeting with his cuffs, and then gazed around at the competitive stage he owned so dominantly a quarter of a century earlier. You won't find any footage of it anywhere, but he bent down to kiss the grass. It was such an emotional gesture to witness. It wasn't actually filmed but it was so very poignant for tennis fans there to see how special it was for him to walk back out on Centre Court. 'I wanted to come back to kiss the grass on the Centre Court,' he told me later.

Until then – after '81, for all those years – I wasn't ready to go back. It wasn't just losing that final. Wimbledon was so special for me. I wasn't ready to go back and see this beautiful place. People wondered why. I was just not ready in my heart, in my mind. But then I took that big step, for me, to come back to Wimbledon. And it was very emotional.

The reception he received was deeply affecting – full of appreciation, warmth, regret, celebration, the Centre Court crowd embracing one of its greatest champions. This time he took it in, and embraced the warmth. 'It felt really good in my heart. I won tournaments all over the world. But those wins at Wimbledon, being there, playing there. It's deep, deep inside my heart. And when it's in your heart, nobody can take it from you.'

4

JOHN MCENROE

If the arrival of Borg on the scene brought box-office popularity to Wimbledon, his ensuing rivalry with McEnroe was the next brilliant instalment of the franchise for Wimbledon fans. Their two back-to-back finals encapsulates a drama that keeps on giving. In 2017 it had a retelling in the film *Borg vs McEnroe*. More recently an episode of the BBC documentary *Gods of Tennis* featured 'the rivalry between sex symbol Björn Borg and tabloid bad boy John McEnroe', billing it as 'the fiercest the men's game has ever seen'. With contrasting characters and physical appearance, they were adversaries from central casting. The Ice Man versus the Volcano. The righty versus a leftie. The enigmatic Swede who never shared his emotions against the irascible, brash New Yorker who could not perform unless he expressed his rollercoaster moods every point of the way. United by a desire to win, their duel between Wimbledon 1980 and the US Open of 1981 – 15 gripping, sport-changing months – fuelled the newfound obsession with tennis as soap opera.

Off the court, to the surprise of many, they were friends. I remember observing their fledgling friendship as a player in their midst. Björn took the maverick Mac under his wing when he first burst onto the scene with a run through the qualifiers to the semi-final in 1977, and helped him feel he belonged. 'In the beginning of his career John was a bit lost,' Björn told me. 'He has a temper and he was behaving badly and the other tennis players said, "We don't like this guy." They didn't accept him as a person or as a player. So I became closer to him.' As a young kid, Borg himself was prone to temper outbursts on court, and at one stage was suspended for several months. At 14 he had been punished for racket abuse and shouting. His parents told him he couldn't continue to play unless he learnt to control his temper. It's said he vowed to himself to keep a lid on his emotions ever after, and I can't think of a single incident when he looked moody on court, let alone questioned a line call or an umpire's decision.

I remember John telling me about one of their early encounters, in New Orleans in 1979. It was a close match and in the final set Mac started kicking off in his usual fashion. At five games all, he had another outburst. Björn stopped and slowly walked to the net, beckoning John to join him. Mac went to meet him at the net, where Björn said very quietly something along the lines of 'John, what are you doing? Why are you behaving like this? We are both playing great tennis, the crowd is loving this match. You don't need to do this. Everything is okay! Just take it easy.' John was shocked that Björn, who famously never broke his focus, would do this in the middle of a match, but he thought about it and agreed. He went on to win the match in a close third-set tie-break. Those words had a lasting effect on him. He felt Björn accepted him as himself, and that changed his mindset and I'm sure contributed towards the way he always behaved with composure whenever he played Björn.

'I think John could feel that I understood him as a person and our relationship became closer and closer,' Björn says.

You could see that respect, I think, whenever we played. It was very rarely against me that he said too many things on the court but, against all the other players, he was going nuts. We had respect for each other, me and John. I could handle him in a different way compared to the other guys when he first came on the tour.

I was amazed to learn from Björn that Mac was always very quiet in the locker room. He saved his words up for the court! 'I'm kind of a private person, I'd sit there and do my thing, but he was the same,' Björn confirmed. 'He didn't say a word in the locker room. As I remember, he didn't say much to anyone in the locker room over the years.'

Off the court – especially after Björn had walked away from tennis – they became even better friends and spent a lot of time with each other, united by those Wimbledon final experiences. 'Even today, we talk to each other, we call each other, we see each other,' Borg says. 'It's a very special relationship and when you look back nearly 45 years or whatever, back to when we battled on the tennis court over who was going to be number one, who was going to win Wimbledon, it's a very special bond we have.' When, in a moment of madness in 2006, he instructed Bonhams, the auctioneers, to sell his Wimbledon trophies, the first person on the phone to him was McEnroe. 'He said, "What the hell are you doing?"' Björn recalls, shaking his head.

'It was a stupid thing for me to do anyway, but the thing was, everything is up here anyway [he pointed to his head]. What I achieved in tennis, what I won, I have all the memories up here and that's what counts, here in my heart and here in my head. Trophies are important too, but not as much as the memories of what you've been through in life. But it was a stupid decision. John was the first to tell me! So I bought them back and it cost me more money to buy them back. Now they are in a safe place.'

That bond stems from being in it together – knowing what it's like to be out there alone on Centre Court, focused on winning. Their rivalry was intense, but short-lived, yet career-changing for Mac. They had never met at Wimbledon before the final of 1980, the battle of physical and mental endurance that Borg calmly won even after that fourth-set tie-break drama. 'Losing to him taught me a lot that day,' Mac told me.

He taught me that even a great champion can find an extra gear, and that he somehow wanted to win it more than me, even though he had won it four times and I hadn't won it once. I was like, how the hell did that happen? I realised I had to get fitter. I had to be tougher mentally. I had to go back to the drawing board in every way. The next time we played I had to make him feel that I wanted it more than he did. It made me a better player because when you're in a one-on-one game it's a very mental game. I learnt that from Borg – and I learnt that from Connors too because I've never seen a guy try as hard as that guy. Those two guys alone forced me to improve in that area. I had no choice.

Rivalries are what every sport needs, and there is no better stage than the Centre Court of Wimbledon to witness two great players pushing each other to ever greater performances. In my memory, we've had the inspiring Laver vs Rosewall and Billie Jean vs Margaret Court battles, but the greatest rivalry in the men's game was Borg and McEnroe's. It was just so intense. They played 14 times on the tour with a head-to-head record that stands at 7–7, but those two Wimbledon finals highlighted the intrigue of an adversarial battle in the era when our sport became a blockbuster attraction. If Borg was the rockstar, John represented the punk era (his friend Chrissie Hynde of The Pretenders was inspired to write the song 'Don't Get Me Wrong' because she felt people only saw one side of his personality). We were so lucky in that the women's game, in parallel, had the epic rivalry between Chrissie and Martina, who played an incredible 80 times between 1973 and 1988, with Martina ahead in the overall wins (43–37), boosted by the number of times she beat Chrissie on the grass at Wimbledon. (How the grass played to suit serve-and-volleyers back then is another story, of which more later.) And many great rivalries have followed: McEnroe vs Connors and Lendl, Becker vs Edberg, Sampras vs Agassi, Graf vs Seles, Venus vs Serena, Roger vs Rafa, Roger vs Novak, Rafa vs Novak, Novak vs Andy Murray …

After the 2023 Wimbledon final, an Alcaraz vs Novak rivalry is a thrilling prospect. That match left us begging for more. In the women's game, no one player has established dominance in recent years. The void left by the Williams sisters is huge. The number of different winners – Garbiñe Muguruza, Simona Halep, Angie Kerber, Ash Barty, Elena Rybakina and Markéta Vondroušová – has certainly given the game variety but sadly the public don't have the same sort of connection with these top players, since they haven't had a chance to develop a relationship with them over the years. Maybe Coco and Iga Świątek can change that.

You Cannot Be Serious

By the time Mac played Borg in the 1981 Wimbledon final, the notoriety that he was receiving for his tantrums and outbursts against officialdom was becoming distracting and energy consuming. I've heard it myself from the horse's mouth. 'Some of it was obviously my fault, but I didn't feel like I deserved the shellacking I was getting,' Mac confided to me.

By the time I got to Wimbledon that year I realised that everything that I was doing was being looked at even more carefully. Especially against Borg, because of the contrast. He never changed his expression.

So everything I said or did was magnified, so I had to be really careful otherwise it would look like I was going absolutely crazy. So I said to myself – well look, we had an incredible match the year before. We have a great rivalry going, so let's just play it out. Just accept whatever happens, which is not the easiest thing for me to do, because I have a tendency to sort of get distracted and lash out at times, at myself or whoever.

Sometimes for the wrong reason. For this match, I was under control. It allowed me, even when it was a set all, 4–5 15–40, I was two set points down, and it could be two sets to one down, and I got a tough call. I just kept playing. Somehow, as Arthur Ashe used to tell me, the calls even out. I'm like, you're crazy. They don't even out, okay? But obviously he had a far better way of dealing with things than I did. So I tried to take some of these things to heart, and in that 1981 final, it worked.

Wearing a white polo-style shirt with a blue stripe across the chest, and a red headband, McEnroe finally ended Borg's Wimbledon reign on 4 July: 'Stick a feather in his cap and call him McEnroney,' quipped Bud Collins, alluding to lines in the popular American nursery rhyme 'Yankee Doodle'. In retrospect, their body language in a photograph of them at the net before the start of the match foretold what was to come. Both are wearing their now iconic zip-up track tops. Looking tense in his familiar red-and-cream jacket with the stripe details, Borg's famous coat-hanger shoulders are up by his ears; Mac, with a hand in one pocket, looks more at ease and up for a battle. It hadn't been a peaceful journey to the final. The first round was when Mac infamously blew up at the chair umpire, Ted James, calling him 'the pits of the world', and then swore at Fred Hoyles, the tournament referee, during his match with fellow American Tom Gullikson. The next day the papers did not shy away from the controversy. 'THE SHAME OF JOHN MCENROE' was the headline on the front page of the *Daily Mail*. A cartoon depicted him sitting at the changeover with a dummy in his mouth.

As he told Mike Dickson of the *Mail* on the 30th anniversary of his outburst (and who knew then that it was destined to get the full commemorative treatment?):

> There was already a lot of pressure I'd put on myself because I felt that perhaps I should have won Wimbledon already by then. It was something when, particularly early in an event, and because this was the first round, it felt like there were so much pent-up nerves and expectation that I put on myself. It had also built up that it was sort of me against everyone else at the time, whether it was the press or the umpires. I had built up this whole scenario and perhaps it wasn't easy, but it wasn't as bad as I was envisioning.

He also remembered thinking, 'If I win this I don't want to come back. This is it. I'll win it, then I'm out of here.' He told Dickson that 'the moment I won the tournament I remember thinking within a few seconds "I want to come back and win it again."'

The reach of the Borg–McEnroe Wimbledon battles was extraordinary. John, who refused all invitations to play in South Africa during the apartheid years, has shown me his treasured photograph of himself with Nelson Mandela, which captured 'one of the greatest moments of my life, bar none'. It shows him with the former South African president and activist, to whom he had given the racket he used in 1980/81. Mandela told Mac he had been listening to his match against Björn at Wimbledon, and John realised he would have been listening to it on a radio in prison on Robben Island. 'I'm complaining about line calls, and this guy spent 27 years of his life in prison.'

Having the privilege of fronting Mac's BBC documentary *Still Rockin' at 60* made me realise just how special that 1981 victory was for John's parents, who had been in his corner through it all, and how much it meant to Mac to have them there for that triumph. The cameras captured his mother with her hands on her ears screaming in disbelief and his father, out of seat, clapping his hands above his head. For the documentary I went to spend time with John in New York City. I visited his beautiful duplex apartment home on the Upper West Side of Manhattan, which has the most stunning views over the city. Mac stretched himself to buy the property during his early playing days and it is now a prime asset, proving what a savvy businessman he was even back then. I met his lovely wife, the singer Patty Smyth, and his family, who were all so welcoming. I witnessed one of his jam sessions with his mates and I'm no expert but he looked like he knew his way around that guitar – when I saw the passion in his eyes, I realised how important music is to him. On that visit,

Mac also took me to his art gallery in downtown Manhattan. Art is another of his great passions. We had a hilarious moment when I held the bottom of a ladder as John climbed up to remove a couple of paintings from the wall. The ladder was a bit wobbly and I felt under extreme pressure. The first painting he handed down I put carefully on the table. The second one I held in my hands, admiring it as John descended. 'How much do you think that one is worth, Sue?' Not wanting to look foolish as I really had no idea, I guessed $100,000. 'Just over a million,' he said – and I almost dropped it. Holding something so valuable was a first for me! I couldn't believe Mac would trust me with handling it at all. I decided to not go near anything else in his gallery, much to his amusement.

Some of the phrases Mac yelled at umpires have gone into tennis folklore. To be fair, he has embraced them and gets paid well for them as part of his entertaining act on the senior tour. He even titled his 2002 memoir *You Cannot Be Serious*; the UK edition was just *Serious*, and a later autobiography was entitled *But Seriously*. They say first impressions are everything, and Mac can blame his unfortunate Superbrat status from the year he burst onto the scene at Wimbledon. In 1977, at the age of 18, he arrived like a tornado of talent, getting through three qualifying matches to earn a place in the main draw, and then went on a remarkable run to reach – and ultimately lose – a testy semi-final against Jimmy Connors, the 1974 Wimbledon champion. It's a feat that has only been matched twice since – by Alexandra Stevenson in 1999 and Vladimir Voltchkov in 2000, who reached their semi-final as qualifiers, but neither built on their unheralded achievement.

The only comparable run at a Slam that I can think of is Emma Raducanu's fairy tale in New York, when she became the first qualifier in the Open Era to go one stage further and win a major singles title. Mac's semi-final match against his fellow American – a player he had admired as a youngster for being 'this incredibly feisty guy ... his whole persona was so intense that it sort of blew people away' – was his first ever match on Centre Court.

Connors was not someone to welcome a rival, let alone a fellow American. Prior to the match, Mac was promoted from the middle to the top dressing room, where there are few players left milling between the practice courts and the locker rooms. 'I tried to introduce myself and he ignored me and then he wouldn't speak to me in the locker room. He just didn't acknowledge my existence,' he told me.

> My legs were shaking because it was my first time on Centre Court. I felt like I had lost before I had won. I didn't even want to win in a way because all of a sudden things were changing so fast. I felt like it would be almost too much. Not that, deep down, I wouldn't have thought, hey, it would be good to beat Connors and Borg and win Wimbledon. This nobody who has come from playing juniors. But it felt like that step would have been too great.

In losing to Jimmy in four sets, Mac also received a warning for his behaviour. This came hot on the heels of a quarter-final against the Australian Phil Dent on No.1 Court, when his antics – arguing with the umpire, smashing a racket – led to the crowd booing him.

And therein lies a story.

Phil Dent is the man we can blame for Mac's outbursts against officialdom. Or so Mac told me. It all started at the French Open, just a few weeks before Wimbledon 1977. 'I lost to him in the second round in five sets, when I'd been two sets to one and had a break in the fourth set,' Mac said.

In my mind, he sort of tricked me. He pretended he was tired, I thought he was done and the next thing I know I look up and I've lost. There were some horrendous calls in that match. He sort of put his arm around my shoulder and goes, 'Son, this is the pros now, so if you want to question a call, you've got to go ask the umpire. Don't look at me.' So this lightbulb goes off in my head.

Ironically, Phil Dent and I played again in the quarters at Wimbledon. I won the first set quite handily, then got frustrated when, after questioning a few line calls [following Dent's advice to approach the umpire], I lost the second set on a tie-breaker. I just couldn't believe I lost this set. I grabbed my racket, a wooden racket obviously, put the head under my sneaker and tried to bend it until it broke. The crowd turned against me. I thought, *Why are they booing? I'm upset at myself!* It was the first time I'd ever been booed. So I decided – just to see if they would react – to kick my broken racket along the grass towards my chair. The boos got louder. That was the first time that I had started to question the umpire about the bad calls, because I was playing the guy who had told me to. I started whining about calls, and complaining, and winning this match – and the next thing I know, I'm being booed and these labels start getting attached to my name.

Wimbledon, though, was where Mac found his self-belief. As an amateur in 1977, he couldn't accept prize money, but for the first time he felt able to play the way he wanted to and make it count. As a junior, he'd never been big enough, strong enough or fit enough before to sustain a run of good results. He played four matches on the outside courts, his quarter against Dent on No.1 Court, then the semi-final against Jimmy on his Centre Court debut. 'So that was like the perfect storm, it all came together there' – unfortunately, the bad-boy label followed him. It would take a long time for the public's view of McEnroe to mellow into an affection. In the papers, he was known as Superbrat, The Incredible Sulk, McTantrum; he was a headline writer's dream. Mac admitted that he would have been a better player had he not been distracted by his behaviour and the response it drew. He thinks he would have won more if he hadn't lost his cool so often. 'It did distract me from my game,' he told me.

Others disagree. They think I harnessed this energy to throw off the opponent or lift my energy. Some of that may be true. I wish I had been able to use 10 or 20 per cent of that energy to train harder, to focus more. Sometimes I was able to focus and keep concentration, but there were times when my tendency to lash out got in the way of things.

In the Booth

When I asked Mac to name his favourite moment at Wimbledon, he didn't pick any of his achievements on court – nothing from his three singles victories in 1981, 1983 and 1984, his rivalries with Borg and Connors, his five men's doubles triumphs (three of them won in the same years he won the singles titles). Instead, surprisingly, he nominated a quiet moment in the commentary booth. 'It would have to be being part of the BBC team for the 2008 final, when Rafa played that incredible match with Roger,' he said.

When it ended, it looked like they couldn't play another point. I do like to talk a fair amount but in this particular case, the tennis was so great that I barely said anything in the fifth set. I let the two guys go at it and speak for themselves. I was proud that I was able to do that. It was also because I've been asked a lot about the 1980 Wimbledon final, and that being the greatest match ever, and I take great pride in other people saying that. But this was the first time, after all the years, that I looked at these two guys and thought, this level of tennis, this quality, this excitement, is as good or better than the final I played with Björn in 1980. They were playing in a different style than we'd grown accustomed to seeing.

You see guys wheeling away from the baseline, giving it absolutely everything they had. Leftie, righty, that obviously reminded me of myself and Björn, but it was the way they played, the way they reacted, their emotions so different. To see them max out and get to a level that no one had seen for a long, long time. That really was a remarkable six or seven hours of tennis. I think, clearly, this is one of the great rivalries ever.

When I asked Mac what thoughts he associates with the word 'Wimbledon', he quickly replied 'a sort of reinvention for me'. It's clear when you look at his story – the journey from his incredible breakthrough as an 18-year-old qualifier in 1977 to the multiple championship titles and then esteemed commentator – that he's had a complex and ultimately rewarding relationship with the Wimbledon faithful over nearly 50 years. A native New Yorker, who was brash and brilliant in equal measures, he was a maverick in the genteel world of tennis (give or take a Connors or Năstase). His love–hate relationship with the All England Club in the early part of his career was fascinating to watch: John versus the Wimbledon committee, with neither prepared to back down. There were times when that backfired on him, such as not attending the champions' dinner in 1981. For that rebuff, the Club refused him an Honorary Membership. 'I wanted to spend [the night] with my family and friends and the people who had supported me, not a bunch of stiffs who were 70–80 years old, telling you that you're acting like a jerk,' he said on ESPN Classic's SportsCentury series. He missed The Championships entirely in 1986 because the constant media spotlight got too much. 'I could've played but I felt I wanted to send a message, so I said I'm going to pull out,' he told me. 'In those two weeks, I noticed that they were still playing. Life goes on [without John McEnroe]. No one's bigger than the game.'

> I enjoy coming to London now. It was hard to relax when the only reason you're here is to try and win Wimbledon. Now, being on the other side, commentating – being a back-seat driver basically – it's awesome. Thinking of the difficulties that I had in the beginning. I had a lot of success but I was struggling with the press and getting accepted the way I thought I should be accepted. Some of it was obviously my own doing, but now it's sort of come full circle. Actually to be given this opportunity by the BBC of all companies, who, when I watched Wimbledon, I saw they approached their commentary and their coverage of tennis in a different way than they did in the States. So to have them reach out to me and say, 'We'd like you to be part of this team,' that seemed rather amazing. And actually because of that, and doing the commentary with the BBC for a number of years, people, I believe, look at me in a different way than they used to. So it wasn't what I expected. But it worked out real well. Sometimes I look around and think, *Is this actually happening?*

Now there's a new catchphrase!

Mac is the BBC's highest-paid employee pro rata, and with good reason: the public love him. He was great to work with, always up for fun, but I had to keep my wits about me. The first year he worked with us full-time at Wimbledon, we had to fill 15 or 20 minutes before going to the *Six O'Clock News* and we had him on for that slot because he's such a good talker. I was told to leave a minute free at the end so we could show a couple of 10-second clips to dot the i's and cross the t's – you know, Steffi Graf is through, Andre Agassi next faces so-and-so, and we've got more tennis for you over on BBC Two – so I was timing the last question for Mac to allow for this summing up. Then I gave him the hand signal to wind up. Bizarrely, he carried on talking with a new burst of energy. I gave the signal again, and he carried on talking. The clock was ticking down. I cut in, 'Mac, sorry, we'll have you on BBC Two, but we have to go now to the news … Goodbye.' We didn't have time to show the clips. Mac looked at me questioningly with a furrowed brow.

'I was giving you the winding up signal!' I said.

'Ah,' he replied, 'but that signal means "keep going".'

He made a cut-throat gesture. 'Why didn't you just do that?'

Wimbledon was always the biggest challenge for me during my BBC career. For a start, my ear was full of studio talkback as we had to convey the live action, results and stories across all the courts, as it happened, and across two channels. Mac and I were often courtside before and after matches when sometimes things would go wrong or plans might change. Mac used to laugh at me trying to get a message to my production team. Because my microphone was live, I had to resort to mime and charades to convey what I needed to and I was obviously useless as very rarely was the message understood. Mac couldn't help me because his mic was live too! The demands of having to be suited and booted for the studio as well could be challenging. Mac and Tim were always amazed that I never wanted protection from the sun. Over the years we often had to broadcast outside in temperatures as high as 40 degrees (in 2013). While Tim and Mac in their dark suits grabbed umbrellas and sometimes the portable fans, I stayed out in the sun, partly because I was more usually wearing pastel colours and partly because I was always busy linking in and out of features so I didn't have a spare hand to hold a sun shade or cooling fan. They were impressed – Tim said I was 'like Federer' in never showing a bead of sweat!

Some of my most treasured interviews at Wimbledon involved John, particularly his ones with Jimmy Connors. I had to be on my toes at all times as their competitive spirit was always on display. Can you imagine? Just about the two feistiest players of all time still trying to trump the other whenever possible. John always begged to see reruns of his wins against Jimmy and vice versa; we could have happily filled two full weeks of rain delays with those two. They were always challenging each other and pointing out the other's losses, but it was obvious there was huge respect too, no matter how grudging! It all added to the fun.

My favourite, though, was having Mac, Jimmy and Björn on Centre Court before the 2012 final between Roger and Andy. There was such a buzz of anticipation for the match and the crowd's reaction to these three giants of the men's game from a golden era was amazing. The sight of them emerging onto Centre from the Royal Box end caused a bunfight as the courtside trench lined with accredited news photographers saw the potential in a rare picture. I was busy on air on BBC One and wondered what the commotion was. Then I saw them … these three gods of tennis, back on *their* stage. I was told by my editor when I spotted them to quickly hand to a three-minute feature as we wanted as much time with them as possible. Let's face it, this was only the second time Björn had come back to Wimbledon since he walked away from the game, and no one had heard from him in years. The photographers were pushing each other, manoeuvring to get the best shot. I had a quick word with Mac, as I guessed (rightly) that he was the ringleader. I suggested I would ask the press to calm down and in return the three of them would stay for photos after the preview. Mac agreed. So I approached the throng of snappers who were delighted with the offer.

Back on BBC One, we previewed the final, which was the blockbuster Roger vs Andy line-up, so we had much to discuss. I've never experienced anything close to that since. Having those three players preview the men's final was the most riveting, insightful 30 minutes I have ever done. We only stopped because we were asked to move from our position by the umpire's chair. (We were always allowed to broadcast previews in the latter stages in the centre of Centre Court, before retreating behind the netting at the far end for the final build-up.) As I thanked the boys, I linked to a long VT to give me plenty of time to unplug and then re-plug behind the netting. I decided this was an opportunity not to be missed. Here I was with these three legends and three of my favourite peers from my playing days, so I jumped in between Jimmy and Mac with Björn on John's left and had *my* photo taken with them. I knew it was not what the photographers wanted, but I thought of my hallway at home and had a vision of how lovely it would be to have this photo in pride of place. I ignored the snappers' pleas to leave. Ha ha! I got the job done and then to the relief of the photographers I departed and they got the shot they wanted. It was on the front page the next day. I should be ashamed of myself, but I'm not, as I have the framed picture up on the wall of my hall and I smile at it every day!

5

VIRGINIA WADE

The best Wimbledons can throw up, in a single tournament, an abundance of enduring stories and cameo moments. Take 1977. For a start, they were The Centenary Championships, which occurred in Queen Elizabeth II's Silver Jubilee Year – and she was due to visit. So the Clubhouse and Centre Court got a new lick of paint for the occasion. On the opening day, 41 surviving singles champions paraded onto the grass under the Royal Box and were presented with silver commemorative medals by the Duke and Duchess of Kent. Wimbledon, with its sense of 'history in the making', is so good at making a special occasion of an anniversary or notable event.

With typical British formality, and the lightest of touches, the official *Wimbledon Compendium* sets out the milestones of the 1977 Championships:

The Band of the Welsh Guards played on the Centre Court, prior to the start of play, for five days of the meeting. A Queen's Silver Jubilee Salver was given to the winner of each Championship event, while all competitors received a commemorative pen and pencil set. Queen Elizabeth, accompanied by the Duke of Edinburgh, attended the meeting on the second Friday and presented the trophy to the winner of the ladies' singles on court, which in this case was, fittingly, the British player, Virginia Wade. The British men could not repeat the trick, Mark Cox the last surviving player in the gentlemen's draw, going out in the fourth round, as the increasingly popular (especially with female fans) Björn Borg reclaimed his trophy. As Rod Laver made his last appearance, an 18-year-old John McEnroe marked his arrival, becoming the first qualifier to reach the semi-finals and the youngest player in the last four for 100 years. Ball girls were used for the first time on the outside courts. There were no poor weather interruptions during the Fortnight, although it was a little chilly in the first week.

It was a little chilly in the second week for me personally, though not in the meteorological sense. It was a great year for British tennis, but 1977 is a tough year for me to look back on. Where the record book says 'fittingly, the British player, Virginia Wade', I have to relive the emotions and reflect on the fact that my name could have been there instead. For, on a personal level, the 1977 tournament was – to adapt one of the late queen's most memorable phrases – my Wimbledon *horribilis*. And yet it started with a lot of excitement. The build-up for the centenary year was hysterical. I was photographed at Hampton Court in an 1870s straw tennis hat and ankle-length petticoat, while the nation's celebratory mood for the Queen's Silver Jubilee prompted a wave of Rule Britannia sentimentality about who would be crowned 'the queen of tennis'. All this coincided with the first time in years that Britain had two female players in the top five, with the press hyping up 'our Ginny and Sue'. Chrissie was No.1 seed, Martina No.2, Virginia No.3 and I was No.4. We Brits were expected to reach the semi-finals and there was no doubt it was a dream for both of us to lift the Wimbledon trophy. Virginia, in her thirties, was possibly afraid that this could be her last chance; I was the young whippersnapper chasing at her heels. The draw worked out well for me. I'd beaten every contender in my half, as well as Chrissie and Billie Jean in Team Tennis (a professional tennis league played in the US). I expected to meet Martina, who I had beaten at the Virginia Slims finals, after, as projected, I had defeated the Australian Kerry Reid in the quarters. I even had a bye in the first round. It couldn't have been a better draw if I had plotted it myself.

Never mind that grass was not my favourite surface, I really fancied myself to do well at Wimbledon, my spiritual home. In the previous year, I had lost a quarter-final against Martina that I should have won, so to avenge that and fulfil my No.4 seeding was a logical progression. (The 1976 quarter-final was a horrible match – Martina was in a foul mood, furious that the crowd was so partisan ... but what did she expect? Despite playing with the crowd onside, I managed to throw the match away when I was serving for a 5–1 lead in the third set. For some reason, I started to play lots of ridiculous drop shots. *The Times* reporter Rex Bellamy wrote that I 'wilted like a flower in a parched land'. I'd suffered a terrible case of nerve-induced capitulation. To this day, Martina reminds me: 'You'd have won if you hadn't started drop-shotting!')

Anyway, throughout that buzzing first week of the 1977 Championships, I loved returning to the locker room, having beaten Helga Masthoff of Germany, my doubles partner Ann and then her fellow American Lea Antonoplis – opponents all despatched in straight sets. In the throng of the competitors' facilities, you'd often hear players say hello to each other and ask each other how their matches had gone. I remember that year a very young John McEnroe asking, after one of my early matches, 'Hi, how'd it go?' Great, thanks!

However, playing under the pressure of being a home player started to affect me in the second week. As I told the journalists, I'd been watching matches on Centre Court since I was seven and the ghosts of past champions seemed to be in every corner. I especially remember being on the phone to Mr Roberts the night before my quarter-final, and he advised me to have a double brandy before I went to bed! He always managed to make me laugh; his dry sense of humour was what I loved most about him. I didn't have the recommended tipple – and I defeated Kerry in straight sets.

The British tennis sages saw this as a good omen because Kerry was an in-form player that season (she ended the year undefeated in singles against both Virginia and Martina, beating both of them three times). The big shock of the tournament was that Martina had been beaten by the unheralded Betty Stove. Having reached the semi-final the year before, Martina was expected to go one stage further. Betty was a formidable physical presence on the other side of the net – six foot one and muscular – but her game was erratic. You never knew what was coming from her end of the court. When Betty found form and consistency, though, you could be sure you were in danger of being on the wrong end of a battering.

Still, it was quite a lift to discover I would be playing Betty, and not Martina, for a place in the Wimbledon final. I had a really good head-to-head record against her. On ladies' semi-final day, Virginia beat Chrissie in the first match on Centre, and all I had to do was beat Betty to make it an all-British final. But on the day of the final, I was to be found not in the Little Waiting Room about to receive a large bouquet of flowers, ready to take on Virginia (who I'd beaten twice that year); instead, I was shopping alone in Bond Street, splashing out on an expensive watch and necklace.

Meanwhile Chrissie, devastated about her own semi-final exit, told Bud Collins that she trashed her hotel room and stayed in her bathrobe for three days eating junk food! My flight back to America was booked for the Monday after Wimbledon, so I couldn't run away immediately and escape. I laugh with Virginia about it now. I spent so much money that day on jewellery – which I took no pleasure in wearing, because of the bad associations! Virginia became Wimbledon champion and made an absolute mint. We talk about it a lot.

I joke: 'Little did I know when you won in 1977, and I lost, that when I joined the Beeb, I would have to sit down every year with you – the last British woman to win Wimbledon – and relive that tournament all over again!' She understands my pain. She's lost matches that she wouldn't like to reminisce about. In her biography, she says she was so pleased it wasn't me she had to beat in the final.

What happened? Virginia had pulled off a surprise victory over Chrissie – a tremendous achievement as Chrissie was so dominant that year and had been the clear favourite for the title. I remember sitting in the locker room thinking, *Oh God, there are only two people other than me left in the draw now – Betty and Virginia – and I have a winning head-to-head record against both of them this year*. I thought, *This is my moment, the Wimbledon trophy is mine*, and that was my mistake. Billie Jean wandered past and ruffled my hair, saying, 'Go for it, Sue. You know, you can do this.' And I thought, *yeah!* On the two occasions I had beaten Virginia that year, I'd won in straight sets. And I really didn't think Betty would pose a problem. She had a bandaged right knee for a muscle injury and I saw her go in to have an ice-pack treatment before she took to the court. I knew she had played well against Martina, so I wasn't going to take it lightly, but I didn't think she'd present insurmountable opposition.

I remember walking on to Centre Court to the most magical reception from the crowd, exuberant after Virginia's win. She'd done her bit to make the dream of an all-British final come true; now it was my turn. I was nervous, but not super-nervous.

Normally I would start a bit shakily in a match, but this was an occasion where I grew more and more tense as the match went on … I found I couldn't control it. I don't want to blame anyone other than myself for losing to Betty that day, but I'd also had the unsettling situation of Mr Roberts not turning up, when he said he would. He never came to watch me play, and he hated the Wimbledon bubble of attention, but this match was so big – everything he'd coached me for since I was 11 – that I had publicly appealed for him to be at my side. I wanted to discuss my tactics with him beforehand and to hear his reassuring voice remind me of what I did well on court. Just to glance towards his presence as the match took its inevitable twists and turns in momentum would have kept me calm. And then, on the day, he never turned up. Where was he? I never really found out. There was a story about him collecting his daughter from the airport and not being able to make it in time; another about him walking through the glass of a French window at his brother's house in south London, where he was staying. This was an era before mobile phones. All I knew was that he hadn't collected the ticket I'd left for him on the gate. As the clock ticked down towards my semi-final, and I could hear the crowd cheering Virginia's performance, my anxiety in wondering where he was, and why he hadn't showed up, was not ideal preparation. I was about to play for a place in what could have been an all-British final, at Wimbledon, the dream, for goodness sake!

As I wrote in my memoir, *Calling the Shots*, Betty played a smart game, using the weight of her shot as an intimidating weapon. She sliced the ball so much and kept hitting it low to my forehand. Because of my extreme grip, it just took my weapon away. I didn't have enough time for my back swing and it totally disrupted my rhythm. There were precious few long rallies. She played cleverly and I didn't. I couldn't find a way to combat her tactics. And I panicked when the momentum of the match switched in her favour. Subconsciously, I was remembering my capitulation of 1976 when I surrendered a winning position to Martina in the Wimbledon quarter-finals.

Maybe I was fearful of another humiliation. I kept on hitting too wide to her. I should have played down the middle and blocked her. 'That's what you normally do,' Mr Roberts said later down the phone. 'Why didn't you do that against her?' My instinct was to keep her running because she wasn't the best mover and she wore a heavy bandage on her leg. But too often she was in control – and I couldn't forget that in the quarters she had beaten Martina, who was practically unbeatable. I knew what I had to do, I just couldn't do it. And then, when the third set started running away from me, I got very nervous. I was inhibited; I just didn't feel like myself out there.

It was a horrible match, traumatising to lose in such a way on such an occasion. In retrospect, though, I can see that in 1977 Betty was playing really well. In fact – and here's the sort of fun fact that I used to pose as a question when I hosted *A Question of Sport* – she reached the finals that year at Wimbledon in singles, doubles and mixed doubles, only to lose them all. I absolutely should have won that semi-final. Three weeks later I beat Betty 6–1, 6–0. I was never the same player again. After that, I always doubted myself. When I got into tight situations in matches, negativity would creep back into my thoughts. I truly felt that was my moment. The opportunity to fulfil my dream was there … and I let it slip away.

That was hard to deal with. But Vitas Gerulaitis, my team-mate in World Team Tennis, was very supportive. He was quick to invite me and Ann Kiyomura (who also played with us for the Indiana Loves team) to sit in the player's box the following day to watch his semi-final against Björn Borg. That 1977 men's semi-final now ranks as one of the all-time classics from Wimbledon – we must have run it hundreds of times during rain delays down the years – and in terms of out-of-this-world tennis and magical shotmaking, it was a great way to stop me brooding over my defeat.

The final score was 6–4, 3–6, 6–3, 3–6, 8–6, and, of a total of 353 points, Björn won 177 and Vitas 176. It was *that* close. Vitas's response to his semi-final loss was an eye-opener for me. Where I was utterly depressed, he was just so happy with his performance. To see how joyful Vitas was – that he had been able to compete against his good friend in a style that made him proud – made me think, *Wow, that's the way to deal with defeat.* Afterwards, he said, 'Come on, we're going out to Tramp!'

It took a bit longer than drinks, dinner and a trip to a night-club, but over the years I've learnt not to consider my match against Betty in a totally negative way, because I think if I'd won it, and maybe gone on to win Wimbledon, I wouldn't have had to find another career – and I wouldn't then have had the most wonderful 37 years in television, working for Channel 7, BSkyB and the BBC.

Queen of Wimbledon

In the course of my time in broadcasting, I went to New York
to interview Virginia, to talk about her memories of being
crowned Wimbledon champion in 1977. Yes, that pain again!
All in the name of duty! Virginia's impact on Wimbledon history
is immense, as she remains the last British winner of the ladies'
singles competition and we are now edging towards the 50th
anniversary of that achievement. There is a commemorative
bust of her on a plinth in front of the All England Clubhouse, the
last in a row of the British women's champions: Kitty Godfree,
Dorothy Round, Angela Mortimer and Ann Haydon-Jones.
Most people, however, recall that iconic image of her receiving
the Venus Rosewater Dish from Elizabeth II, whose pink tweed
dress coat and matching hat happily coordinated with Virginia's own dress and an old rose cashmere cardi that she thought
would go nicely with it. Teddy Tinling, she told me, had made
her four dresses that year. 'There was always this concern that
if you wore Teddy's clothes, it would be a little too flashy, but
he always dressed me very demurely,' Virginia said. 'And this
particular one with the pink piping, I was winning in it, so I had
to wash and hang it up every night, and wear it again. I decided
it was my lucky outfit and it was dead easy to wash.'

On the day of the final, Virginia couldn't resist a peek out
of the dressing-room window to watch the royal party arrive
in time for lunch in the Royal Box. She wanted to spend a few
minutes soaking up the atmosphere. 'There were so many fans
cheering and waving Union Jacks as her beautiful car pulled

up,' she recalled. 'It was cool because I saw that the Queen was dressed in the same colour as my cardigan, and I took that as the biggest omen.' At 31, playing in her 16th consecutive Wimbledon, Virginia was admirably philosophical, both before and during what turned into a three-set match. 'In tennis, you have to work hard. You have to do all the groundwork. You have to practise and you have to dedicate yourself mentally. Once in a while, it all falls into place,' she argues.

> After I won, everybody asked me if winning had changed my life, and I said I had changed my life before Wimbledon. My attitude had become so much more professional, and that's why I could win Wimbledon. I think I was ready to win two years earlier, but I played Evonne Goolagong in a long match on Centre Court and I had some chances, but she came up with the magic. I didn't do anything wrong. I came off court thinking it just wasn't meant to be. Two years later, it was meant to be.

In terms of her changed attitude, Virginia explained that she had learnt not to dwell on bad line calls. She'd realised that you have to expect both the very best and the very worst to happen in a match.

> So, if you win the first set 6–0, that's not very realistic. If you lose it 6–0, that's also not very realistic. You have to be prepared for every eventuality. I had matured to

the extent that when I lost the first set, I thought to myself, okay, we have three sets. That's the beauty of tennis, it's very forgiving. You have time to work it out. First of all, I had no intention of losing that match, and I felt I had done a lot of good work against her. Betty was difficult to play because she gave you no rhythm, but you had to bide your time and hope that a few errors would come in. I just thought, play one point at a time. You prepare for things going wrong, you prepare for things going right.

With that approach, she went on patiently to win 4–6, 6–3, 6–1.

The press had noticed that Virginia arrived at Wimbledon that year with a new, sharper haircut.

I'd been itching to cut my hair, and finally I thought, I'm going to cut it. Everybody has a little something they do when they want a change, and it's very often to do with their hair. It's the same with the guys, Federer and Nadal, it just got shorter and shorter!

As she says, her new look worked. But she also confessed that the pressure of being the favourite did not affect her unduly.

It was one of those strange things. I know everyone tries to tell themselves all the time that things are going to go right, but that year I honestly felt it was my tournament to win. I had to play Chris, and that was the best match of my life, really good tennis. I thought, I've now won six matches, one more to go. I had a very good record against Betty and I was quite relieved that it wasn't a certain Sue Barker who won that semi!

Virginia prepared for the final by watching the 'mesmerising' Borg and Gerulaitis match, then did some visualising work and drove herself to Wimbledon for a quick hit on the practice courts. Looking back, she also recognises a few moments that she regarded as 'signs'. For example, later in the day, after the Champions' Parade on Centre Court, she bumped into Maria Bueno at Queen's, where she had gone to practise.

I said to her, 'That was fantastic, that parade,' and Maria said, 'You'll be in one next.' Things like that make a difference. I had a message from Arthur Ashe, who had won Wimbledon two years before, and we'd both won the US Open in 1968, and we shared a birthday. He left a message for me saying, 'Just camp out at the net, and you'll be alright.' So there were meaningful things and by the time I played Betty, I was in my cocoon.

The Venus Rosewater Dish

Virginia is only the second British woman to win Wimbledon in the Open Era (the other being Ann Haydon-Jones in 1969) and the only one in history to be a champion at all four majors, having won the singles at the US Open and in Australia, as well as the ladies' doubles at the French Open, where she paired up with Margaret Court to defeat Françoise Dürr and one Betty Stove. All the Grand Slam men's and women's singles trophies are classic cups with handles, except for the holy grail for women at Wimbledon. When I was presenting *A Question of Sport*, I used to do a lot of quizzes from the website Sporcle with my producer, and there is a question that challenges you to match the eight Grand Slam singles trophies with their major. The Venus Rosewater Dish, Wimbledon's ladies' singles trophy, stands out by a mile. Unique in shape and style for a tennis prize, it's instantly recognisable as the Wimbledon trophy. Another reason why it feels so special to win it. A sterling silver salver, partly gilded and 18.75 inches in diameter, it was first presented to the champion in 1886. It is actually a reproduction of an item in the Victoria & Albert Museum called The Temperance Basin – a serving platter that would be piled with food at a buffet. Taking my role as a Wimbledon historian seriously and moving into *Antiques Roadshow* mode, I can give you all the facts about this most iconic of trophies in women's sport ...

The theme of the decoration is mythological. The central figure is Temperance – a virtue promoting modesty and restraint – seated on a chest with a lamp in her right hand and a wine jug in her left, with a sickle, fork and a heraldic wand around her. The four sections around her each depict a classical god, together with the four elements air, water, earth, and fire. Around the rim, the goddess Minerva presides over the seven liberal arts: astrology, geometry, arithmetic, music, rhetoric, dialectic and grammar. The trophy has no words on it other than the engraving showing the dates and names of all the champions.

The V&A has fifteen reproductions of the original design, which dates from 1585, but the one held up in triumph by Wimbledon champions represented the height of nineteenth-century modernity when it was first crafted by Elkington & Company of Birmingham in 1864. Like players wearing Teddy Tinling dresses in cutting-edge fabrics, the champion's trophy was at the forefront of technological innovation. But what makes it so very special is that it has been engraved with the name of every champion since 1884. The winners from 1884 to 1957 are inscribed around the inside of the bowl and champions from 1958 onwards are around the outside of the bowl.

I've seen the thrill in the eyes of players from Venus Williams and Petra Kvitová to Simona Halep and Ash Barty when they realise their name will forever be commemorated on it as a champion who has added to the drama and history of Wimbledon. And how nice for Venus that there was a dish with her name before she ever struck a tennis ball!

The trophy remains at the Wimbledon museum and the champions take home a 14-inch replica. Unfortunately I am not among those who have one in my trophy cabinet, but I do have a framed photograph of myself holding it up as if in a moment of glory on my wall. The trophy came over to the BBC studio for a feature and I wasn't going to let it go without pretending it was mine, just for a few minutes!

6

CHRISSIE EVERT

For the ten years following Virginia's Wimbledon victory, only three different names were engraved on the Venus Rosewater Dish: Mrs JM Lloyd (Chris Evert's married name) and Mrs R. Crawley (Evonne Goolagong's married name) appeared one more time each, while the engraver was kept busy etching the letters for Miss M. Navratilova eight times. The Evert-Navratilova rivalry remains the standout era in the history of women's tennis, and for tennis fans of a certain generation it defines their memories of Wimbledon. Remarkably, five of the ten Wimbledon finals from 1978 to 1987 were contested between the pair and none of the ten were without one or the other. Theirs was an astonishingly enduring dominance of the game. And it was just my bad luck that my career was forged in parallel to these two all-time superstars! Those of us who were ranked No.3 in the world – and that included me in 1977 – had to consider ourselves No.1 in the rankings of mere mortals.

Before I met Chrissie in person, I had read many articles about her and followed her results. She is two years older than me, and I watched her rise with awe. By 1969 she had already started breaking records as the No.1 ranked U-14 girl in America. I remember reading how, as a 15-year-old, she beat Françoise Dürr and then Margaret Court, who was No.1 in the world, in an event in North Carolina. I saw photos of this very composed young girl with long, straight, dark blonde hair, parted in the middle and tied in a ponytail with a big white ribbon. I read how unflappable she was when playing her first Grand Slam at the US Open aged just 16. We had no television at home, but I remember reading and re-reading newspaper reports about how, match after match, she came back from a set down to win, getting through to the semi-final to play Billie Jean King. The tennis world knew a special player had arrived.

Chrissie's 1971 US Open debut really was something else. As Steve Tignor of the tennis.com website recapped the phenomenon in 2015,

New fans tuned in to see old legends like Rod Laver, who generated mass interest with his Grand Slam run in '69, and Pancho Gonzales, who proved to be a must-see star even into his 40s. But none of the game's greatest players could match the appeal of the little blonde teen with the big backhand, who was taking two weeks off from Ft. Lauderdale's St. Thomas Aquinas High School. When the world watched 'Chris America' coolly reduce her older opponents to tears on her way to the

semi-finals, usually with a dramatic comeback thrown in
for good measure, the boom was on.

In ten days she had become a national sensation. Her arrival on
the scene was an era-defining moment in tennis and the start
of a golden era for Wimbledon. Nine months later, I remember
watching Wimbledon at home on the television – at last we'd got
one! – with my family when she made her debut on the grass. She
was the No.4 seed and reached the semi-finals. I will never forget
my first impressions of her in that summer of 1972. She looked so
cool and calm; she never showed a flicker of emotion. I thought,
How does she do that? Her outfit, the three red stripes across her
shoulders and the red trim around the flared skirt, was as impeccable as her tennis. She wore hoop earrings, bobby socks with
little pom-poms at the heel to keep them from slipping down,
and her hair was tied back with a pretty ribbon. She was on every
front page. Every young girl wanted to be gorgeous Chrissie – so
ruthlessly good at tennis, so cool in demeanour, so feminine.

Mr Roberts was mesmerised by the way Chrissie constructed
the points and told me to study her. But the big difference
between the two of us was patience – I had none! My biggest
problem was always forcing the point too early; I loved trying to
make things happen, even when it wasn't the right thing to do.
Mr Roberts said that I had the fitness to last in long matches but
it was always my patience that let me down.

Chrissie's father, Jimmy Evert, was a professional coach who,
when she was just five years old, started giving her lessons at the
tennis centre he ran in the Holiday Park in Fort Lauderdale. All

her siblings played. I would play against both Chrissie and her sweet younger sister Jeanne on the tour and in Wightman Cup matches. Their brothers, John and Drew, and youngest sister Clare were all US college tennis scholarship players. Four out of five of them won titles at the prestigious Junior Orange Bowl in Florida. The Everts were a star family – the tennis equivalent of 1970s TV shows like *The Brady Bunch* and *The Partridge Family* – and all so nice. None of them ever gloated when they won or became moody when they lost. Jimmy Evert taught Chrissie not to reveal her emotions because it would give an opponent insight into what aspects of her game to exploit. He said matches are usually lost, not won; and that if you keep composed and control the tempo, then opponents become vulnerable and start making errors. Chrissie was a good student. After her remarkable run to the semi-finals, aged 16, in that 1971 US Open, *Sports Illustrated* described her as 'the poker-faced 16-year-old Florida ingenue with a two-fisted backhand and nothing to lose'.

I had wonderful battles with Chrissie, quite a few of them going the full three sets ... which she won (eventually). She was a brutal opponent and I treasure my straight-sets victory over her in Boston in 1979 when I played the perfect match. She got her revenge quite soon after though. What made her so difficult to beat? She had perfect ground strokes, powerful, accurate and reliable on both wings, and astonishing mental resilience. Her confidence, composure and competitive instinct were second to none, and so off-putting to her opponents. Always unruffled, she was given a lot of nicknames that she didn't like – Ice Maiden, Little Miss Icicle, The Ice Princess and, in Italian,

Signorina macchinnetta (the Little Machine). In the early days she was accompanied by her mother, Colette, but behind the scenes, I gradually got to know Chrissie and discovered her great sense of humour.

I did bemoan the fact that I was born into the era that included two of the greatest ever in Chrissie and Martina, but looking back I wouldn't have missed it as it was a privilege to play with them, and against them, and both have become super friends. I wonder how many players from other eras could say that? Of course, I must include Billie Jean too as she is still a big influence in my life, but she has always been more of a mentor and I didn't play against her that many times. Chrissie and Martina, so opposite in their styles of play, were the standard-setters and through our years of shared experiences we became closer. Both of them were happy to come in to the BBC studio to be star guests when I was hosting Wimbledon. Our camaraderie, which extended to Tracy Austin and Pam Shriver, too, added a popular dimension to our coverage.

My chats with Chrissie were so well received, largely because she took the mickey out of me, which my team thoroughly enjoyed. She was also a great student of the game and her assessments were so incisive and informative. I loved talking to Chrissie whether on air or not. One time when we were passing in the crowd at Wimbledon, I shouted to her, 'Thanks for popping into the studio yesterday. Everyone loved our chat and how we kidded each other.' To which she replied theatrically, 'That's because we had that wonderful affair years ago.' Everyone's eyebrows, including mine, were raised, but she was still waving and laughing as she disappeared out of view, leaving me with a shocked crowd of people. I couldn't say anything. My floor manager, Liz, was in hysterics.

For a long period Chrissie was an ever-present star at Wimbledon. She took pride in her consistency, and her record in the Grand Slam tournaments was incredible. She reached the semi-finals or better in 52 of her 56 majors. She never lost in the first or second rounds and only twice in the third. Of the 18 years she entered Wimbledon, she reached the semi-finals in 17. She finished as champion three times, runner-up seven times and semi-finalist seven times. The one anomaly was her exit after losing a third-round match against Kathy Jordan in 1983. Naturally, there were mitigating circumstances. Having been struck by a stomach virus, she had requested to have her match moved to the following day, but was denied. That loss marked the first time in Chrissie's career that she lost prior to the semi-finals of a Grand Slam.

But only three Wimbledon titles? Of course, we were all up against Martina, who became one of the greatest grass-court players of all time. It's significant that Chrissie never beat her in a Wimbledon final; her titles in 1974, 1976 and 1981 came after defeating Olga Morozova, Evonne Goolagong and Hana Mandlíková. I never played Chrissie on the grass at Wimbledon, but we have talked about it a lot and we both feel the same about the surface. The low-bouncing grass suited the serve-and-volleyers. The speed of play made it difficult for more defensive players like Chrissie, who relied on getting into a rhythm before unleashing her winners with exceptional depth and shot placement. Her game was built on great timing, but on the grass she always felt she was digging out low balls. Certainly I felt I never had time to get my racket back before swinging through. We always moan about how much more successful we'd have been if only the Wimbledon grass played like today's virtual hard courts. Our records might be a different story.

The Head Groundsman would back us up. Until 2002 the grass played fast and low. After the 2001 Championships, the All England Club initiated a change to its court cultivation to bring Wimbledon more in line with how tennis was played around the world. The traditional mix of 70 per cent ryegrass and 30 per cent creeping red fescue switched to 100 per cent perennial ryegrass, which allows the ground underneath to stay dry and firm, resulting in slower, slightly higher and more consistent bounces. It meant a different type of player could do well at Wimbledon. The 2001 men's final was a relentless serve-and-volley rollercoaster between Goran Ivanišević and Pat Rafter; after the switch in grass mix, the 2002 match featured two baseliners, the Australian Lleyton Hewitt and David Nalbandian of Argentina. I've read statistics that show how in 2003, Roger Federer served and volleyed on 48 per cent of his service points en route to his first title. Nine years later, when he claimed his seventh title, that figure was less than 10 per cent, but that probably had more to do with who he was serving to! Rafa, Novak, Andy ... three of the greatest returners.

Chrissie had a glamorous presence on court. Only she could stop a high-profile match at the US Open and look for the diamonds that had scattered across the court when her bracelet broke! This actually happened during an early round at the 1978 Open, the year the event moved from Forest Hills to Flushing Meadows. Thereafter a diamond line bracelet, which had become popular in the 1920s, was known as a 'tennis bracelet'.

Away from the court, Chrissie's glamour brought a different kind of attention. In 1974 Chrissie won her first Wimbledon title while her fiancé Jimmy Connors was crowned the men's champion. The sport of tennis could not have hoped for a more telegenic It Couple when the American duo became engaged. She was 19; he was 21. After their dual success at Wimbledon – and a champions' dance – they were hailed as the 'Love Double'. (They occasionally played mixed doubles together, too.) The press intrusion was intense. Jimmy thrived in it; not so Chris. The wedding that was planned for 8 November 1974 was called off. When I sat down to talk to her for my 2017 documentary, it was interesting to hear her open up about that time, but it was difficult to hear how the media attention affected her. 'It bothered me when the facts weren't right. I mean, if they printed something that was completely wrong, yeah, it did bother me,' Chrissie said. 'It bothers me to this day. But if something was right, like, if Jimmy and I were dating, we were spotted having dinner, then you know, how can it bother you if it's true? I think you become a little hardened to it, but I still was sensitive to it.'

The romance did not last and the next one guaranteed a similar level of media intrusion. By the 1978 Wimbledon final, Chris was falling in love with John Lloyd, the pin-up of British men's tennis. Today, Lloydy reckons Martina owes him dinner. 'I helped her win her first Wimbledon,' he says mischievously.

Chris was 4–2 up in the final set but could not summon her usual killer instinct to finish off the match, not even for a third triumph at Wimbledon, the greatest prize of them all. Martina was quick to capitalise and won an emotionally charged first Wimbledon title – 'the happiest I've ever been on the court', she said. Fans will remember how thrilled Chrissie looked for her friend as she ruffled her hair and smiled indulgently at their sporting exchange at the net. She and Martina bantered affectionately as they stood courtside before the trophy presentation.

'How come you're not crying?' asked Chris.

'I don't know,' replied Martina, adding: 'I don't want to, not in front of all these people.'

'I did, the first time,' Chris said, remembering 1974.

Then she quipped, 'I can't believe it. I hit you in the head with the ball, and you started playing better.'

Almost 40 years later, Chrissie admitted to me: 'I was not upset at all losing that final, which I should have won.' She added, 'And I should have been upset, but I was in love.'

7

MARTINA NAVRATILOVA

Martina and Chris had the perfect rivalry. Whether they were in form or not, their match-ups were always guaranteed to be pure theatre thanks to their opposing styles of play: the left-handed, attacking and athletic serve-and-volleyer against the right-handed, counter-attacking baseline player with impeccable footwork. Martina was so emotional and distractible on court, Chrissie so calm and self-contained.

Their deeply competitive nature drove each other to become better players. When I recall their matches, I think of Martina rushing forward, arm outstretched to put away a sharp-angled volley, or Chrissie on the baseline defying her with a clean, whistling passing shot. They had to work hard to find the precision to outwit each other and that made their encounters mesmerising to watch.

On an emotional level, they were initially good friends and a great doubles pairing, winning the Wimbledon ladies' doubles in 1976 by beating Billie Jean King and Betty Stove in an exciting three-set battle. Those were the days when all the top singles competitors loved to play doubles, too. Chrissie had the upper hand and the world No.1 ranking – that is, until 1981, a watershed year when Martina hired American former professional basketball player Nancy Lieberman as her coach. Lieberman is said to have urged her to 'hate Chris, and you'll play better'. Thereafter, with Martina's killer instinct sharpened, she became the more dominant player. For an incredible 12 years between 1975 and 1987, one of the two of them was ranked No.1 in the world, all bar 23 weeks. And in that period, only three players beat them back-to-back in a tournament – Evonne, Tracy Austin and Hana Mandlíková – but no one ever managed that at Wimbledon.

I first met Martina when she was 13, when I practised on the adjacent court to her at the Palace Hotel in Torquay, where she came to play in an international junior competition sponsored by BP. That was my very first view of her. I saw this incredible athlete with a huge, swinging, leftie serve, charging to the net and unleashing killer volleys. She made her offensive game look so easy. I thought, *Oh dear!* Not only would I need to compete against the unbreakable Chrissie, but now this powerhouse from Czechoslovakia, who I could see was going to cause me major headaches! The only way to play her was to keep her away from the net. If you hit a ball short, or tried to lob her, that was it, she could jump like a gazelle and end the point with a powerful smash. Once she was at the net, she was almost impossible to pass.

Martina didn't speak a word of English then, but at the tournament we acknowledged each other with a nod. We were the best players in that pool of junior talent, so we guessed we'd be seeing a lot more of each other in the future. She had an aura about her, even then. Martina wasn't expressive; she didn't give a lot away. She could look quite stern and serious. But when she smiled – just as now – her face lit up. We met in European competition a lot when we were 14, 15 and 16, in the Princess Sofia and Annie Soisbault cups. In a way we grew up together, playing with and against the same cohort of players, so I had respect for her, but no fear – compared to Chrissie, who I'd seen in newspapers and on TV when she was already hailed globally as a prodigy, and who I was in awe of. Chrissie always seemed to be on a higher plane, destined to date a Hollywood actor and a son of a US President, and be painted as a cultural icon by Andy Warhol. 'The sports stars of today are the movie stars of yester-day,' the artist said, and Chrissie was our sport's leading lady.

I've already mentioned the drop-shot debacle of my horrible 1976 Wimbledon quarter-final against Martina, when I was only 20 years old. Unfortunately there is footage of it ... of me, stomping off the court with a face like thunder, with my towel and rackets gathered up in one arm and a prim little bag on my shoulder with my player accreditation pass fluttering poignantly as I made my exit. To my horror, it was replayed once by the BBC team during the No.1 Court roof opening event. Mac was merciless.

'Your *handbag*!' he laughed.

'Your face may have got you through the gates,' I said, 'but I needed my competitor's badge and it was tied to my handbag!'

Chrissie went on to beat Martina in the semi-final and it was another two years before Martina would win her first

Wimbledon against Chrissie (thanks, in some part, to John Lloyd!). The year 1978 is significant in being the first of what would turn out to be a record nine Wimbledon titles for Martina, but it was a bittersweet achievement. To win on Centre Court had been her dream since she was a little girl. It was the prize she sought when she defected from communist Czechoslovakia at the age of 18, seeking political asylum in the United States in order to pursue her goals. All she wanted was to play tennis, but the authorities in her home country thought she was becoming too 'Americanised'. She requested a permit to play in the 1975 US Open. It was granted, and on the night before she flew to America, she walked along the river in her home town with her father, and resolved to emigrate. They agreed she would say nothing to her mother. Martina was so close to her mother, Jana, but she had to leave without saying goodbye to her and without knowing when she would ever see her again. I just can't imagine that. 'Leaving my family was the hardest thing I ever had to deal with,' she later told me. 'After that, playing a match, coming out, a piece of cake. I didn't know if I was going to see my parents again. I didn't know if I was going to see them alive.'

When she was presented with the trophy in 1978 by the Duchess of Kent, Martina told her a little about the political situation and why she could not share the dream she had long nurtured with her family, and the Duchess promised to try to help.

Martina was stateless; she had been stripped of her citizenship and her parents, sister (also called Jana) and half-brother were not permitted by the Czech government to travel to London. Before the match, Martina wasn't even sure that they would be able to watch the final as Czech TV didn't show it. 'They'd show Wimbledon until I started winning and then they wouldn't show it. That's how people knew I was in the finals.' So, her family drove to friends who lived near to the German border, where they managed to receive a German transmission and crowded around their small television to watch her play. As Jana recalled, 'We were so nervous. Mother had a Cognac and father a little brandy.' A couple of hours later, they all spoke to Martina on the phone. Everyone was thrilled.

The following year the Duchess of Kent intervened on her behalf and implored the Czech government to grant Martina's mother a visa so that she could watch her play. Jana was permitted a two-week visit. It was the first time mother and daughter had seen each other for four years. Imagine how overwhelming that must have been for Martina. 'It was like some long-lost reunion after a war. At some point we didn't even know if we would ever see each other again. To this day, I don't know how I played tennis, I wanted to win so badly in front of her,' she told me. Naturally, she was to face Chrissie – now Mrs J.M. Lloyd on the scoreboard and backed by a home crowd keen to claim her as British. In front of 13,600 spectators, Martina beat her arch-rival in straight sets, 6–4, 6–4, taking exactly one hour to defend her title and accept the trophy again from the Duchess. Then she blew a kiss to her mother in the crowd. I recall her taking her mother with her to pose with the trophy outside the front of the Club – her mother was smiling with pride, Martina looked absolutely dazed.

Immediately after the match, Martina was asked which victory made her happier, her first or her second. According to the *New York Times*, she answered that you cannot compare joy. 'This was more a relief than joy,' she said. 'I was happy not to lose, especially with my mother here. It seemed harder this year – I've had tougher opponents this time – but I wanted to win this year more than last year.'

Later, I spoke to both Chrissie and Martina about that match and its context. Another contrast in their many-layered relationship was that Chrissie's mother, Colette, was a regular presence at tournaments, travelling with Chrissie in the early days. She was well-known for her kindness and interest in her children's opponents. Martina never had that comfort and security. Still brimming with emotion years down the line, she told me it was 'magic' that she had been able to share that 1979 Wimbledon title with her mother. And Chrissie didn't see her loss on that occasion in terms of career statistics and head-to-head records; she was happy for the rival who had beaten her. 'That [moment] is greater than the game of tennis.'

I was there throughout Martina's defection, her memorable Wimbledon victories, her coming out, all the big headlines in her life. One of the most moving documentaries I made was reliving her story with her. For *Just Call Me Martina,* she invited me back to her home in the Czech Republic, in Řevnice, a market town 10 miles southwest of Prague, to see where it all began. She was born Martina Šubertová in Prague in 1956. Her parents divorced when she was three years old, and three years after that her mother – who excelled at gymnastics, tennis and skiing – married Mirek Navrátil, who became Martina's first tennis coach. She took her stepfather's name (adding the -ova to create the female surname). One positive aspect about growing up in a Communist country, Martina told me, was that women athletes were encouraged and respected. Indeed, her maternal grand-mother, Agnes Semanska, was a top-ranked tennis player for the Czechoslovak Federation before the Second World War. So top-level tennis was in Martina's DNA – her granny had caused quite a stir by beating the mother of Věra Suková, a Wimbledon finalist of 1962, in a national tournament – and her desire to improve was a family effort. Like so many of us, she started at an early age by obsessively drilling tennis balls against a wall. By seven years old, she and her stepfather were working hard on her technique and footwork. At the age of eight, she announced she wanted to win Wimbledon. By 15, she was Czech national champion, and a year later turned pro.

When she first visited America in 1973, the contrast between life in the West and at home startled her. As well as marvel-ling at the size of American cars, she just could not believe oranges grew so abundantly on trees in Florida and that you could just pick one off a branch to eat; in Czechoslovakia, she'd have oranges once a year, at Christmas. Nor could she get over the door-stopper wedge of ham you'd get in a $2.50 sandwich compared to the wafer of meat she'd get at home. Two years later, with Czechoslovakia under Soviet control, the 18-year-old Martina defected to the United States, shortly after losing the US Open semi-final to Chrissie.

Much of the focus of sympathy for Martina's decision has been on her separation from her mother but, as she pointed out, when she defected she also lost the treasured guidance of her stepfather. 'He was my coach, so no coach for six years,' she shrugged, when I spoke to her for our 2016 BBC documentary, *Just Call Me Martina*. Few, if any, of us had coaches that travelled on the tour but Chrissie could go home to her father to reset, just as I went back to Torquay as often as I could for Mr Roberts to cast his eagle eye over my game. Martina couldn't even contact her stepfather long-distance about her game; her matches were not shown on television so he had little to observe and comment on. All this meant she had to redefine her approach herself, all while continuing to play in the tense, competitive environment of world-class tennis. She pinpoints the moment she started to evolve from a top-level contender to the dominant player of the era to when she met fellow athlete Nancy Lieberman in 1981.

'We started training that summer and the idea was to leave no stone unturned,' she said. With Nancy overseeing her fitness, Martina took her training off the court as well as on it. She played basketball, she skied, she scuba dived. A typical day would be four hours of tennis, two hours of drills, two hours of sets, sprint training and weights. If she wasn't playing basketball for 90 minutes, she'd be running on the track – ten 100-metre sprints or (with a groan) four 250 metres. She expounded on her approach in *Conversations with Tyler*, the podcast series created by Tyler Cowen to explore the minds of 'underrated thinkers'. 'I worked harder than I needed to,' she admitted. Martina started the craze for cross training, using skills honed in other sports to sharpen her tennis, both physically and mentally. If you are physically strong, you feel indomitable mentally. In addition to Nancy, she had Renée Richards as a coach and a nutritionist to overhaul her diet. When she first took sanctuary in America, she made up for lost time by enjoying the novelty of fast-food outlets such as McDonalds and Baskin-Robbins ice creams. Those excess pounds were soon burnt off or converted to muscle. There's no doubt that Martina revolutionised women's tennis by raising standards so high. With her aggressive style of play and goal-setting mentality, she made striving for excellence every single day – rather than getting ready to go out to compete – the norm. The women's game has never been the same.

The Duchess of Kent

The elegant Duchess of Kent was a regular feature of Wimbledon trophy presentations from 1969, the year Rod Laver sealed his second Grand Slam, right up until 2001, when she congratulated Venus Williams on a successful defence of her title. Alongside her husband, the Duke of Kent, who was president of the All England Club from 1969 to 2021, the Duchess attended Wimbledon every year to present the winners' trophies to the ladies' singles champions at the end of the tournament. It was a role she clearly loved. One year, she handed out prizes despite having her foot in a surgical cast.

It was a private gesture, but the compassion she showed towards Martina in helping her share her triumph with her family projected a wider understanding of the sacrifices made by champions on their paths to success and just how much the fulfilment of long-held dreams mean. Not just a royal figure to curtsy or bow to as players walked on and off Centre Court, the

Duchess acquired something of an aura of being a fixer of broken dreams and a conjuror of heartwarming cameos. She is probably best remembered for being a comforting shoulder for another Czech star to cry on, when Jana Novotná burst into tears after losing the 1993 final to Steffi Graf and was utterly inconsolable. Novotná had led 4–1 in the final set, and dramatically surrendered with an all-too-visible show of nerves under pressure that was almost unbearable to watch. One look at the runner-up's plate in the Duchess's hands and her bandana-ed head bent low, racked with sobs. The Duchess was nonplussed and offered soothing words of comfort. Four years later, Jana lost again on Centre Court in three sets, this time to the 16-year-old Martina Hingis, but she seemed to accept her lot – even whisking the trophy from Hingis and pretending to run off with it.

Presenting her with another runner-up's prize, the Duchess assured her, 'Don't worry. I am sure it will be third time lucky.' And when Novotná's dream finally came true in the following year, after she survived a tie-break scare to crush French player Nathalie Tauziat in straight sets, the Duchess handed her the Venus Rosewater Dish and said, serenely, 'What's all the fuss about? I told you last year you would come back and win.'

What Makes Wimbledon Unique?

As the only Grand Slam tournament played on grass, Wimbledon is unique and romanticised for the All England Club's immaculate cultivation and care of the emerald-green 'living surface'. Visit the Club in the winter or very early spring, and you might happen upon a delivery of hundreds of bags (totalling 9 tonnes, to be precise) of perennial ryegrass seed piled up ready to be planted for the new lawn tennis season. The ground staff follow a precise timetable: the courts are seeded in April, then cut once the new grass reaches 15mm; in May the grass is continually cut three times a week to keep it at 15mm. During The Championships, the grass on each court gets a closer cut so that its height is only 8mm. It has to be cut every day to maintain that height. At the end of summer 6 tonnes of soil are applied to the courts to make sure the playing surfaces are level, ready for the next sowing of seed.

At one time all the majors staged in a sport traditionally known as lawn tennis were played on a natural grass surface – except the French at Roland-Garros, who have always played on their distinctive red clay or *terre battue*. When Chrissie made her breakthrough in the 1971 US Open, she played on grass at the West Side Tennis Club in New York. The US Open didn't switch from grass to green clay until 1975; it then moved to hard court when the tournament moved to Flushing Meadows in 1978. The Australian Open persisted with grass until 1988 before adopting its current hard surface. So the grass is only one aspect of what has made Wimbledon special down the years.

What I think really makes The Championships unique is its history and particularly its long association with royalty. No other Grand Slam has a Royal Box attended daily by members of a royal family and their guests. The *Wimbledon Compendium* – a meticulously compiled and edited record book of every fact and figure imaginable – details the event's association with royalty, which started in 1907 when the Prince of Wales, accompanied by Princess Mary, visited the old Worple Road ground. They were met by the Committee and entertained in the courtside Committee Box, which had been temporarily dressed as a Royal Box. 'They stayed until a thunderstorm put an end to the day's play, having watched the last of W.V. Eaves v L.H. Escombe, Miss M.G. Sutton v Miss A.M. Morton and part of a doubles contest,' the record book states.

> Before leaving the ground the Prince accepted an offer of the Presidency of the Club and declared his intention of donating to the Club a challenge trophy. The Prince remained President until his accession to the throne as King George V in 1910. He then became Patron of the Club, a position subsequently maintained by succeeding monarchs.

And so it was that Queen Elizabeth II served as Patron from 1952 until the end of 2016, when she stood down and was succeeded by the then Duchess of Cambridge, now the Princess of Wales.

When the new All England Lawn Tennis Club grounds were constructed at Church Road in 1922, it was King George V who oversaw the official opening. Rain delayed the ceremony, naturally, before the king banged a large gong to signal the start of a new era. Queen Elizabeth's tenure as Patron spanned a fascinating tranche of Wimbledon history. Did her visits always coincide with milestone moments, or does Wimbledon serve up milestones every year? It's a moot point! The late queen first attended The Championships in 1957, when she presented the Venus Rosewater Dish to Althea Gibson, the first African American player to win the ladies' singles. Five years later she was back to present the trophy on court to Rod Laver in the year of his first calendar Grand Slam. In 1977 the tournament provided a quintessentially British backdrop to Queen Elizabeth's Silver Jubilee celebrations, when she and Virginia posed for that iconic image in their colour-coordinated outfits. Her last visit came in 2010. I remember that day so clearly as we peered out of the BBC studio's prime viewing spot to see a tiny figure in a turquoise hat and dress coat with white trim touring the grounds, walking past Henman Hill and down St Mary's Walk, led by chairman Tim Phillips. She watched some tennis on Court 14, an outside court, and then went up to the competitors' facilities and met Roger Federer, Serena Williams, Novak Djokovic, Andy Roddick and Venus Williams, before crossing the bridge to the main Clubhouse and eventually settling down in the Royal Box to watch Andy Murray play the Finn Jarkko Nieminen. Andy turned and gave the monarch a very impressive bow as he walked onto Centre Court!

Catherine, Princess of Wales, is an inspiring Patron of the All England Lawn Tennis Club. I loved the way she donned her official Wimbledon tennis kit to go on court with Roger Federer last summer and hit a few balls to highlight the hard work put in by the ball boys and girls during their eve-of-tournament training. She has spoken to me about her love of tennis and how watching Wimbledon every summer was very much part of her childhood. 'It's such a quintessential part of the English summer, and I think it really inspires youngsters,' she said. 'It certainly inspired me when I was younger to get involved in the game. Wimbledon hasn't changed either, I think that's what's so wonderful.'

During the filming of my *Our Wimbledon* documentary, I interviewed both the Duke of Kent and Catherine, now Princess of Wales. It was obvious to me how much Wimbledon meant to the Duke and his family as his parents presented the trophies before him – so it was very much a family tradition. His love for the game and the place came across and also how much he had seen it evolve. Wimbledon combines tradition and innovation with ease. Catherine was so lovely to talk to, too. I waited in a room in Kensington Palace with producer Carl Doran and the camera crew. We were all a bit on edge and then in she came and put us all at ease, even saying she was a bit nervous as she hadn't given many interviews. (I'm sure she said that to make me feel better.) She was a natural in front of the camera and what came across in the interview was her obvious love for the game from an early age. Tennis is a family passion and the Middletons came to queue and watch Wimbledon most years. She told me how mortified she was when her father once mistook Tim Henman for Pete Sampras. 'My father is not going to appreciate this, but we were walking past Tim Henman and we had just seen [Pete] Sampras play. And dad said very coolly: "Hi, Pete." I was mortified!' She also revealed her mother has a bit of a crush on Roger Federer! She's not alone …

Just as she attended with her parents, Carole and Michael – who occasionally now join her in the Royal Box – so she is clearly sharing her love of the game with her own children.

It was lovely to see Prince George and Princess Charlotte make their debuts in the front row of the Royal Box as they accompanied their parents to see Novak and Carlos Alcaraz fight for the men's singles title, mirroring the year Princess Diana brought along the nine-year-old Prince William.

Diana was a familiar face in the Royal Box. She was famously present when Mac had his meltdown in the semi-final against Rod Frawley in 1981 and much was made of her departure in the middle of his match. This was the notorious occasion when he called the umpire, who was a wing commander in the RAF, a 'disgrace to mankind' and ranted, 'I always get robbed because of the umpires in this place.' He was later astonished when he met her and she displayed empathy for him playing under such scrutiny at Wimbledon. 'She said, "Oh God, the pressure must be unbelievable",' he recalled. 'And I thought, she's under 100 times more pressure than I'll ever be and she still said that.'

I remember being so jealous that Virginia always got invited to have tea with Princess Diana – another perk of being a British Wimbledon champion, and another reason to regret my 1977 semi-final! I once passed Diana on the stairs up to the Royal Box as she was being escorted out to her car. I stood back to let her through and stood to attention; I was so in awe. She smiled and said, 'Hi, Sue, how are you?' I mumbled something ridiculous which I can't now recollect but I was so thrilled she even knew my name. That is a favourite Wimbledon memory.

Catherine said she and William often enjoy playing doubles and that they are quite competitive. When I received my CBE in 2021, it was Prince William who presented it to me, which I was thrilled about. He was so easy to talk to and knew so much about my career, I was on cloud nine. He, too, mentioned how much they loved the game as a family. The Wimbledon royal connection is in safe hands.

• • •

Back to tennis royalty in the shape of Martina. Wimbledon is the platform on which tennis fans saw the unparalleled achievements that mark her out as surely the greatest grass-court player of all time. From 1973 to 2006 – that's 33 years! – tennis fans watched her game evolve on the grass, her trophies pile up and her records become ever more impressive. As well as her nine singles titles, she was three times a runner-up, five times a semi-finalist and three times a quarter-finalist. I mean, that is a stunning record. Add in seven ladies' doubles titles and four in the mixed doubles and her Wimbledon trophy tally is 20, a figure that equals Billie Jean King's. Her longevity is extraordinary – away from Wimbledon, she won her 59th and last Grand Slam title, in the mixed doubles with Bob Bryan, at the US Open, when she was nearly 50. She is the only player ever to have won Grand Slam titles throughout four decades. To think her life in tennis started when she was just four, hitting a tennis ball against a concrete wall in Řevnice.

While the rest of us went for a run to build up our fitness, she introduced the idea of working with weights for conditioning, sprint training for speed, eating well for overall health, and cross training, which involved playing a host of other sports like basketball to improve footwork and extend reach. As a result of this disciplined approach, she was in a different league from the rest of us. Her reaction time was lightning quick, she had incredible stamina and she became even more powerful.

At Wimbledon, she always seems totally at home. Fans have told me they once saw her cycling in and she just stopped for a chat, which made their day. The local greengrocer would deliver boxes of healthy fruit and vegetables to the house she rented close to the All England Club. She would even bring her dogs! I was always grateful that she, like Chrissie and Tracy, would pop into the BBC studio as my guest. There's nothing she doesn't know about how to play the game at Wimbledon. She was my unfortunate guest one year when I nearly burned down the studio and possibly the whole media centre. It was another rainy day, and I was in the studio trying to fill hours of time. Martina came in to help. I always had loads of research notes on all the players and coaches with me. I tried to keep them out of sight but close by in case I needed to refer to them when we were showing a VT. My producers always liked the desk to be as tidy as possible, which wasn't always easy for me! As Martina and I were chatting away I suddenly saw my floor manager Liz looking worried and talking in an animated fashion to the gallery; the next minute I heard Martin Hopkins, the producer, say, 'There's a smell of smoke in the studio.' Everyone was looking concerned. Martin told me to link to a VT, but the only one available was one that Martina and I had to talk over – but at least it would give Liz and the team a chance to do a sweep of the studio. Just as Martina and I started talking over the footage, I was aware of an intense burst of heat around my legs. Flames started flickering up from under my desk. Stupidly, I had put my spare notes on top of the 'hot' lights instead of on the shelf next to them. There was chaos as we fanned the flames and threw the remaining notes on the floor. I still carried on commentating over the footage, slightly breathlessly, as Martina and I wrestled with the flames. Liz joined in, stamping on them. One of the crew rushed in with a fire extinguisher (which wasn't needed, thankfully).

I'm pleased to say the flames were put out, but the smell of smoke lingered for some time. No one at home would have known of the drama, but we had a good laugh when finally we handed back to live coverage of Centre Court. My laughter soon departed when the health and safety team told me in no uncertain terms how dangerous my inadvertent action had been. And I had no excuse as I was always given a safety briefing prior to The Championships and these lights were the number one priority. Needless to say my whole studio crew were relieved when LED lighting came in.

I've said before how lucky I feel to have been on the tour with the likes of Chrissie and Martina, Tracy and Pam Shriver, Virginia, Ann and the rest. We were friends, rivals, confidantes and companions during the endless waiting for matches or practice courts, empty evenings and flights out to the next tournament. Virginia taught me how to do cryptic crosswords. When the board game *Trivial Pursuit* came out in 1981, a lot of us would sit down around the board and entertain ourselves by challenging each other's general knowledge. I played a lot of backgammon with Jimmy Connors. During the Italian Open in Rome one year he was wandering around asking the guys if they knew how to play, or wanted to play, and no one was up for it. Rather forlornly, he looked questioningly at me. 'Yes, I'll play,' I exclaimed, and it became a regular pastime for Jimmy and me at the majors. I remember one Wimbledon when his girlfriend, Patti McGuire, then famous as a former Playboy model (whose now been married to Jimmy for more than forty years), surprised me by coming up to me and enquiring how my match had gone. We'd never met but she was so friendly, telling me Jimmy had told her I had a big match. In the whirl of emotions that sport evokes, we were all family in the broadest sense. Chrissie later spoke via satellite link when I was the subject of an episode of *This Is Your Life* in 1996. And when I started hosting the BBC Wimbledon coverage, many of my old tennis peers popped in to help me out during rain breaks, as a favour to a friend really, and people loved the informality of our chats and the insight of these great champions. Soon our guest panel of stars-turned-pundits became more formalised – an extra dimension I'm proud to have brought to the BBC job.

As with everything they gave to tennis, Chrissie and Martina's enduring friendship is the quintessence. As the last two in the dressing room preparing before and after for a final, they saw each other at their lowest and at their happiest. Over years of deep rivalry and friendship, they came to understand each other in ways no one else can. Most recently, that meant supporting each other through gruelling treatments for cancer. Tennis has a way of bringing people together in the most extraordinary ways and Chrissie and Martina's friendship is a beautiful example of this.

8

BORIS BECKER

No balls were struck in official competition at Wimbledon in 2020. The world was locked down under strict social-distancing rules to try and prevent the spread of COVID-19. Wimbledon, our timeless bubble of balls thwocking off rackets and champagne corks popping among chattering picnickers, was set to be shrouded in silence. It was the first time since the Second World War that The Championships had been cancelled. We had to acknowledge grim, unprecedented times even though the grass courts and English country garden grounds of the All England Club stood expectant, cultivated to perfection, ready for the hordes to arrive and witness another year of history-making competition. Alas, it was not to be. 'This is a decision that we have not taken lightly, and we have done so with the highest regard for public health and the wellbeing of all those who come together to make Wimbledon happen,' said Ian Hewitt, the Club chairman.

It has weighed heavily on our minds that the staging of The Championships has only been interrupted previously by World Wars but, following thorough and extensive consideration of all scenarios, we believe it is ultimately the right decision to cancel this year's Championships, and instead concentrate on how we can use the breadth of Wimbledon's resources to help those in our local communities and beyond.

The year 2020 was one we'd all like to forget, but the Cancelled Championship was not without its entertainment. BBC Sport planned for more than 50 hours of programming following a much-reduced familiar format for the fortnight. I was asked to front a highlights programme looking back at some of the most memorable Wimbledon matches with the help of some familiar studio guests. Of course I said yes. The All England Club offered me a place to stay that backed onto the grounds, as I couldn't travel to and from the Cotswolds, where I live, every day, which was so kind of them (and the home was beautiful). Looking back on some of the most memorable matches from the archive was so much fun. The only complaint from me was that the format chosen for the 'Wimbledon Recreated' theme meant showing the best matches from the round that would have been shown on that day of The Championships: in other words, two days of first-round matches, two days of second-round matches and so forth. This meant only one day of men's and ladies semi-finals and finals. Most of the matches I would nominate as the greatest came in the second week and it was hard to select just three for each day. Imagine trying to choose just three men's finals since television coverage began! Impossible, but it had to be done. We narrowed it down to Borg vs Mac in 1980, Nadal vs Federer in 2008 and Murray vs Djokovic in 2013, but there were so many more we could have chosen.

We had satellite link interviews with Mac, Chrissie, Billie Jean, Martina, Simona Halep, Rafa, Coco Gauff, John Isner, Virginia, Andy and more, reflecting on life suspended from competition during the pandemic. Our tennis family tuned in and everyone entered into the spirit. We had Andy talking about entertaining his kids, Rafa trying to sort out the best place to put his iPad camera while discussing his pasta recipes, John Isner having to pause the interview for an Amazon delivery and Martina giving us a tour of her menagerie of dogs and birds. Chrissie and I had a very amusing, risqué pre-recorded chat, none of which we could use on air, but it certainly entertained the crews in London and Salford. We eventually had a chat we could use but everyone preferred the first! Studio guests included Tim, Boris, Jo Konta, Heather Watson, Jamie Murray, Dan Evans, Sam Smith, Annabel Croft, Andrew Castle and Pat Cash. For those of us who were part of the on-site team it was a bittersweet experience to be back under such circumstances in a place so familiar we could probably all walk around it blindfolded. We were not allowed into the Broadcast Centre; we had a makeshift studio on the balcony of one of the corporate suites opposite, so we were presenting outdoors against the familiar backdrop of the show-court silhouettes of Centre Court, No.1 Court and Henman Hill. We had to keep metres apart from each other and operate with minimum interaction with the studio team. This meant no make-up artists, so we were given online tutorials on how to do our own hair and make-up. Boris Becker came in a few days after we'd all had our lessons, and we cried with laughter as we watched a very patient Tim try to teach Boris the finer arts of how to apply concealer and anti-shine powder, and instruct him in hair management. The things you never thought you would see behind the scenes at Wimbledon! I so wish I'd recorded that, but I was laughing too much.

For people tuning in in need of light-hearted entertainment, we really did our bit with the Wheelie Bin challenge. This very quickly became the viewers' favourite feature. The challenge involved the surprisingly tricky art of trying to hit six balls into a wheelie bin in 30 seconds from 30 metres away – it proved exceptionally entertaining. Andy and Jamie Murray started it with fellow British players who were competing in the Battle of the Brits tournament masterminded by Jamie. It began as a fun contest while killing time in between practice at the National Tennis Centre. Jamie and Andy showed off the challenge when they were guests on *The One Show* – Jamie 1, Andy 0. They then urged me to get involved and *The One Show* team got in touch and asked me to do it in my back garden. Lance, my husband, was referee and cameraman. He placed the bin about 25 metres away – which wasn't cheating, it was just the furthest distance my garden could cope with. I didn't have any tennis balls, only the balls I threw for my dog Charlie, so he was my ball boy, charging after every missed attempt before at last I got one in. And I celebrated like I'd won Wimbledon. Little did I imagine the impact this challenge would have when we introduced it into our Wimbledon coverage. It became a nightly event, hosted by Rishi Persad, and staged up on the flat lawn where, in normal years, queuers inch towards the Ticket Resale cabin. We had Jo Konta, Annabel Croft, Andrew Castle, Anne Keothavong, Pat Cash. Everybody's competitive spirit came out, including mine, as they only placed the bin 15 metres away, not 25. I got very depressed every evening as people beat me. But no one was more competitive than Tim. He scored four and cheered every missed attempt for the next week. Pat did well with three; so did Annabel. Tim was still top of the leaderboard when we brought out the big gun ... Boom Boom Boris.

Could Boris defeat Tim and rob him of his first Wimbledon trophy?! The big wheelie showdown was broadcast on the day that would have been the men's singles final – and it was tense stuff. Boris scored 3 from 5 balls ... would it be a tie-break or would Tim claim the crown? Boris choked on his final ball, so Tim was the champion. We went to the trouble of getting a very cheap *Blue Peter*-style homespun golden trophy made in the shape of a wheelie bin, which was presented to him on a racket with an exceptionally long handle, a bit like a pizza-oven slider, to meet the social distancing rules. One of Tim's daughters said it was the trophy she was most impressed with from his entire career. Poor Tim! But it caused quite a stir around the country with people taking on the challenge in their own gardens – a bit of light relief in difficult times.

Boris, a born entertainer with his big serve and explosive energy, carried his on-court persona into his broadcasting role.

He was always game for a laugh when he joined the BBC team in 2002, three years into his retirement. From the moment we first saw him burst into the top flight as a teenager at Wimbledon in 1985, he was set to be a huge presence, ushering in a special era. The tabloids styled him Boris 'Boom Boom' Becker – and many other names to mirror his off-court life, but we won't go there … His place in the record books is enshrined as the youngest player ever to win Wimbledon – at 17 years and 227 days old – and he's always had a mature perspective on his achievement. Reminiscing in 2010 with Mark Hodgkinson of the *Telegraph*, he said:

> What I remember most was that people suddenly looked at me differently – they thought I was from planet Mars, and that I had done something I wasn't supposed to do, something that shouldn't have been possible. But I did it. And then I did it again at 18, just to make the point.

The extraordinary thing is that even by 1985, the schoolboy Boris had already had a turbulent introduction to Wimbledon and its hallowed grass courts. Two years earlier, at 15, he had been steamrolled by Stefan Edberg in the first round of the junior competition. A year later, in his first professional outing, his career in tennis could have been over had he not been forced to consider his motivation, and re-fire himself up for a future in the game. Racing in for a volley in a third-round match against Bill Scanlon (the American player who was known for his combustible encounters with Mac), Boris tore ligaments in his ankle. This was on Court No.2 – the so-called graveyard – and as if to emphasise its reputation Boris hopped to the net for a sportsmanlike handshake with Scanlon and was then carried off motionless on a stretcher. When he called his mother, she simply said, 'I told you, you should have stayed at school.' When I later sat down with Boris to reflect on his Wimbledon years, he revealed that it was during the long rehab after the operation on his ligaments that he realised how much he wanted to make a go of life as a professional. And, boy, did he bounce back ...

Charismatic, thrilling to watch and often somewhat controversial, Boris appeared on the scene with a super-confident presence, some would say borderline arrogant. His manager, the droopy-moustached Romanian Ion Țiriac, added to the mystery and enhanced his aura. The words 'pot' and 'kettle' spring to mind, but Mac remembers how Boris had the confidence to complain to umpires throughout the clay-court season in the months leading up to the 1985 grass-court season. 'I remember saying to him at the time: "Why don't you win something, before you start complaining?" Little did I think that at 17, four months later, he would take me at my word.'

Prior to Boris coming to the traditional men's warm-up event at Queen's Club in 1985, there had been much talk about this wonder kid with the thunderous serve and sublime diving volleys. When I first saw him on the court, I was amazed at his physicality for a 17-year-old. He was a muscular six foot three inches, all spring and athleticism at the net. Off court, he looked wide-eyed and innocent. 'When I came over to London I didn't think about winning Wimbledon,' he said of his breakthrough year.

At 17, you live in the present, you don't think about tomorrow. My luck was that I won the Queen's Club tournament so I felt good about myself. I was unseeded at Wimbledon but I was number 20 in the world. I didn't imagine myself winning the title but I also didn't feel nervous at all. I did have a sense of anticipation and of something positive changing about myself, especially in the second week of Wimbledon. More and more people wanted to talk to me! The press conferences were getting longer and longer!

When the unseeded Becker beat the South African-born Kevin Curren to become the youngest player ever to win Wimbledon, the tennis world realised it was witnessing a special moment. He kissed the trophy and put it on his head ... When told he had won £130,000 in prize money, a wide-eyed Boris said, 'That is a lot.' He added: 'Perhaps my victory will change the position of tennis in Germany because we have never before had an idol in this sport.' From the word go, Boris was an endearing combination of youthful innocence (it was said he had only recently stopped asking his coach for pocket money) and a certain savviness. He was unusual in wearing a big gold watch on court. 'It's because I have a contract with the watchmaker,' he replied when questioned about it during a press conference.

Boris's first win always ranks among the top five 'Best Moments at Wimbledon' polls. The crowds always love a breakthrough, and his was particularly stirring. The scoreline reflects a tight battle across four sets: 6–3, 6–7, 7–6, 6–4. Curren may not have a high profile as a household name in tennis history, but he grew up on grass and was one of the very best players at the time, ranking no.5 in the world and reaching the finals of both the Australian Open and Wimbledon. As Boris said, 'He had beaten John McEnroe in the quarter-final in straight sets, and he beat Jimmy Connors in three sets in the semi, and those two guys were the best on grass for many years.' Curren himself was pretty relaxed about the match-up against the unseeded young German; he went to a Bruce Springsteen concert on the night before the most significant match of his life on Centre Court. Everyone thought Boris would crumble under the pressure. But that's when he showed the fighting spirit that would characterise his greatest victories: the bigger the occasion, the brighter the spotlight, the more Boris seemed to bring to the court. The only time he says he was aware of the pressure was when he came out to serve for the Wimbledon title, and yet I remember him looking nerveless. 'I sat at the changeover with the towel over my head just imagining what might happen and I had to stop my mind from racing,' he recalled. 'First point, double fault immediately. My arm became heavy. Then three big serves, 40–15. Then another double fault on my first match point … I just prayed, "God, give me one more serve."'

The Almighty delivered. From the moment Boris did that wide-legged celebratory shuffle and lifted his arms to the sky in victory, he had no doubt his win was life-changing.

I saw my father holding this little camera trying to capture the moment and forgetting that left, right and centre there were millions of pictures now being taken of his son! As I walked to shake Kevin's hand, I knew something had changed and that something dramatically was not going to be the same any more. I didn't know in what way, but I knew my life would change.

Boris now calls the day he became a Wimbledon champion – 7 July 1985 – his second 'birthday'. Like Borg and McEnroe before him, he found it hard to deal with the limelight away from his antics on court, starting with the welcome party of 50,000 his father had organised when he returned to his home town of Leimen in Germany.

> I felt like the Pope in his Popemobile, waving to all the people. Obviously my father and mother were proud, but I was only 17, I felt uncomfortable. I was paying my respects to the people who had come out to celebrate, but the adulation was overwhelming ... Because it's not why you get involved in tennis in the first place. You get involved because you love the game, you want to compete and ideally to win. I was not comfortable being in front of so many people, questioning me about my emotions, my thoughts and fears. That was something I had to get used to over the years.

Although the first win was Boris's most memorable, for me 1986 was more impressive, coming back with all the pressure and expectation to win Wimbledon again. It's so much tougher to defend a title than to win one first time round. And he was still only 18. 'If I had won it for the first time in 1986 I would still have been the youngest [male] player ever to win Wimbledon,' he said. 'I had a lot of maturing to do. Of course I couldn't win every tournament before '86 and the press just killed me, saying I'd had the classic 15 minutes of fame and I was never going to win another Grand Slam.' Weeks after his Wimbledon victory, he fell in the fourth round at the US Open, and was knocked out of the 1986 French Open in the quarters.

> I felt a lot of pressure from the media – and I wasn't sure 1985 wasn't a one-time win either! Could those two weeks be repeated again? Am I good? Am I that good? So for me, personally, the defence was much more important than the first time around because it instilled in me an inner belief that I belong to this tennis world.

Watching the media scrum around Boris reminded me of the chaos around Björn. To be that young and to have that level of intrusion … I understand why he's talked about how difficult it was back then. Time and time again we see those who were thrust early into the limelight struggle to deal with the consequences that come with fame. 'The tennis bit is the easiest!' Boris laughed as we discussed the situation he found himself in.

> It's the before and after that you have to get used to. Expectations are sky-high to accomplish everything you are supposed to. Of course you get criticism if you

don't win every match, and then ultimately you are just a human being with emotions and if somebody says or writes something bad about you, you don't like it. That's normal, and the only way out of it is up. You have to win and you have to defend titles and come back again. And that's difficult.

By 1987, two consecutive Wimbledon victories intensified the stakes for a potential hat-trick when Boris returned to the All England Club as No.1 seed. Would he be the first man since Borg to nail three in a row? Could he ultimately go on to better the Swede's record, given his young age? He couldn't, and his riposte to journalists poised to criticise him after his shock loss in the second round of that Wimbledon to the Australian Pete Doohan suggested he had been musing on the pressure he found himself under for some time. 'It was not a war,' he famously said in the press conference. 'No one got killed. It was a game of tennis and I lost. I'm not immortal. I knew I would have to lose some time at Wimbledon. Sometimes in this game it is sunny, sometimes it is cloudy.'

Like all players following the protocols in the walk from the locker room, down the stairs and onto Centre Court, Boris would have passed under the lines on the wall from Kipling's poem – 'If you can meet with Triumph and Disaster, and treat those two impostors just the same'. From his post-match philosophising, it was clear he had not only taken this declaration of sportsmanship fully on board, but he had embraced the opening lines of the poem, too: 'If you can keep your head when all about you, are losing theirs and blaming it on you'. When he relived that moment in our interview, he went on to expand on his response. 'Of course I was upset to lose but it wasn't something I dwelt on. I thought, I have two titles, let's continue on this journey of becoming a better tennis player without the constant burden of always having to win Wimbledon.'

'Always having to win Wimbledon': that's a phrase that speaks of the pressure that the world's best players take head-on each year when they start their campaign to do just that. 'Always having to do well at Wimbledon' is a phrase that British players know as a pressure to be shrugged off as they strive to do their best in front of the home crowds. Being a professional athlete brings with it extreme emotions. There's no grey area between the highs of success and the devastation of defeat no matter how much coaches talk of taking the positives. There is never a compromise, never a draw. Everyone deals with disappointment differently. Many mask their feelings brilliantly, but everyone goes through some inner turmoil because every individual player cares. I wish I'd handled the 1977 Wimbledon loss differently, and more along Boris's philosophical approach. Mistakes are necessary if you want to learn and improve; psychologists will tell you to try and focus on the process rather than the outcome, but that's easier said than done. I'm not sure I ever achieved that!

Losing a close match, one in which you've had chances to win, is the toughest kind to deal with, so spare a thought for the Frenchman Nicolas Mahut, who lost the longest ever match in tennis history to John Isner on Court 18 in 2010. Their 11 hour and 5 minute marathon match played out over three

WIMBLEDON: A PERSONAL HISTORY

days with the score finally being settled to the American, 70–68 in the fifth. It was a battle that transcended sport; in the 'decider' – more of a 'sit-on-the-fencer' – neither could find a way to break the other's serve. Around the media centre, we joked that this match was wallpapering each day's schedule. It was stuck in a loop, like some sort of tennis *Groundhog Day*. There was always one monitor playing this match. As the fifth set went on, and on, commentators stopped talking so much about who might win and dwelt on the devastation the losing player would inevitably feel after so much effort. Tennis is such a psychological battle; you put so much of yourself on the line when you go out to compete. That fate was Mahut's. He has been open about how the loss was initially so devastating for him and, even a year later, it was hard to talk about. But time heals and he has since said the memory of that match inspires him. To have shared that unique experience in history with Isner has forged a bond between them that can't be broken. On one level, that might seem like a heroic case of the psychologists' advice to look for the positives, and yet I think Mahut really can take immense pride from a competitive battle that tennis fans look back on fondly. Neither player was prepared to give an inch and their match remains the embodiment of a never-say-die attitude, until fatigue inevitably started to creep in. To this day, the plaque on Court 18 that commemorates the match remains one of the most popular points of interest in the official behind-the-scenes tour of the grounds.

As Boris was inferring, the journey up the world rankings is fun and exciting but the pressure to try and stay there is intense.

Players face other distractions the more successful they become that make staying at the top even harder, such as the loss of privacy. (This is something 22-year-old Iga Świątek has admitted struggling with: 'People recognise me almost everywhere. It's difficult for me to live in peace and quiet,' she said in an interview in 2022 with German publication *Tennis Magazin*.) As Boris said to me,

> The price is high for the stars of today or yesterday. We love our fans, but not 24/7. There are times when we want the sanctuary of being private citizens to spend time with our family and friends, and that's not possible. A lot of people don't understand the flip side of winning a trophy. Everything has a price. If you win out there, you lose your privacy. Period. That's the price you are going to pay. And then you question who you hang out with. You have trust issues with your family, your friends or your girlfriend about how this story came out. You start to trust no one. It's a problem. Your circle of friends becomes very very small. And you always double check, you always question. It's a high price.

From 1985 to 1995, Boris's Wimbledon record was superlative. He was seven times a finalist – three times the champion and four times a runner-up (twice to Stefan Edberg, once in an all-German contest with Michael Stich and once to Pete Sampras). In that same period, he also reached the semi-finals twice (losing to eventual champion Sampras in 1993, and to Goran Ivanišević in 1994) and was knocked out in the last eight (losing to eventual champion Andre Agassi). But it's not just his achievements that stick in my memory; it's the style with which he achieved them. Has anyone ever brought so much energy to the court? Like a marauding bull let loose on Wimbledon's pristine lawns, he would hurl down a menacing serve, driven with the full force of his legs, and then sprint towards the net as if his life depended on it. There, in the blink of an eye, you'd see all 85 kilograms of him flying horizontally through the air to score a winner from seemingly impossible angles.

Those diving volleys, complete with brutal landings, were his trademark, and they required the physical resilience of a rugby forward or a wrestler. Talk about commitment! The fast grass of Wimbledon showcased his talent to perfection. Anyone who got to see him play there was lucky to see the best of him. His win-loss statistics stand at 71–12, which translates into an 86 per cent win record. For a glorious period, he was part of the Wimbledon furniture – and he made sure that was quite literally the case. When the All England Club constructed the new No.1 Court, he took home the original tennis net and net posts from old Court No.1 and installed them on the court at his villa in Majorca.

With the understanding he gained from his experience as a player – and his fabulous sense of humour, even in his second language – Boris became an outstanding broadcaster. He was always game for a laugh and took part in so many memorable opening videos for our broadcasts, before and after the COVID pandemic. He once did a hilarious voiceover about who is 'the

GOAT'. With typical Boris humour, this skit involved real mountain goats, as few people at the time, when the phrase was first being bandied about, knew what it actually meant! On another occasion, the cameras panned up his body as we previewed the day's play, the voiceover ending with the line, 'It will be hair raising'. To accompany this, Boris had combed and gelled his hair so that it stuck upwards and his eyes, comically pantomime, were bulging. He was always one of the most popular members of the BBC team, always available for filming at any time, and loved by everyone in the office and studio.

One lasting memory I have comes from the Parade of Champions on the first Saturday of the Millennium Championships when 64 former players were invited back and presented with a memento by H.R.H. The Duchess of Gloucester, who is honorary president of the Lawn Tennis Association. Boris strode on to his beloved Centre Court wearing a sharp suit, with his chest puffed out; no one looked prouder to be there.

Awesome. Memories like this make it even more sad to see what has happened to Boris over the past few years. Deportation after a conviction and prison sentence in England for tax evasion means he is currently barred from entering the United Kingdom. So often I have seen youngsters who were thrust into the limelight at a young age suffer later in their careers. They earn too much money too soon, and sometimes receive bad financial advice. These teenagers are money-making machines without the knowledge and experience to manage their finances and deal with all the pressure that comes with it. Boris, who coached Djokovic from 2013 to 2016, recently stepped down from his role as coach to the young Dane Holger Rune. He is unable to attend Wimbledon until the term of his sentence is over. I hope to see him back at Wimbledon in the future. To not be at Wimbledon will hurt him massively.

Stefan Edberg

We often talk about Wimbledon and the great rivalries, and one that was played in an admirable sporting spirit was between Boris and Stefan Edberg. For three consecutive years, from 1988 to 1990, their finals were a joy to watch, a great display of serve-and-volleying and a clash of opposing personalities. They both clearly liked and respected each other. 'Usually it is easier if you don't like the person you are playing, it stirs up emotion and you want to beat him and motivation goes through the roof, but I like Stefan,' said Boris.

> He was a nice guy before and after matches. Ours became this great sporting rivalry, we fought our tails off on the court but afterwards, we gave each other a hug and said well done and joked, 'Next time I'm going to beat you!' or something like this. Being friendly wasn't off limits. Before our Wimbledon finals, we were sitting across from each other in the locker room and chatting … you know, whoever wins, wins. It was unusual, yes. And it was rare because not only did we play three consecutive finals when we were No.1 and No.2 [in the world rankings] for many years chasing each other, but also, even

later, when Stefan became a coach of Roger and I became
a coach of Novak, we had our friendly rivalry back.

Like with Borg and Mac, and Chrissie and Martina, the appeal
of their rivalry was rooted in a contrast of styles: brash Boris
with his brawn and puppy-like exuberance and serene Stefan
with his cat-like grace. 'His footwork always reminded me of a
ballet dancer, he was so light on his feet,' Boris said. 'I was the
power guy, with the big serves.' They first met across a net at
Wimbledon in 1983, drawn against each other in the first round
of the boys' singles. Stefan was top seed; it was the 15-year-old
Boris's debut at the All England Club. The Swede won easily and
went on to win the title. I doubt if the audience that day knew
they were witnessing the start of a fascinating rivalry, but that's
undoubtedly the magic of watching the juniors at Wimbledon. A
match that might not seem particularly special at the time could
hold plenty of retrospective history. I remember watching Stefan
that summer, in the year when he won all of the Grand Slam
junior trophies and ended the season unbeaten. Even as a junior,
he had that majestic air that he always brought to the court; he
played with effortless ease. I admired his game. He didn't possess
the bullets that Pete Sampras made so familiar to Wimbledon
spectators a few years down the line, but his serve was incredibly
effective. The wonderful kick serve gave him time to get to the
net, where his volleys were sublime. He just made it look so easy.

As an all-conquering junior, Stefan suffered from the weight
of expectation, particularly in comparison to Becker, whose
career trajectory was practically vertical and who of course had

gone on to win Wimbledon at a precocious age. For an hour on 23 June 1987 – when he was only 21 – Edberg's tennis was pure perfection. In the opening round of Wimbledon, he doled out a crushing 6–0, 6–0, 6–0 victory over his namesake and compatriot Stefan Eriksson, becoming the first man to inflict the humiliation of a 'triple bagel' scoreline on an opponent at Wimbledon since 1947.

Poor Eriksson only managed to claim 35 points. 'I thought about giving him a game in the end, but then I thought I may never get a chance to win like this in a Grand Slam tournament again,' Edberg said. 'I felt sorry for him, but he only laughed afterwards.'

In massive contrast to Boris, you never knew whether Stefan was winning or losing – even in that match. He had a true poker face. His untroubled facade made following his matches easier for his fans – why get upset if he doesn't appear to be? – but it also left him open to accusations that he didn't play with courage or show a burning desire to win when it mattered. In one notable match at Wimbledon, however, he was down a break of serve in the fifth set, and despite never revealing a flicker of anguish, he dug deep to silence his critics on that score once and for all. This incredible fightback came in his 1988 semi-final against the tricky Czech player Miloslav Mečíř, who had deposed Stefan's compatriot, the No.2 seed Mats Wilander, in the quarter-final. The press had billed it as a spicy match-up as the Czech player had become known as the 'Swede Killer' for the bizarrely comprehensive success he had against Swedish players, not just Wilander but also Joakim Nyström and Anders Jarryd. But Edberg battled back to win a place in his first Wimbledon final. When he chased down a lob on match point and struck a forehand that Mečíř could only volley into the net, he threw his arms up in a rare expression of emotion. 'It's hard to believe I came back from so far off,' he said. 'I got my act together and felt better and better. If I didn't have guts today, I wouldn't have won. I gutsed it out.'

As history relates, Stefan went on to beat Boris at Wimbledon that year (as he did two years later, sealing his second triumph on Centre Court with a second tremendous Wimbledon fight-back). The 1988 match was a magical display of volleying, with Edberg getting the edge thanks to his ability to handle tough low balls. In 1990, Becker broke serve to go up 3–1 in the final set but, by his own admission, started imagining himself holding the trophy. He thought, with that break of the Edberg serve, he could serve the match out. But Stefan had other ideas, break-ing back immediately and unleashing clever shots – notably a backhand lob that left Boris stranded in no-man's land, unable to retrieve it. It was the sort of outwitting shot that drains confidence in an opponent.

My playing career was coming to an end just as his was taking off, so I mostly observed him as a broadcaster. The year of his junior title win at Wimbledon was also the one I was knocked out of in the first round by 16-year-old Bulgarian Manuela Maleeva, with the *Daily Mail* printing a picture of me looking out of the dressing room window, with the caption, 'Sue Barker, eyes blurred red with the tears of defeat, left Wimbledon yesterday afternoon with a tennis career to sort out.' Too right! Thanks to a catalogue of injuries, my world ranking had tumbled from top 20 to 70th in the previous 18 months. In 1994, having hung up my racket ten years earlier, I was covering the Queen's Club Championships for the BBC – it was my first year working a full tennis summer for the Beeb, so I was desperate to please. I raced down to interview the top three seeds for *Grandstand* on the Sunday before the start of the tournament. Pete Sampras was courteous and positive, as always. Michael Stich was also interesting and generous in his interview. When I asked about Stefan, I was told he had 'already done the BBC'. I said that I'd only just arrived that day, so when I saw Stefan I asked him for the interview but he said no, he'd done the BBC. After investigating further, I found out that he'd spoken to Rob Curling for the local London news station. This meant I had to return to *Grandstand* one interview short, which was devastating. I understood Stefan completely, but it made me aware just how difficult it was to secure a one-on-one when there are so many broadcasters milling around putting in interview requests. Sadly I didn't get to interview him many times after that, so that lost opportunity still disappoints me.

9

STEFFI GRAF

When Boris Becker said he hoped his 1985 Wimbledon win would change the status of tennis back home, his wish was doubly fulfilled – and then some – as along came Steffi Graf, giving the German nation two outstanding role models. Both were child prodigies whose periods of dominance roughly overlapped, give or take a few years. On the tour in 1982, I'd heard a lot of excited talk about this young girl who had won both the U-12 and U-18 titles at the European Junior Championships. Two years later, I played her in her first Wimbledon when she had just turned 15 and I was trying to prolong my career after battling injuries.

Our second-round match was scheduled on Court 14, which was then a small show court at the southern end of the grounds. A fiercely patriotic crowd filled the stands to cheer me on. From the first point, I was blown away by Steffi's speed and athleticism as well as her ability to read the ball. My forehand was my big weapon, and so was hers – she soon came to be celebrated in the tabloids as 'Fraulein Forehand'. She struck her forehand with a huge wind-up, which made it not only powerful but difficult to read. She was tall and wiry and I felt her power even though it looked like the wind might blow her away – she hit the ball with such great timing. As for that backhand slice ... well, that was always effective against me as it took away my most potent shot on the low-bouncing grass. I recall there were some shocking line calls at crucial moments, which unsettled me, and I lost 6–7, 3–6, despite having a set point in the first set and leading 3–1 in the second. I didn't know it at the time, but it was my last ever singles match at Wimbledon – though looking back at newspapers from the time I see now that it was on the cards. As Rex Bellamy wrote in *The Times* after my match with Steffi, 'Miss Barker is such an engagingly jolly woman that her defeats are always unwelcome, though we are getting more accustomed to them.' If there was any consolation, it came in retrospect, knowing I had experienced at first hand a tantalising hint of the greatness to come from Stefanie Maria Graf.

Steffi, the youngest player in the tournament in 1984, went on to reach the fourth round, where she faced another home player, Jo Durie, and lost a close match in front of another partisan crowd. You could tell by the cursory handshake she gave Jo at the net how tough the young Steffi was on herself. She had saved two match points and literally stamped her feet before coming up to the net; she looked so unhappy to lose. But her incredible footwork and elegant athleticism, the flourish of the racket head as she swung through her ground strokes, the winning angles she found, the tactical finesse ... her all-court game would develop a lot and increase in power over the next few years, but there was already a lot to admire.

As a broadcaster, I came to see the incredibly modest side of Steffi, who was pretty inscrutable on court. She was almost embarrassed by her success, even late in her career. On occasion, she drew criticism for a cool handshake at the net after a rare loss, but that was her perfectionism. She was cross with herself, not being disrespectful to her opponents. 'I was shy and I just didn't make friends very easily,' she admitted in a 2022 interview with American sportswriter Peter Bodo (the co-author of Sampras's 2009 autobiography).

> I loved the playing and I loved the training. I enjoy performing before a crowd, even though you wouldn't know it from my face or my body language. I took the game the only way I knew how, seriously, and it wasn't in my personality to be smiling on the court or getting involved with the crowd.

I remember enjoying a fun dinner at San Lorenzo during Wimbledon in the mid-1980s with four mates. On another table we spotted Steffi sitting silently on a large table with her parents, her coach, her agent and others, but without anyone her own age to chat with. We thought, *How sad, that can't be much fun.* But Steffi has also said that for her, a life in tennis was always about the time on court, where she let her tennis do the talking. She didn't loiter in the competitors' facilities at tournaments. She wasn't one for making a statement with tennis dresses; she preferred a practical polo shirt and skirt, simple pearl earrings with her hair held back in a bandana. In between points she'd hoick up her sleeves on her shoulders in a let's-get-down-to-business way. Her introverted personality is what made her reaction to the famous Centre Court marriage proposal so funny in 1996. She was bouncing the ball ready to serve to the Japanese grass-court supremo Kimiko Date in the semi-final and a voice from the crowd shouted out, 'Steffi, will you marry me?' She smiled, paused to prepare again to serve, chuckled again to herself and then, with brilliant comic timing, looked shyly up and called back, 'How much money do you have?' This rare chink in the Graf focus endeared her to the crowds and created one of those much-replayed iconic Wimbledon moments.

Between 1987 and 1989, Steffi and Martina came face to face in three Wimbledon finals in a sort of prolonged changing of the guard. (Almost in parallel, her fellow German Boris was embroiled in his three consecutive finals with Edberg.) Though Steffi was 12 years Martina's junior, their rivalry would actually go on to span nearly ten years, a fact which speaks volumes about two of the most impressive athletes the women's game has ever seen.

Martina got the better of Steffi in 1987, but in 1988 Steffi arrived in SW19 determined to claim her first Wimbledon title. She was 19 years old, and a Centre Court triumph was not the only ambition on her horizon. She was on track to achieve a 'Golden Slam'. Tennis was again an official Olympic sport at the 1988 Games in Seoul that were due to be staged shortly after the US Open, having been left out since the 1924 Summer Olympics in Paris. A new, tantalising target loomed – could anyone win all four majors and an Olympic gold medal? Steffi had beaten Chrissie in Melbourne, the first year the Australian Open switched from grass to hard courts. In Paris, she inflicted a stunning (and humiliating) double bagel on Natasha Zvereva to add the French Open title. Zvereva, a brilliant doubles player and no slouch in singles, had beaten Martina in the fourth round but was on court against Steffi for just 32 minutes, winning only 13 points. To this day, Steffi's dominance on the clay courts of Roland-Garros makes it the shortest ever Grand Slam final in the Open Era, and the only 'double bagel' in a major final since 1911.

This collection of Slam wins set Steffi up nicely for stage three of the 'Golden': Wimbledon. She and Martina were seeded No.1 and No.2 respectively, which presented an interesting dynamic. Martina had won six consecutive titles and was set on securing a seventh, which would take her to a record tally of nine Wimbledon titles. Steffi was looking to avenge her loss of the previous year and to swap the runners'-up plate for the Venus Rosewater Dish. Walking out under the Royal Box for that 1988 final (her sixth final in what would be a run of 13 consecutive Slam finals), Steffi had been the world No.1 for nine months. The match started well for her. She went up 5–3 in the first set, but Martina took the next six games to leave Steffi trailing 7–5, 2–0. The loss of the first set – the first she had lost at a Slam that year – could have been a psychological blow, but in her six matches en route to the final Steffi had lost just 17 games and it looked like she was able to just click back into that ruthless mindset.

'The first set made me very angry. I just wanted to hang in there, to show I could play much better than I was,' she said later. Competitive fury drove her on to win the next nine games. Martina then broke back, but still trailed 3–1 in the final set, and then … rain stopped play. 'I saw her in the locker room and she was so down,' Steffi said. 'I thought, if she's going to play like she looks, she can't win.' Three more games sealed it, and Steffi was a Wimbledon champion – and had moved one Slam away from achieving a clean sweep. 'If you have to lose, you might as well lose to the better player on the final day,' said Martina in the post-match press conference.

> This is the end of a chapter. Passing the torch, if you want to call it that. I could feel what she was feeling, have that same joy because I know what the feeling is. Steffi is a super player and a nice human being. If she can keep winning, great.

The focus of a Wimbledon fortnight is in watching a singles draw narrow from 128 competitors in the first round to the ultimate champion. In the women's draw of 1988, however, Wimbledon was significant not merely as the stage for the emergence of a first-time champion on the grass; it also represented the cornerstone of a unique piece of tennis history. The Wimbledon title was a crucial step in Steffi becoming the only player ever to complete the 'Golden Slam'. Having beaten Martina to win her third consecutive major title, the challenge only grew harder. In New York, she had to beat the only player who had defeated her that year (twice) – Argentine player Gabriela Sabatini.

Again, Steffi rose to the occasion and came through another three-set effort to secure her Grand Slam, a feat only previously recorded by 'Little Mo' Connolly in 1953 and Margaret Court in 1970. And just to put the icing on the cake, Steffi's 1988 Grand Slam remains the only one in history completed on three surfaces (grass, clay, hard court). Three weeks later, she again beat Sabatini to win the Olympic gold medal.

When Novak Djokovic declared that in 2024 his aim was to achieve a clean sweep of the four Grand Slam tournaments as well as the gold medal at the Paris Olympics, the record he was hoping to match belongs to Steffi Graf – the only player to achieve the so-called Golden Slam. Djokovic's defeat in the semi-final of the 2024 Australian Open put paid to that dream.

• • •

Thanks to the good old British weather, there are a couple of generations of tennis fans who are supremely well versed in Wimbledon highlights of the past. Before the arrival of the retractable roofs on both Centre and No.1 courts, rain delays had to be filled with a variety of studio chats, replays of classic matches (as well as some novelty moments, such as the visits from Hacker, the dog puppet from CBBC). Among the classic matches we dug out of the archives was one extraordinary game between Steffi and Arantxa Sánchez-Vicario in their 1995 final. For Steffi, a sixth Wimbledon title was at stake; for Arantxa, it would have been a dream first victory on Centre Court. With the score level at 5–5 in the third set, the pair of them served up a scintillating game that featured 32 points, 13 deuces and a breathtaking display of power, guile, spin, slice, drops and lobs. Arantxa, who was serving, ended up sending down 44 serves (which is a Herculean effort when you consider that to win a match 6–0, 6–0, without a loss of a point, a player need only serve 24 times).

The marathon game lasted nearly 20 minutes and ended to the advantage of Steffi – who allowed herself a rare fist clench of triumph as she headed back to her chair with the prospect of serving out the match – and with the Centre Court crowd jumping to its feet in ovation. Thus fired up, Steffi won the next four points and her sixth Wimbledon title.

She ended her career with seven Wimbledon titles (and 15 other major titles) and became the only tennis player to win each Grand Slam at least four times (Serena 'only' managed the French three times). I was in awe of her versatility and the effortless way in which she masterfully adapted her movement for all four Grand Slam surfaces, but interviewing her later in my career was always a challenge as she really didn't want to give much away. I admire her for that and, having known her for years, understood that any press intrusion was painful for her.

Her manner of retirement was in keeping with her straight-forward approach. It was 1999 and, having lost the Wimbledon final to Lindsay Davenport, Steffi announced she was bowing out. She was only 30 years old and weeks earlier had won her sixth French Open title. Knee and back injuries had left her on the sideline for much of 1997 and 1998, but she had returned to winning ways and retired when she seemed to be back at the top of her game. 'I suppose people were surprised when I said I wouldn't be back after I lost to Lindsay in the final, but to me that definitely was the end of something,' she confirmed to Bodo.

> I felt so much joy after expecting so little. I was so satis-
> fied. That's probably why my motivation finally left me
> for good when that great run ended. When I went home
> after Wimbledon, I felt empty toward tennis, and that
> sensation didn't change.

Still, it is hard not to wonder how many more titles she might have won had her hunger for success remained.

The highlights programme we put together at the end of that Wimbledon produced my most mortifying gaffe. I was asked to close the show by linking to a montage of Steffi's greatest moments. At the end of every show I hear a hard count through my earpiece to the moment when I should stop talking. It is unprofessional to underrun or overrun, and I needed to be saying goodbye as the count went from one to zero. In those 10 seconds, I decided I would close with the line, 'After a magnificent career, Steffi waves a final farewell to Wimbledon and her beloved Centre Court, but at least she walks away with some great memories.' In my ear, I could hear the producer Sharon Lence ask where the closing montage was … this was 10 seconds to go before I would deliver my line. Adrenaline was running high. Where was the montage? Would my words work if we didn't have the clips? Needless to say, with seconds to go, the video compilation was ready – everyone had played a blinder to put it together on time – and I ploughed on and delivered my line: 'After a magnificent career, Steffi waves a final farewell to Wimbledon and her beloved Centre Court, but at least she walks away with some great mammaries.'

I lay my head on the desk as there were huge gasps from the gallery. Martin Hopkins, the daytime producer, burst through the doors in hysterics. 'At least you were factually correct,' he roared. We all burst out laughing. The next day I got a message from the men's locker room thanking me for 'stating the b*****
obvious'. My embarrassment was complete.

Steffi Graf beating
Martina to claim her first
Wimbledon title in 1988,
the year she achieved the
Golden Slam, winning
all four majors and
Olympic Gold.

One of the most iconic
images of Wimbledon
is Jana Novotná crying
on the Duchess of
Kent's shoulder after a
heartbreaking loss to
Steffi in 1993. There
wasn't a dry eye in the
locker room when her
dream of lifting the
trophy came true five
years later.

My favourite Tim Henman moment! Saving match point against Paul Haarhuis in the fifth set on People's Sunday. It was Wimbledon but not as we know it. Magical.

Pete remembers the 1999 final win, his sixth title, against Andre as the 'Perfect Day', the best match of his career.

Pete's most emotional Wimbledon moment: hugging his parents after his seventh and final win a year later. It was the first time they had travelled to London to see him play.

People's Monday in 2001 was a day to savour when a career that looked over was reborn. From wild card to Wimbledon champion, Goran Ivanišević embarked on one of the most unlikely and yet remarkable Wimbledon triumphs as he defied the odds to lift the trophy.

The Williams sisters = the History Makers. The sisters met for the first time in the semi-final of 2000, who would have imagined the impact they would have on the game?

Venus celebrating the first of her five singles titles in 2000.

A year later, in 2001 Serena collected the first of her seven... The Williams's dominance had begun and women's tennis changed forever. Their drive to succeed was impressive but always most important to Venus and Serena was ... family.

Roger Federer's first Wimbledon title was back in 1998 when he won the boys' singles without dropping a set.

Winning the final in 2003 is Roger's most cherished memory. It's also when his love affair with Wimbledon and the Centre Court crowd began.

Was the 2008 final the greatest match of all time? Rafael Nadal ended Federer's unbeaten run of 65 matches at Wimbledon. The rain delays and late-night finish just added to the drama.

Wimbledon favourites, husband and wife: Andre and Steffi returned in 2009 for a special ceremony to celebrate the new Centre Court roof.

The moment in my broadcasting career that I would love to relive. Walking onto Centre Court to announce Andy Murray as the first British men's champion in 77 years. He had nerves of steel that day. Take a bow Andy.

The nation celebrated again as Andy won Wimbledon again in 2016.

Federer won his eighth title in 2017. His graceful style and flawless reputation on and off court has left a lasting legacy.

An 18-year-old Emma Raducanu sweeping the competition aside in her third round against Sorana Cîrstea in 2021.

The man who has dominated Wimbledon in the last decade, winning his seventh Wimbledon crown in 2022. Novak Djokovic.

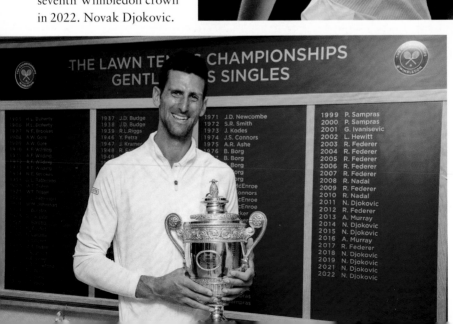

THE LAWN TE... CHAMPIONSHIPS
GENTL... S SINGLES

1937	J.D. Budge	1971	J.D. Newcombe	1999	P. Sampras
1938	J.D. Budge	1972	S.R. Smith	2000	P. Sampras
1939	R.L. Riggs	1973	J. Kodes	2001	G. Ivanisevic
1946	Y. Petra	1974	J.S. Connors	2002	L. Hewitt
1947	J. Kramer	1975	A.R. Ashe	2003	R. Federer
1948	R. Falkenburg	1976	B. Borg	2004	R. Federer
1949			B. Borg	2005	R. Federer
			Borg	2006	R. Federer
			org	2007	R. Federer
			org	2008	R. Nadal
			cEnroe	2009	R. Federer
			onnors	2010	R. Nadal
			cEnroe	2011	N. Djokovic
			cEnroe	2012	R. Federer
			ker	2013	A. Murray
			ker	2014	N. Djokovic
				2015	N. Djokovic
				2016	A. Murray
				2017	R. Federer
				2018	N. Djokovic
				2019	N. Djokovic
				2021	N. Djokovic
				2022	N. Djokovic

10

ANDRE AGASSI

In 1974 the Wimbledon crowds embraced the 'love double' of the newly crowned champions Chris Evert and Jimmy Connors. Eighteen years later, in 1992, the seed of a longer-lasting romantic attachment began between Steffi Graf and Andre Agassi at the champions' ball. Agassi was six years into his career as a pro and in the ascendancy. Despite reaching the finals of the French Open (twice) and the US Open, and also being a four-time semi-finalist at those tournaments, he boycotted Wimbledon for three years from 1988 to 1990. One early visit in 1987, when he was 17, was enough to put off a rebellious soul. 'It's my first time at the most hallowed venue in tennis, and from the moment we arrive, I dislike it,' he wrote in his autobiography *Open* (2009).

> I'm a sheltered teenager from Las Vegas with no education. I reject all that's alien, and London feels as alien as a place can be. The food, the buses, the venerable

traditions. Even the grass of Wimbledon smells different from the grass back home.

It was the dress code rules that really offended him.

> I resent rules, but especially arbitrary rules. Why must I wear white? I don't want to wear white. Why should it matter to these people what I wear? Above all, I took offence at being barred and blocked and made to feel unwanted.

Agassi went through many changes of appearance, but in his early days he had a long mullet with beach-blond highlights (which we later learnt was a wig) and wore a dangly earring. He also loved sporting a pastel-coloured kit and a flamboyant bandana. Not for him, traditional tennis shorts; he was more likely to be in denim-look cut-offs over purple lycra undershorts. His clothing brand was a big part of who he was and he thought players should have the freedom to express themselves. 'Without colours I'd still be me, but I'd be more boring,' he said.

Reading his autobiography makes us realise he was a troubled soul for much of his early career. To learn that he hated tennis because of the constant pressure he felt under was a huge shock to everybody. He was so exciting to watch, different from any player before him, and he had a charisma that was second to none. By taking a stand against officialdom, though, he attracted more intrusive attention and publicity and maybe that added to his dislike of the sport. What a shame, because he inspired so many to take up the game.

Thankfully however, Andre eventually conceded to enter Wimbledon in in 1991, when he lost a tough five-set battle with fellow American David Wheaton in the quarter-finals, and in 1992, when he fulfilled his incredible talent and won the tournament. I remember feeling so excited by the way he competed, not just beating Goran Ivanišević in the final but also defeating Becker in the quarter-finals and a 33-year-old Mac in the semi. 'I used to watch John play Björn Borg on TV,' Agassi said at the time. 'I just always remember seeing McEnroe-Borg, McEnroe-Borg on that scoreboard ... It's almost like they edited my name up on the board.'

It turns out there was one Wimbledon tradition Andre was willing to embrace. In *Open*, he describes how he was very aware of the tradition whereby the Wimbledon men's and ladies' singles champions danced together at the ball. Steffi had already beaten Monica Seles to win her fourth Wimbledon title when Agassi, on the eve of his final against Goran, decided to go out shopping to buy a tuxedo in case he won and got the chance to 'twirl her across a dance floor'. He later revealed that he had harboured a crush on her since he saw her being interviewed after the previous year's French Open.

A dance with Steffi as his incentive, Agassi fought hard to beat Goran – it took him five sets – and win what would be his one and only Wimbledon title. Duly attired in his smart tux at the ball, he arrived excited for his turn on the dancefloor, but was dismayed to learn that the traditional champions' dance had been cancelled for the first time in history as players were thought to be no longer keen on the custom. (Ever the perfectionist, Steffi joked on a BBC *Inside Sport* programme that she had 'worked them real hard to cancel it ... I've never learnt how to dance the proper way. I wasn't looking forward to it in that sense.') So Andre did not get to dance with Steffi that night, but he made sure the pair were formally introduced and they posed for photographs with their trophies in tuxedo and white dress. 'For a long time, I admired her and respected everything that I could sort of see in her from a distance, the pillars of her life, the loyalties, the relationships,' he later said. 'It all got my interest ... and also the looks.' Nine years later, the popular champions wed and, at the time of writing, have celebrated 22 years of marriage.

Against the odds as a baseliner up against some of the greatest serve-and-volleyers, Agassi had won Wimbledon at the age of 22 – not that far removed in time from the boy sitting in front of a television at 6am at home in Las Vegas or from the 13-year-old at the Nick Bollettieri Tennis Academy in Florida watching NBC's 9am show *Breakfast at Wimbledon* (with flamboyant commentator Bud Collins talking about Wimbledon's history and legends). It was a victory that shows how Wimbledon has the power to change the world's opinion of a player in one day. 'I thought I was famous long ago,' he wrote in *Open*, 'but now I discover that I was actually infamous. Wimbledon has legitimized me.'

Two months later, after an unremarkable first-round match at the US Open (a straight-sets victory over Mikael Pernfors), Frederick Waterman, a Boston-based journalist with United Press International, started his question at Agassi's press conference with the statement, 'Andre, the major that you were least likely to win was Wimbledon.' Agassi started smiling. Waterman continued, 'Do you get up in the morning, look in the mirror, and think, *Holy cow, I'm the Wimbledon champion!*?' Agassi, now grinning, began gesturing excitedly. 'That's exactly it! I still can't believe it! I won Wimbledon!' And he went on for several minutes about how astonished he was and how much it meant to him.

Agassi's strength was his baseline game at a time when Becker, Edberg, Sampras and Pat Rafter were blitzing the grass courts with their serve-and-volleying prowess, so the Wimbledon crowds were never likely to see the best of him even before his career turned into a bit of a rollercoaster. After his breakthrough as a teenager, his appearance in the finals at Roland-Garros and Flushing Meadows, and that astonishing victory on Centre Court in 1992 – not until Lleyton Hewitt, ten years later, would another baseliner triumph at Wimbledon – Andre's results became increasingly erratic. I recall the shock engendered by the revelations in his autobiography *Open*: his troubled relationship with his father, his 'hate' for the game and his admission of taking crystal meth in 1997. With his marriage to the actress Brooke Shields failing, too, Agassi seemed at odds with himself and the sport as his career and personal life hit an all-time low. He looks back at being No.1 seed at Wimbledon in a rainy 1995 and recalls the queue.

It rains every day, but still the fans mob Wimbledon. They brave the rain, the cold, they line up all the way down Church Road, for the love of tennis. I want to go out there and stand with them, question them, find out what makes them love it so much. I wonder what it would feel like to feel such passion for the game.

Pete Sampras was as shocked as everyone when Andre's book came out with the admission that he had 'hated' – strong word – tennis from childhood. He said to me when I interviewed him for my *Our Wimbledon* documentary:

> I always had a sense that Andre was a little tortured, even on the tour it was a lot of work for him, a lot of stress, a lot of nerves. In the locker room he was always fidgety. We all get nervous, but you could see the fear in his face. I don't know if that was from his childhood and his dad's pressure, I don't know him that well, but I think he resented the sport a bit, what it took out of him.

Andre's huge turnaround from 1999 says so much about him as a player and a person. To come back and have so much success, winning five more Slams (three Australian Open titles, the French and beating fellow American Todd Martin to take honours for a second time at the US Open) was a stirring achievement for which he is greatly admired. For us at Wimbledon, he was a star attraction for three consecutive years, providing sensational entertainment and endearing himself to the crowds as he emerged a valiant loser – succumbing to Pete in the 1999 final, and twice in classic five-set tussles with a determined Pat Rafter. Although he didn't quite reach the heights we first thought he would, he is still remembered as one of the greatest entertainers ever to play the game and certainly one of the most popular off the court. His innate ability is underlined by his achievements on all surfaces. He was the first man in tennis history to win all four Grand Slam titles on clay, grass and hard courts (followed by Roger, Rafa and Novak) and the only player to enter the Guinness World Records for recording a 'Career Super Slam' – winning the four Grand Slam tournaments, an Olympic gold medal, the Davis Cup and the ATP World Tour Finals – which he completed when he won the French Open in 1999.

In 2009 Steffi and Andre came back for the official opening of the Centre Court roof. It was lovely to see them together, these two players who loathed the media spotlight but through tennis had found each other and happiness. Although they seemed opposite personalities on the outside, they in fact had so many similarities and forged a future valuing privacy, loyalty, family and togetherness. Three years later, on the 20th anniversary of Steffi's fourth and Andre's one and only Wimbledon title – his first Grand Slam win – they again returned to the All England Club, this time as guests in the Royal Box. Sitting in the same front row as Prince William and the Duchess of Cambridge, they created a picture of tennis royalty alongside true royalty. Andre, dressed in a pale suit, white shirt and purple-and-green club tie, was very much in elder statesman mode. 'Now I've come back to the beginning and it's quite a moment,' he said. 'I have been blessed. It was here where I did a lot of growing up.' As if to emphasise his status, Mikhail Youzhny, playing Roger Federer in a quarter-final match on Centre Court below, playfully looked up at the Royal Box and asked Agassi, 'Can you tell me what I'm supposed to do out here. Please tell me?' Another great Wimbledon moment.

In 2017 Andre returned as a coach in Novak Djokovic's camp and came out with one of my favourite quotes. '[Wimbledon] is the place that first taught me to respect the sport, to really appreciate the opportunity and privilege it is to play a game for a living.' Long gone was that rebellious teenager who boycotted the All England Club.

11

PAT CASH

The legacy of a Wimbledon champion tends to be statistical – a record number of titles to beat (Roger Federer's eight and Martina Navratilova's nine) or longevity in terms of the greatest number of appearances in a Wimbledon draw (Jean Borotra of France was crowned singles champion on Centre Court in 1924 and 1926 and competed in 35 Championships over a period of 43 years between 1922 and 1964). The official *Wimbledon Compendium* even has a section immortalising individual players' choice of equipment, including a list entitled 'Champions who wore headgear in a singles final', where the standout entry is Miss S.R.F. Lenglen and her cloche hat.

I can only think of one player whose legacy has been to initiate a ritual that has become a cherished part of a Championship – one which already is not short of traditions – and he also happens to be on the list of champions with notable headgear. Stand up Pat Cash, who was wearing a distinctly rock'n'roll-style black-and-white chequered headband in 1987 when he embarked on his infamous cat-burglar climb up over rows of seats and a commentary-box roof to reach his player's box and celebrate his triumph with his girlfriend, family, coach and friends. 'I remember thinking, *What in hell is he doing?*' said Darren Cahill, who had practised with Cash before the final against world No.1 Ivan Lendl. 'But it was great ... spontaneous and emotional ... very similar to the way Cashy has always lived his life.'

The Climb, as it is now known, turned out to be the peak moment in Pat's injury-plagued career, even though he was then only 22, but his response to winning has become an integral part of a newly crowned champion's celebration routine. His decision to scale the courtside structure to get to his box was not as spontaneous as it looked. 'I thought about it the night before. It seemed the most natural thing in the world to do but nobody had done it before,' he said to viewers of *Tennis Channel Live* when reminiscing in 2021.

> I'd shaken hands with Ivan [Lendl] and the umpire and, if you've been on Centre Court for a final, you know how quickly the trophy ceremony gets under way and before you know it, the carpet has been rolled out, the ball kids are lined up and the royal family are half way out on the grass. I thought, wow, if I don't do it now, I'm never going to do it. So off I go!

Pat clearly hadn't done a recce. Once he'd committed himself to this course of action he discovered that his ascent was thwarted by a lack of seats to clamber over. Until his climb, there was an area of standing room on Centre Court. (After his daredevil climb the All England Club had to replace the standing room with seats to comply with new laws following the Hillsborough disaster.)

> I got to that area and I realised, Oh my goodness, there are no more seats … I was trying to get up on the roof of the commentary box and I looked down and saw a priest. He said, 'Stand on my shoulder, my son.' I thought, well, this is divine intervention, and I stood on the guy's shoulder and I got my way up there. I only found out later that it was a guy dressed as a priest.

The Climb has become a defining moment in the crowning of new champions, and some have made the move their own. In 2008 Rafael Nadal – despite looking as if he could not play another point after his epic battle with Roger – somehow found the energy to clamber up and celebrate with his family, and even included a diplomatic swivel to walk along the roof above the commentary teams towards the Royal Box in order to greet the Spanish Crown Prince Felipe and his wife Letizia. And who can forget Andy Murray's victory climb in 2013, when he embraced everyone in his player's box, started to leave but was called back sharply because he had forgotten to thank his mum, Judy!

By 2014 the tradition was honoured with the introduction of a small official gate, to give the victorious players an easier pathway to celebrate with their families. The so-called Champion's Gate is painted in the same distinctive green as the

Centre Court masonry (Permaglaze Spruce Green, code 14C39, if you're curious). Instead of having to scramble over spectators' seats and over roofs, players could henceforward simply skip up the steps to a walkway that leads to the gate. 'That's really taking the challenge out of it!' Cash joked to listeners on BBC Radio 5 Live. 'If they're fit enough to win Wimbledon, I think they should climb up or have some other sort of challenge. It's way too easy now!' The new gate was christened by Petra Kvitová, who became the first player to use the gate after her win the year it was introduced – and would have had plenty of energy to spare for the original-style scramble, having crushed Eugenie Bouchard, Canada's first ever Grand Slam finalist, 6–3, 6–0.

Ash Barty must have committed her fellow Aussie's original climb to heart. I was very worried in 2021 when she headed up to her friends and family looking set on doing a bona fide Pat Cash impersonation. I said to her in the interview that followed on the court, 'I wanted to shout, "There's a gate there!" but eventually you found it.'

'It was a little bit of a wobbly step there,' she laughed. 'I probably should've taken the elegant road but that's okay.'

A video posted to Wimbledon's TikTok account showing the 2023 ladies' champion Markéta Vondroušová climb up and share an embrace with her sister Julia, friends and her husband Stepan Simek went viral. There have been a few who haven't scaled the sides of Centre Court – Novak Djokovic famously ate the grass, and Roger Federer said he felt it was unfair to leave the runner-up alone on court.

12

PETE SAMPRAS

One name dominated the Wimbledon men's honours board during the 1990s and that was Pete Sampras. He won seven out of eight consecutive tournaments in an astonishing run from 1993 to 2000, proving himself to be the greatest male grass-court player of modern times. He had to beat all sorts of challengers for his Magnificent Seven – fellow American Jim Courier; the fast-serving Goran Ivanišević; Boris, by then a seven-times finalist; the all-court French shot-maker Cedric Pioline; Agassi in his comeback year; and the athletic and brilliant volleyer Pat Rafter – and he did so with bucketloads of pin-point aces and totally without fanfare. Roger Federer would go one further, garnering eight titles in total, but Sampras's winning record on the grass of SW19 is actually higher – 90 per cent wins to Federer's 88 per cent. We're talking about the nuances of genius!

Although Pete made his Wimbledon debut in 1989 at the age of 17, I had made sure I saw him play earlier in the year as there was already talk about a future great rivalry between him and Andre. The Sampras family had moved to California when Pete was a young kid so that he could play all year round at the Jack Kramer Club, a facility just west of Long Beach that also nurtured Tracy Austin and Lindsay Davenport. Pete idolised Rod Laver and, like me, had the opportunity to meet and play with Rod as a junior. Though his wasn't a tennis family – Pete discovered the sport for himself – watching Wimbledon became a family ritual. When he was ten years old, he remembers getting up at 6am to sit around with his parents and siblings to watch The Championships final. 'It was exciting. I loved the court, loved the atmosphere, the echo of the ball, the royalty in the box, it was different. It had a huge effect on me as a kid,' he told me.

Even at 16, there were signs that his serve-and-volley game would be superb and certainly suited to the quick, slick grass courts. However it was at the US Open in 1990 that he first triumphed in a major, beating Agassi, and it wasn't until 1993 that he claimed his first Wimbledon title and his businesslike dominance of Centre Court began. Apart from his fast, accurate and well-disguised serve – he was soon nicknamed 'Pistol Pete' by the media – and his crisp volleys, Pete also had a dangerous forehand. He was super-calm and focused on court; he rarely showed emotion or lost his focus. In contrast to Andre, he didn't play to the crowd or indulge in showmanship. Typically in a baggy top and shorts, he saw himself purely as an athlete, not an entertainer. As such, he wasn't everyone's favourite.

'I loved the winning, but the aftermath of the interviews and talking about how great I am? I just felt like I wanted to win and leave!' he told me when I interviewed him for my *Our Wimbledon* documentary.

> I know there was a responsibility to talk about it but I almost felt embarrassed and sheepish when I walked into a press conference. 'You've broken this record, how do you feel?' 'Well I've worked hard.' I found it almost uncomfortable, some of my success. I was all about winning and working hard and achieving goals, but the attention and the stardom? I grew to accept it as I got older, but I didn't enjoy it. I liked keeping it on the down low, keeping it simple and not letting anything distract me.

On one level, it was about being fearful of losing his edge. 'When I was the best player in the world, something was going to make me fall,' he reasoned.

> That's why I always had this recipe to keep it the same, not do too much. I saw that with Andre a little bit, trying to be the best player in the world and do all these other things off the court. It's hard to do both.

Rather like Borg, Pete took his time to learn to love the grass and the way it played.

> I'm a California kid, I want the ball right there every time on a nice hard court, but the grass? It was too fast. The bad bounces. I didn't return well. I didn't move

well. I was holding serve easy, but couldn't break serve – I was losing tie-breakers. I had a really negative attitude towards the grass, I just didn't feel it was a fair surface. It took a couple of bad calls or a bad shot and I lost the set. I went out there in a negative frame of mind and it affected me during the first couple years I'd played Wimbledon – I struggled. I loved Wimbledon and what it meant to me in my childhood, our sport's Super Bowl, but from a game standpoint, if you can't break serve at Wimbledon, you're not going to win. I didn't have a grasp of how to do that, my movement was unstable and my attitude was horrible.

Pete told me it was John McEnroe who called him out.

I said, 'I can't play on this stuff, all the bad bounces ... and it rains.' He said, 'I don't want to hear that. You're a great athlete, what are you complaining about?' He put me in my place. I was ranked sixth in the world and I realised I shouldn't be talking like that. It was a combination of John and his comment that made the difference. He didn't have to say much but he gave me that look, you know that look he gives you? I didn't want to hear what he said and it woke me up. Then I needed to work on a few things in my game, but mentally I was getting more positive about the grass – come '93, everything just clicked, my mind was right, I learnt how to move on the stuff and return on it better. From '93 onwards, I owned it. I felt like I figured it out, but it took me a few years.

He nominates his final against Andre in 1999 as the favourite match he played at Wimbledon.

> It was just perfect tennis. I got into the zone, and played flawlessly. He'd just won the French and I just got in the zone at the Wimbledon final. I'd never had that feeling before and that was the best tennis I've ever played.

As Pete told me, he wanted to keep everything to do with his tennis simple. His routine was uncluttered by obsessive rituals:

> I used different toilets in the locker room, different towels on court, but I did use the same racket all tournament! The racket I started with in the first round was the one racket I'd play with. I'd get it re-strung, but it was always the same racket. That was my one superstition.

I was a huge admirer of Pete's shot-making artistry and I respected the way he didn't change himself to court popularity, even though it left him more admired than loved by the Wimbledon crowds. I feel that if he'd had the chance to speak to the spectators after his matches, as is standard practice today, his warmth, humbleness and amazing insight into the game would have won him a legion of fans. He was always focused on results, not style. Not for him the court as the big stage for entertainment; he just didn't want to interact with the crowd during a match. Jon Wertheim wrote a great line in an article in *Sports Illustrated* contemplating the quiet champion at 50: 'Sampras was the GOAT. But with the public disposition of a turtle.' That ability to remove emotion from his game was his psychological strength, but when I visited him in California to interview him after his retirement, he admitted his regret at not having the opportunity to engage more with fans. It was only in 2000, the year of his last victory on Centre Court, that we started doing the on-court interviews after the final ... and that exchange after his record seventh Wimbledon crown shows just how emotional he was about The Championships and how much his era of dominance meant to him.

> When I was winning my [early] Wimbledons, you took your trophy, shook hands and kind of walked off the court. The nice interview afterwards was a better production. I wanted to share my trophy moment with the crowd and show how much I enjoyed playing there and say what a great event I think it is and thank the club.

As well as being a year of millennium celebrations, 2000 was a personal milestone for Pete. Thank heavens for Pat Cash initiating The Climb as a new Wimbledon tradition thirteen years earlier because, quite out of character, Pete climbed up through the spectators to hug his shy, rarely seen parents, Sammy and Georgia. When I asked Pete to relive the moment he got to celebrate with them, he welled up, swallowing hard to prevent tears from flowing. His parents had never seen him play at

Wimbledon. 'I was always nervous bringing them over if I'd lost – my dad is superstitious,' Pete said, but his fiancée (now wife), the actress Bridgette Wilson, phoned his sisters and the three women organised flights for his parents. They weren't in the player's box. Thoughtfully, he got them tickets for seats to the right of the Members' Stand to keep them off camera and allow them to watch him in peace. 'They got on a plane and made it – and it was an amazing time after [they'd watched me win a then record seventh Wimbledon title]. They were emotional, I was emotional ...'

We had to stop the cameras to give Pete time to compose himself. 'Sorry, I still get emotional,' he said.

> It's tough times seeing your folks get older. I think about my dad in those moments – I wish he could've seen me play more often. My kids are 14 and 11 now, you want to be part of those moments – my parents weren't part of those moments enough for me. I carry that a little bit today. Because of whatever decisions I've made in my life, they weren't part of the story or part of me winning. If my son won the Masters in golf, and I wasn't there, I'd be disappointed. For my parents with Wimbledon and the Open, I feel their pain.

I consoled Pete when he cried as I understood exactly what he was feeling. I have similar regrets to Pete – but on a much smaller scale – as I didn't allow my parents to be part of my moments either. I'm pleased I made sure they had tickets at the Royal Albert

Hall in 1978 for the Wightman Cup, when they saw Virginia and me beat the unbeatable Chrissie Evert and the young Pam Shriver in the decisive doubles match to take the honours for Great Britain, but I didn't ask them to come to Paris in 1976 or to any of my Wimbledon matches. I, too, live with those pangs of conscience about not involving my parents enough and I know many other players feel the same. It's tough, but sadly we can't go back. It just wasn't a regular occurrence back then and, of course, we didn't have the same level of help – from the Slams, from the player associations and from a vast team that the top players have today to help arrange things like transport, hotels, tickets and so on. I'm so glad Pete had his moment with his parents amid the Centre Court celebrations in 2000 and I had mine on that electrifying night in the Albert Hall in 1978. We can cling on to that.

Not surprisingly, people often ask Pete how to win Wimbledon. What's the secret? For him, it was all about the second serve.

> That's your key shot. You can hit 30 aces and win your service game to love, but it's that second serve at 30–all when it's 4–4 in the fifth set that makes the difference. I just felt like when push came to shove, I was the guy to hit my second serve. That's why I won seven Wimbledons. My movement, my return ... but my second serve became a weapon. It takes good technique and it takes courage to go for it. My second serve was how I did it.

In matches involving a big server, you used to be able to rely on a second serve to initiate a point that might extend into a rally and lead to a more balanced exchange across the net rather than a brutal barrage of aces, mis-struck returns or returns into the net. But the big servers could also unleash an explosive and accurate second serve, which meant that every point in a match was potentially short and quick – and not exactly box-office theatre. Boosted by the new graphite racket technology and improved fitness levels, players like Goran Ivanišević, Greg Rusedski, Andy Roddick, Marat Safin and Mark Philippoussis as well as Pete could rely on their weapons-grade serves, which gained them 20 to 30 points a match purely through aces. The 1994 Wimbledon final between Pete and Goran – two of the biggest servers of all time – proved the danger in the way the men's game was embracing power over guile. Under the strapline 'Pete Sampras wins tennis matches with such brute force that fans might find it boring to watch', the Associated Press news agency baldly served up this match report:

> Sampras played the power game at its best – or at its worst, depending on your point of view – as he beat Goran Ivanišević 7–6 (7–2), 7–6 (7–5), 6–0 for his second straight Wimbledon title and fifth Grand Slam championship. There was little subtlety in this match. Both men fired serves at close to 130 mph, with Ivanišević hitting 25 aces and Sampras 17. The Croatian served 16 aces in the first set, with at least two in each game.

For fans seeking immersive entertainment on Centre Court, the stats given by AP told a bleak story:

There were no breaks of serve until the third set, when Ivanišević wilted and Sampras broke three times. On more than half of the 206 points in the match, the serve was not returned in play. Few points had rallies of more than three shots and none more than six.

I remember interviewing Pete when he came off court after this final. I can't remember my exact question but it prompted him to protest that this was grass-court tennis, and he went on to say that, by contrast, clay courts could have matches where the rallies were 'too long'. For the next seven years, a big server crash-bang-walloped their way to the title – Sampras five more times, Richard Krajicek in 1996 and Goran in 2001. From 1994 onwards, however, the Wimbledon committee initiated some attempts to slow play and prompt more rallies – a softer ball, a different cut of grass – until 2001 when the composition of the grass changed to 100 per cent perennial ryegrass. It's no coincidence that in 2002 the Wimbledon final was contested between baseline counterpuncher Lleyton Hewitt and the Argentinian David Nalbandian, whose game was built around a tremendous return of serve that was a 'bigger' weapon than his own serve.

'Pistol Pete' was greatly admired by youngsters growing up. He was a role model to Novak, and Andy Murray said Pete was a favourite of his. Some champions stay in the game, returning as coaches or television commentators. Not Pete. Perhaps we'll get to see him sitting in the Royal Box next to Roger soon. Right, Tim?

13

GORAN IVANIŠEVIĆ

While Pete Sampras made winning Wimbledon look effortless, other champions have made their fans gasp, flinch, forget to breathe, destroy fingernails and shake heads in disbelief at their heroics every point of the way. I'll get to Andy Murray later, but Goran Ivanišević in 2001? Every element of his eventual title was simply incredible. As he said afterwards, 'Why do it easy, if you can do it the hard way?'

Three times the Croat, now a familiar figure in Novak's coaching team, reached the final in his prime, and three times he fell dramatically short. In 1992 he seemed indomitable. Unleashing his devastating leftie serve – delivered with a simple action that looked not unlike someone swatting a fly with a frying pan – he swiped aside Lendl, Edberg and Sampras (Pete didn't manage to get a single break point in their four-set match!) to set up a final against Andre Agassi. Goran was gunning for his first Wimbledon title, but so was Andre. The battle was won by the Las Vegan in his baseball cap and trademark dangly earring (inspired in part, as I wrote earlier, by the prospect of a dance with the ladies' champion at the champions' ball!). Goran's fans watched in dismay as he failed to convert a break point at 3–3 in the fifth set, then double-faulted twice in the final game – by a player who had only served five double faults in the six matches that got him to the big one.

Two years later he was back for the Centre Court serve-athon with Pete, when he capitulated 0–6 in the third set. He didn't get his hands on the trophy, but he put his name in the record books by bettering his previous year's record of the most aces in the tournament, increasing the number from 206 to 213, the highest in Wimbledon history at the time. Roll on another four years, and Goran was again in the spotlight up against Pete, who was focused on a target of equalling Borg's five titles on the grass. Goran started well. Could it be third time lucky? No. Having failed to convert set points to give himself a two-set lead, he again ended up with the runner's-up plate. To lose when he had been in a winning position seemed like a cruel stroke of fate. Thereafter, troubled by a shoulder injury, his ranking slipped inexorably downwards. Clearly, with a game built for the fast surface, his failure to land a Wimbledon title rankled. After that loss, things started going downhill. 'I couldn't get over it,' he said. During a match in 2000 in Brighton, ranked 134th in the world, he was so frustrated with himself that he smashed every racket in his bag, rendering him unable to play. He had to default, telling the press, 'At least when I've finished playing tennis they'll remember me for something. They'll say,

"There's that guy who never won Wimbledon, but he smashed all his rackets.'"

Hmm ... that sounded like unfinished business.

The very next summer Goran was back, still labouring with a shoulder injury and with a world ranking (125th) that was not high enough to earn him a place in the main draw. As a three-time runner-up, however, he was awarded a wild card. Having cast himself as The Man Who Couldn't Win Wimbledon, he had a lot of fun with the media. He had discovered the BBC children's television show *Teletubbies* – four toddler-type characters who speak in gibberish – and tuned in every morning as a ritual to calm the three warring inner Gorans (the Good, the Bad and the Crazy 911 one). The man from Split in Croatia turned his reputation for a fiery temper and eccentricity into his 'Split personality'. His press conferences were guaranteed entertainment. As Pete Sampras wrote in his memoir, *A Champion's Mind: Lessons from a Life in Tennis*:

> In the locker room, the players all stopped whatever they were doing and gathered around the television sets and turned up the volume when Goran was giving a press conference. He handled those sessions like a guy on a psychiatrist's couch, but always with great wit and charm. You just never knew what was going to come out of his mouth next.

And who could have guessed how his Wimbledon campaign would pan out? Calmed by his morning sessions with Tinky Winky,

Dipsy, Laa-Laa and Po, he reeled out a string of impressive wins over Carlos Moyá in the second round, Andy Roddick in the third round and Marat Safin in the quarter-final – all former and future world No.1 players – and beat one home favourite, Greg Rusedski in the fourth round, on his way to setting up a semi-final against another, Tim Henman. And what an emotional rollercoaster that was. Five sets, played over three days. Had rain not prevented the match from finishing on Friday, Tim might just have won. Back on Saturday, he lost the tie-break for the fourth set and had to walk out again on Sunday down in the final set. Goran aced his way to victory. 'When I served for the match I was so tight that my arm felt like 10 kilos,' he said. 'I felt sorry for Tim because of all the pressure he has been put through, but this was destiny. God wants me to win. He sent the rain on Friday.'

On the day of the final, I remember driving to Wimbledon and passing the thousands who had queued overnight as more than 10,000 Centre Court tickets were being offered on a first-come, first-served basis. How I miss those days now that everything is digital! If the queuers weren't lucky enough to get a seat on Centre, they could get access to the grounds to watch on the big screen on Henman Hill. The momentum had really built up for this finale and everyone wanted to be there to share in the occasion. It was a very special atmosphere and one of my favourite Wimbledon memories, not just because of the fans, but also because of the two competitors in the final. Both Goran and Pat Rafter had the game for grass and deserved to be a Wimbledon champion. Goran was good-looking; so was Pat. Goran had failed at the final hurdle here; so had Pat. Goran was adored by the fans; so was Pat. It was hard for us to pick a favourite that day. We had started to forgive Goran for ending Tim's best chance of winning the title. He was the unlikeliest fairy tale hero of The Championships – the sore shoulder, the fact that he had run out of kit and hadn't brought enough rackets. His success was a media dream to follow from the first round to the final. He gave us great quotes, with his dry humour and brutally honest take on everything. It was so refreshing; he never spouted out the tried-and-tested phrases.

What an atmosphere, too. The perpetual rain meant that the final had to be played on the third Monday. With outbursts of chanting and raucous singing, it felt more like a football match. Goran had come to the fore at the same time as the exciting Croatia football team did well at Euro '96 and in the 1998 World Cup, and he was followed by an army of all-round sport fans draped in the red-and-white chequered flag of the new nation. As for Pat, with an Australian win ending the first Ashes Test a day early, the Aussie team decided to take a day off and descend on Wimbledon to support their compatriot. Their emergence on Centre Court coincided with me coming on air on BBC One. As I started my hello and welcome, a chorus of loud boos rang out from around the stands, which confused all of us until the camera panned to the Aussie team arriving in their seats – obviously some irate England cricket fans were in the crowd, too. I was somewhat relieved as I didn't think my opening link was that bad. Fans who had flown in to follow the Ashes descended on Wimbledon as well, to cheer on another of their favourite heroes. It was mayhem.

Whoever won or lost, I remember dreading how to conduct these two players' interviews as this final was so emotional for both sides. Goran and Pat were both nearing 30 and playing their hearts out trying to win their first Wimbledon. Inevitably, it went to five sets and I had more than three hours to contemplate the pair as Goran sent down a barrage of ferocious serves and Pat looked commanding at the net. In this now-or-never scenario, it could have been either man's title until 7–7 in the final set. Goran broke and then had to simply serve for his dream. Simply? Of course not. An ace gave him Championship point, but he double-faulted. Another Championship point, another double fault. Pat saved a third Championship point with a brilliant lob. One more serve and there was Goran sobbing on the grass. He'd done it. Pat looked distraught. He knew it was the 'one that got away', but as always he was charming and gracious. 'Someone had to lose, and I'm the loser again,' he said, inspiring a resounding 'Awww' from the crowd. Goran was in a trance. I don't think he knew it was me asking the questions or what I was even asking. He was lost in the emotion of it all. He and I had enjoyed a number of funny interviews during the tournament, and I still had another couple of questions for him, but he'd had enough and just raised the trophy aloft and headed off around the court!

Outside of Andy's win in 2013, this final was competed in the most amazing atmosphere and it's one I was so proud to be a small part of.

14

TIM HENMAN

We all have a Wimbledon match that got away from us that we would love to play again. I have the 1977 semi-final; Tim has that semi-final against Goran. I am sure that if the match had not been stopped on Friday, Tim would have won, as he came from a set down to take control with some scintillating tennis. He had the final in his sights. In the third set, Goran had no answers – he won just four points in six games and he looked thoroughly demoralised. The rain that had helped Tim in previous matches worked against him in the important match. It certainly broke his rhythm and it couldn't have been better timing for Goran. You have to admire Tim, he always gave his best and that's all you can ask of a player. Over the years he gave us so many thrilling matches, including four Wimbledon semi-finals, which is the third best record post Great War for a British man behind Fred Perry and Andy Murray.

I first met Tim when he was ten years old and I watched closely as he rose up the rankings. By 1994 it had become obvious that he was maturing physically and mentally as a player and began to climb up the world rankings. I was confident he would have a successful career but he exceeded my predictions, and that was because of his ability to play pressure points well. Before Tim, and then Andy, the home crowds would get incredibly excited if a player got anywhere near the middle Saturday of the tournament, let alone the second week. Then along came Tim and it all changed.

Suddenly, we had a player that could beat the best. He had a superb game for grass and wasn't daunted by the pressure put on the home players. This was highlighted by his first-round match in 1996, at the age of 21, when he made his Centre Court debut. He was up against the newly crowned French Open Champion Yevgeny Kafelnikov. Tim relished his time on the hallowed stage and fed off the crowd's energy. If we needed any proof as to whether he had the right mentality for the fight, he proved it when 5–3 down in the fifth set, facing two match points at 15–40 on his serve. Cool as a glass of Wimbledon Pimm's, he produced two aces. That spoke volumes to me. Tim made it through to the quarter-finals that year. The era of Henmania had begun and what a rollercoaster of emotions he took us through. Come on, Tim!

Now to my favourite Henman moment, a classic torturous watch. It remains one of the most memorable matches I've ever witnessed, even though I was glued to it from my studio chair and not courtside. The rain is never a welcome visitor at Wimbledon but in 1997 it did us a favour of sorts. Two washed-out days in the first week meant that we would have play on the middle Sunday for only the second time in the tournament's 120-year history. It was dubbed People's Sunday. Fans queued for hours, a line marshalled by the honorary stewards that stretched back three miles.

For many, Tim's exploits had inspired a first-ever visit to Wimbledon and their vitality created the most incredible atmosphere, with Mexican waves, songs and a buzz that was energising in itself. This was Centre Court as I'd never seen it before. The tournament couldn't have provided a better Wimbledon showcase match as the people's champion Tim strode out to face the cool, calm Dutchman Paul Haarhuis. It may not have been tennis of the highest quality but the tension and drama was second to none ... an absolute thriller! 'The noise was at a different level,' Tim said after the match. 'Every time I won a point it felt like the roof was going to come off.'

It was Wimbledon but not as we know it. For four hours, the twists and turns of the score had us on the edges of our seats. I had to take regular walks outside the studio. I couldn't bear to watch at times. In the BBC office that backs up the studio action, everyone was glued to the TV screens, just as they were at home. More than 14 million viewers suffered along with us. In typical Tim fashion, he saved a match point on the Haarhuis serve at 5–4 in the deciding set and on we went into one of the most dramatic final sets ever seen, with Tim ultimately clinching victory, 14–12. He proved what a fighter he was, how calm he was in the heat of battle. He was the coolest head anywhere in Wimbledon that day. How his parents sat through those matches with such serene expressions I don't know. I would have been jumping up and down screaming ... which I did in the studio!

Tim and I are still firm friends today. We've both come a long way from the days when I used to drive him and the other boys in his junior training squad back to school. Auntie Sue is very proud of his achievements. I believe he made the most of his ability and always gave 100 per cent. You can't ask for more than that. When I had my wobble at Wimbledon in 2017 and asked to quit my role at the helm of the BBC coverage, Tim did the equivalent of providing me with the chocolate treats and hamburgers I used to sneak him and the boys in defiance of their strict training diets when they were juniors. I decided to return as Wimbledon host if my hours were cut. The agreement was that I would finish at six o'clock after handing over to the BBC One news. At 6.01pm I would get a text from Tim – if he wasn't commentating – inviting me to join him for a glass of champagne in the Royal Box area. We used to have such fun chatting to the guests, the former players, celebrities, even royalty. It was a wonderful way to end the day before I'd have to head home to write scripts and notes for the next day.

One day I had been watching Rafa Nadal vs Nick Kyrgios before signing off at 6pm and venturing down for a drink with Tim. He could see I was captivated by the match, as they are two of the most watchable players Wimbledon has ever seen. Tim said he would ask Debbie Jevans, who was overseeing the Royal Box, if I could sneak in the back row. Debbie said that was fine as some of the day's guests had left. I made sure my phone was on silent but I was still wearing my talkback earpiece, although I had the volume turned down low. I did this so that I could still follow all the stories that were unfolding that evening that would inform my scripts for the next day. Debbie joined me for a few games and it was lovely catching up with her – we go back a long way to our junior playing days, so we have a lot in common. Just as I was thinking I should return to my rented flat to start my research for the next day, the All England Club chairman Philip Brook asked me to join him in the front row as his special guests had departed. This was a first for me, not only in the Royal Box but now in the front row. I had to turn my talk-back off as the abusive banter I was getting from commentators and production staff was proving a little difficult not to react to. They were hilarious. Then my phone started vibrating in my pocket, over and over again for an hour until Rafa won in four sets. I thanked Philip for the honour of sitting in the front row and spent the evening going through my messages. They came from America, Australia, family in New Zealand, all around the world. That's the reach of Wimbledon. Apparently Mac, commentating on ESPN, was saying, 'And there's Sue Barker in the Royal Box. How has she got time off? Get back to work, Sue!' Andrew Castle, another of my mates, was being mischievous, calling me a part-timer! I'd only been live on air for eight hours that day!

Tim may go down as one of Wimbledon's most memorable players who didn't win the title, but he's in honourable company. Pat Rafter, Ivan Lendl, Ilie Năstase, Andy Roddick … they have all evolved into new roles at The Championships as commentator, pundit, coach, invitation doubles player. Tim is on the board of the All England Club. Roddick joined the BBC commentary team in 2015, and he won all the plaudits. Always witty and self-deprecating as a player, he continued in that vein and we had a lot of fun during the rain delays. In one of them – a 20-minute delay in Andy Murray's quarter-final against Vasek Pospisil – we discussed the various diets of the top players, including Novak's then novel gluten-free diet. 'I didn't even know what the word "gluten" meant when I was playing,' he said. 'Maybe I should've!' We then talked about menus for gluten-free and vegan diets before deciding we would both be going off for a burger when we were done!

We found him hilarious. He had the timing of a comic genius. Spotting David Beckham on the screen, he said: 'I think he makes a splash anywhere he goes. Just look at that bone structure. I haven't (met him) yet but I have long been an admirer ... (pause) ... of his hair.'

During one of Murray's matches we were in the studio with Tim and I cheekily got Roddick involved in the debate about whether Henman Hill should remain immortalised with that name or whether it was time to change it to Murray Mound. Quick as a flash, Andy quipped, 'I can moonwalk better than Michael Jackson, but he did it first.' Fair point – and Tim was delighted with that answer.

15

THE WILLIAMS SISTERS

Few champions become legends in their own lifetimes, let alone have an equally talented Grand Slam-winning sibling and an Academy Award-accoladed film made about their childhood and breakthrough, but everything about the record-breaking Williams sisters has been achieved on a blockbuster level. Between 2000 and 2016, the devoted sisters, who were drilled on run-down courts in Compton, California (often starting at 6am and returning after school to keep practising until dark), won an incredible 12 Wimbledon titles – Venus five, Serena seven. Those titles are just a fraction of their combined total of 62 Grand Slam titles (including singles, doubles and mixed doubles) and eight Olympic gold medals. Both players made an impression when you first saw them, whether that was, like me, on a practice court in Florida when they were barely teen-agers or when they first ventured onto the match courts at the majors. They were smart, athletic and played an exciting brand of tennis with an aggressive mindset – and both were supremely grounded and confident on and off the court. As Venus said in 2021, in response to Naomi Osaka's announcement that she was to take a break from tennis to prioritise her mental health, citing media pressure, 'For me personally, I know every single person asking me a question can't play as well as I can and never will. So no matter what you say or what you write, you'll never light a candle to me.'

As superlative athletes with a sense of responsibility about how they competed and how they carried themselves in and around their match schedule, they are the absolute fulfilment of the WTA's founding ideal for women's tennis. As Billie Jean says in a piece on the WTA website,

> Venus and Serena transcend tennis and have ushered our sport into the 21st century. From the first time I saw them in 1988 at a World Team Tennis clinic, I knew they were special, and they have both led tennis with grit and grace. They don't look like the tennis establishment, and they brought a style of play that focused on power and passion. Even with all their championships, their greatest contribution, in and out of tennis, will forever be opening doors for others, particularly people of colour.

When Venus arrived at Wimbledon in 1998, having just turned 18, she had already blazed her way to the US Open final as an unseeded 17-year-old, but her dream had always been first and foremost to win on the Centre Court grass. I was fascinated to sit down to interview her. She had asked if she could bring along her younger sister, which I agreed to. On camera, Venus introduced Serena to everyone and with unabashed confidence told the world to look out because Serena was going to be better than her. I remember laughing out loud, thinking, *Oh yeah?* Venus herself, with her long legs and broad reach, was so competitive, so powerful and so tactically aware, it seemed unthinkable that the little sister she was so protective of could be even more formidable. What were we to know? Everything they did seemed unprecedented. What was also impressive was that neither sister shied away from the media pressure and expectation. In fact, they embraced it and seemed to enjoy it, particularly in the early years. Racket in hand, they took courage and commitment to new levels, and responded to their victories with endearing pirouettes and girlish curtsies. The fashion, the hair, the jewellery: their impact was huge.

Most remarkably, perhaps, Venus and Serena were actually born of tennis. The sisters may never have come into existence were it not for someone I knew well from my playing days, the Romanian star Virginia Ruzici, who more recently has been Simona Halep's manager. Famously, in 1978, Richard Williams had been watching TV and idly channel-hopping when he happened to see Virginia picking up a $40,000 cheque at Roland-Garros after winning the French Open. *Wow*, he thought, that much money for winning a string of tennis matches? He said that right there and then he became inspired to raise top-performing tennis players. His wife Oracene already had three daughters, but he hid her birth-control pills and the result was Venus, who was born in June 1980. Serena came along 15 months later. As Virginia recalls, 'The story came out when Venus first won Wimbledon and it is incredible. What is amazing is the fact that Venus and Serena were born because of the sport. It was a miracle!' Having only heard this story in the media following Venus's landmark maiden Wimbledon title, Virginia introduced herself to Richard Williams. He confirmed it was true and then introduced her to Venus. Venus later came up privately to say hello again and have a chat with Virginia. 'It was very emotional to tell you the truth. In those days everyone was looking at Chris and Martina Navratilova, these big champions, and this time it was me!' she recalled. 'Venus gave me a hug and I wished her luck.'

Who can forget Venus's jubilant jump in the air when she won that first Wimbledon in 2000? 'I've been working so hard and I was determined to get this,' she said, tightly hugging the Venus Rosewater Dish. 'This is unbelievable and I just have to say that it is better than the men's cup in my opinion!' She had beaten a tough rival in Martina Hingis in an enthralling quarter-final, defeated her sister in the semi-final (the first time in history that two sisters had faced off in a Grand Slam semi-final) and then out-hit fellow Californian Lindsay Davenport to become the first Black woman to win Wimbledon since Althea Gibson in 1958. In our interview on court, Venus also shared her strong sense of fashion-consciousness with the revelation that she had come to Wimbledon with an evening gown ready to wear at the annual Wimbledon champions' ball. Many players might have been superstitious about such forward planning, but she said she did it because 'I was determined to get this.'

The following year she successfully defended her Wimbledon title, beating Justine Henin in three sets, and again brought fashion into her victory speech. Embarrassingly so for me! I was wearing a beige striped trouser suit with some gold sparkly Armani shoes, which I thought was fitting for the occasion of ladies' final day. Venus was so thrilled to win, clutching the trophy close to her and laughing with joy as she sauntered towards me. Her first words into the microphone? 'Great shoes, Sue!' That threw me. She'd just won Wimbledon and I was poised to ask her about her emotions and what it meant to her, the key points in the rollercoaster match, and she'd just made my choice of expensive designer shoes a focus for the packed Centre Court crowd and 500 million television viewers worldwide! Three more times I interviewed her in the same victory bubble and she never mentioned my choice of shoes again – which was quite demoralising!

Following Venus's second win, a BBC Sport online forum asked the question, 'Can Venus be truly great?' It's quite something to see that there was genuine belief that this ground-breaking talent might not want to stay on the scene long enough to become a Wimbledon legend. An early departure from the game was certainly not in Richard Williams's plans. He became a familiar figure at Wimbledon. Dressed in shorts and a polo shirt, with a camera fitted with a long lens strapped across his shoulder, he would walk around keen to talk about his prodigy daughters, and was often to be found sitting on a bench outside the entrance to the media and broadcast centre, opposite the referee's office. What an incredible journey for him to see the fruition of his 75-page master plan, a document he famously drew up as a blueprint to lead his girls to become the best in the world – before they were even born. He didn't play tennis himself so he committed himself to research, reading books, studying videos and approaching members of the US Tennis Association for discussions. Nothing was going to derail his ambition. He even chose to move the family from the comfortable community of Long Beach in California to Compton, because he wanted his girls to develop a fighter's mentality. In his own memoir, *Black and White: The Way I See It* (2014), he wrote: 'What led me to Compton was my belief that the greatest champions came out of the Ghetto, I had studied sports successes like Muhammad Ali and great thinkers like Malcolm X. I saw where they came from.' He fought off gangs and drug dealers who saw the dilapidated courts as their territory and his persistence paid off. He also hired children to surround the courts and heckle and jeer at Venus and Serena to accustom them to adverse environments. In her life story, *On the Line* (2009), Serena described hearing gunfire as they played on the courts at Tragniew Park, which were in a 'sorry shape. There was broken glass every here and there. Cracks in the cement. Weeds poking through. Soda cans, beer bottles, fast-food wrappers.' Not exactly Centre Court at Wimbledon.

Richard referred to the sisters as 'Ghetto Cinderellas' and he was keen for them to understand their future place in history. 'Coming up in the late '80s, there weren't many African Americans playing, so you wanted to learn the history of them,' Serena said. 'I wanted to know everything they went through, and it motivated me. We're all here to inspire each other and lift each other up.' The unorthodox coaching he and their mother Oracene Price gave them was questioned time and time again, including by me, but look at the fairy tale it worked out to be, not just for one child but two. Single-minded tennis dads have been a blot on the tennis landscape for some time, but Richard, while being a hard taskmaster – sometimes not allowing the girls to finish until they had returned 500 volleys, according to their own accounts – was admired for wanting his girls to enjoy their childhood while still being driven to success. Determined for them to enjoy the simple satisfaction of hitting the ball well as long as possible, he removed them from the junior circuit and only let them play matches once they turned pro.

Venus and Serena were both executive producers on the recent biopic *King Richard* (2021), in which Will Smith won an Oscar for his portrayal of their father and his maverick style of coaching. Only after seeing the final cut of the movie did they give their endorsement to ensure it was an accurate portrayal. 'I think it was a great opportunity to see how amazing African-American fathers are. A lot of Black men aren't seen in that light,' said Serena. 'And a lot of people think that my dad was a different character. He wanted us to have fun first over anything. That's the thing that I loved most.'

By the time Venus and Serena were both vying for the No.1 world ranking, it was inevitable they would meet each other across the net at the sharp end of the draw at Wimbledon. Of their six meetings, four were in singles finals – and these were always bittersweet competitive storylines for tennis observers who wondered how these close sisters could possibly apply their trademark ferocity to each other. In 2000 Venus won her first Wimbledon title, having seen off Serena in the semi-final with a muted exchange at the net (neither sister ever wanted to revel in beating the other). Two years later, the younger sister had duly matured as Venus had predicted and it was Serena who danced on Centre Court with the Venus Rosewater Dish for the first time. A year later, Serena again beat Venus, this time requiring three sets to win and make it two Wimbledon titles each. In 2008 Venus came into Wimbledon on opponent-crushing form and in that same spirit beat Serena; she didn't drop a set during her entire Championship run. A year later, it went the other way again, and it was Serena whose name went up in gilt letters on the honours board. The last time they met was in 2015, in the fourth round, when Serena – en route to her sixth title, and gunning for a calendar Grand Slam – beat Venus in straight sets.

However much admirable tennis there was on display, their matches lacked the passion and ruthlessness of two intense rivals battling it out. Without a strong sense of rivalry between the players, there was little emotion pulling the fans to root for one sister over another. The crowds for these finals were always unusually quiet, but they served up plenty of scintillating matches against other opponents. Venus's fifth appearance in a Wimbledon final, against Lindsay Davenport in 2005, was an absolute thriller that many people still consider to be the best women's Wimbledon final in living memory. It was certainly the longest, and the most intense. Over the course of two hours and 45 minutes, the pair – two of the cleanest strikers of the ball to have played the game – traded ferocious ground strokes, trouncing each other after long rallies with sharply angled attacking shots and down-the-line winners. When they missed, it was by a tiny margin. Neither of them ever wanted to give an inch. The standard of tennis was just phenomenal. Lindsay, the 1999 Wimbledon champion, served for the title at 6–4, 6–5, but Venus's response was a ruthless reeling off of three consecutive winners. In the next game, she broke to love and then took the set with a determined 7–4 tie-break. Ditto, in the third set, when Lindsay took a 4–2 lead, only for Venus to turn it around. Even after Lindsay took an injury timeout and was clearly in pain, her own fighting spirit took her to 5–4, with Venus double-faulting at 30–30, leaving her one point from a well-earned victory. But Venus battled on to win the decider 9–7 and became the first woman since Helen Wills in 1935 to win the title after saving a Championship point. 'Every time the chips were down for Venus, she played unbelievably,' Lindsay said. 'It was great, and it was exhilarating. Even after losing the second, I felt like, God, this is a good match, and wow, she really played well to win that set.'

Venus, the No.14 seed, had come into Wimbledon after a patch of poor form, desperate to get back to winning ways. The cameras beautifully captured her reaction after the final point: the look of utter disbelief on her face. Then she literally jumped for joy tens of times. How she had the energy, I'll never know, and my first question to her after she had received the trophy was, 'Have you stopped jumping yet?' To this day, people tell me this was the match that made them fall in love with tennis. It had all the ingredients that the Williams sisters seemed to bring to the Wimbledon stage – the toe-to-toe fighting, comebacks, drama, speed and power, but most of all their desire to acquit themselves to the best of their ability on the best stage of all. And Venus's matches against Lindsay, who could put so much pace on the ball, were always exciting.

Astonishingly, on the eve of this biggest of matches, when other players might be resting and fine-tuning their tactical approach, Venus accompanied Larry Scott, the then head of the WTA Tour, to a Grand Slam committee meeting that included top Wimbledon officials to press for equal prize money. Wimbledon may have been a pioneer in accepting professionalism but it was the last Grand Slam tournament seen to offer equal prize money to men and women. Wimbledon actually announced equal prize money before the French did in 2007, but because Roland-Garros took place first, Wimbledon has been incorrectly perceived to be last. By all accounts, Venus spoke with eloquence and emotion to make her point. A year later, she argued the case in an article in *The Times* under the headline 'WIMBLEDON HAS SENT ME A MESSAGE: I'M ONLY A SECOND-CLASS CHAMPION'. The All England Club went on to announce equal prize money in 2007 and it was only fitting that Venus defeated Marion Bartoli that year to scoop the prize she fought so hard for.

In 2011 Venus received the devastating news that she had a chronic illness, Sjögren's syndrome, a long-term autoimmune disease. Such a diagnosis would be a huge blow to anyone's life, but to a professional tennis player it was potentially career-ending as well. She had started experiencing symptoms such as fatigue and shortness of breath in 2004 but didn't get it fully checked out until seven years later. With the help of medication and lifestyle changes, including a vegan diet, Venus has been able to continue in the sport she loves and is still looking forward to playing in 2024. In an interview with CNN in 2014, she said, 'There's only so much I can do, so I've definitely had to adjust a lot but I just see it as a challenge because in my life I've never been defeated by anything.' That attitude is why she is the champion she is.

As for Serena, one of the matches I wish I could watch all over again – though it was ultimately heartbreaking for the home crowd – is the 2015 third-round match when our own Heather Watson fought back to have a 3–0 lead in the final set and then serve for the match at 5–4. Sadly for Heather, who responded heroically to the hopes and expectations of the Centre Court crowd, the sentence continues with a BUT ... as Serena somehow, amid a series of nerve-fraying match points, pulled it out of the bag. What a match. So near and yet so far for Heather, who grew up with a poster of Serena on her wall. But what courage and composure she showed playing not just a five-time Wimbledon champion with 20 majors to her name, but also an unforgiving opponent who was on a mission to become the first player since Steffi Graf to win a calendar Grand Slam.

The sisterhood was very much showcased in the doubles competitions – and what luck for Wimbledon spectators when the day's order of play revealed an evening match featuring Team Williams – a chance to see not just one icon, but two, and observe their close bond and exuberant skill. Again, their record playing alongside each other is just astonishing. They emerged winners of all of the 14 Grand Slam doubles finals they reached, including six at Wimbledon, where they scooped victory in straight sets each time. Imagine walking onto court with that kind of record; imagine their opponents preparing to face a peppering of power played with all the intensity Venus and Serena instinctively bring on court.

I don't know who first mooted the idea of the Serena and Andy Murray mixed doubles pairing in 2019 – or Team MurRena, as it became known – but it was brilliant dose of fun for The Championships that year – and, I dare say, a tonic for both players in their senior years as the reception these great champions got was special. Serena was trying to regain form following a knee injury and was still on the trail for the elusive 24th Grand Slam title (which, if she won it, would have equalled Margaret Court's all-time record) while Andy was gingerly returning to the game after his 'retirement' in Melbourne and then hip resurfacing surgery, and the running gag of their press conferences was a report into how their bodies were holding up. Three times they hit the court and thrilled the crowds before they lost nobly in three sets to top seeds Bruno Soares and Nicole Melichar. Beyond sharpening up their games, the experience showed the fans another side of their personalities. 'We had so much fun,' Serena said to the gathered journalists at Wimbledon after their last match.

> We aren't ready for it to be over but we both are obviously focused on our health. We're celebrating the fact that we're feeling better. We want to just continue to do

better. I just love Andy's spirit. It's so fun to play with him. He's so calm and chill. I loved having the support of the crowd. Hopefully I can still have it. To play on this stage with Andy, who has done so well here for so many years, it is literally a lifetime experience. I'm so happy that I got to experience it.

Injuries and health issues have dogged both Venus and Serena, but their longevity in the game is proof that a love for tennis underpins all they have achieved. Serena announced she would 'evolve away' from tennis after losing in the third round at the 2022 US Open, when she was just a few weeks from turning 41. At the time of writing, Venus is targeting a comeback after injury in spring 2024 in the year she will become 44. To be still playing in their forties, when everyone felt that business opportunities, particularly in fashion, would tempt them away, is a wonderful example for them to have set. To me, their greatest achievement has been the 'Sister Act'. The unbreakable bond between them has never wavered, no matter who beat who or who won more. All the titles, the records, the firsts they achieved, the cultural forces they became: they did everything as a unit. It wasn't about the numbers or their individual stature in the game. Even when Serena leapfrogged Venus to become No.1 in the world – and, in my view, the greatest champion of all time – she described her big sister as her 'guiding light'. All the two Williams cared about was family and that is to be hugely admired. Venus's agent, Carlos Fleming, gave an insight into their dynamic, marvelling at how they continued to share a house for years and travelled, practised, ate and roomed together even on the nights before they would battle each other for titles. They'd be the only two in the locker room getting ready for the final, walk on and off the court side by side, and after the match see the flowers left for the winner. 'Can you imagine doing all that?' he said.

The Big Shriekers

In fulfilling their father's no-stones-unturned blueprint for sporting success, Venus and Serena Williams turned women's tennis into a power game. The serve – which in my day was more often than not simply a way of initiating play and now looks shockingly timid in old footage – became a red-hot weapon. Obviously, racket technology and ball pressure play their part in this development, but that doesn't explain how Venus, standing at six foot one, could fire down the fastest recorded serve in the women's game of 129mph at the 2007 US Open. (This remained a record until the German Sabine Lisicki recorded 131mph seven years later during a WTA tournament in Stanford.) With her first serve averaging at 113mph and the clever options of a kick and slice as a second serve, Venus was always hard for an opponent to break.

Serena's serve, as well as being powerful, was just so consistent, smooth and relentlessly precise. Her coach from 2012 to 2022, Patrick Mouratoglou, hailed it as the best serve ever. I read an extraordinary statistic that showed that at the Australian Open in 2021, Serena's fastest serve equalled Nadal's, and registered higher on the speed gun than 52 men in the draw.

When asked about her fastest recorded serve – 128.6mph at the 2013 Australian Open – she quipped it was 'my fastest *that went in*. I've hit some 150s, but of course, they're, like, in the sky!'

With the power game came the surround-sound of the off-putting shrieks of effort behind each howitzer of a shot, with certain players particularly criticised for their grunts and yells – and Maria Sharapova, Monica Seles and Victoria Azarenka top of the list of offenders. In the hushed show courts of the English country garden atmosphere at Wimbledon, such sounds are amplified and can cause a kerfuffle among fans, who complain that it detracts from their experience as spectators. Some of the shriekers' peers complained about it being a deliberate tactic to annoy or distract them – a clear case of gamesmanship. I recall telling the *Sunday Times* that I had lost count of the number of people who had written to me saying grunting spoils their enjoyment of a match, spelling out how unattractive and distracting they found it to be. In 2013, an off-the-scale match between Sharapova and the Portuguese player Michelle Larcher de Brito – whose 109-decibel shrieks were deemed by the *Telegraph* to be 'only slightly quieter than a chainsaw' – turned the problem into an issue on which the All England Club had to comment. I agreed with chief executive Richard Lewis's view that

> grunting is something that the game recognises ideally would diminish rather than increase. But I think equally it's fair to say if you're a top, world-class player and that's the way you have competed for 20 years, then I think it's difficult to force them to change.

The appeal to quieten down had little effect and certainly didn't stop the tabloids having fun with their gruntometer listings and surveying 'grunt merchants' with a hand-held decibel-measuring device. Larcher de Brito's 109 decibels were deemed 'only 11 decibels short of the sound a plane makes when taking off' while Marion Bartoli's typical 81-decibel grunt was said to be on a par with a vacuum cleaner.

The power game is an all-court show of strength. As well as the whistling serves, there are the blitzing ground strokes, which require opponents to have a lot of physical resilience to do more than just attempt to keep the ball in play. It was no surprise that on the grass at Wimbledon smaller players like Martina Hingis and Justine Henin were up against it and players who reached the finals, and made inroads into the Williams's dominance on the honours board, were hard-hitters like Lindsay Davenport, Maria Sharapova, Petra Kvitová, Amélie Mauresmo, Marion Bartoli and Garbiñe Muguruza.

When Chrissie, Tracy and myself burst on to the scene, we were players of average height at five foot six inches. Evonne Goolagong measured the same while Billie Jean stood at five foot four and Rosie Casals was just under five foot two. But how times have changed. We would now all count as notably small – and that's a problem for players of similar physical stature in the modern power game. Let's look at the smaller players who lit up the grass courts with their own unique brand of guile, athleticism and pinpoint accuracy to triumph.

First, Justine Henin (just under five foot five), a supremely gifted player who really struggled with the power of her opponents. She was in a very different era to the likes of me and Billie Jean, and up against the big-hitting 'giants' of the game, including Venus, Serena, Lindsay, Maria Sharapova and Kim Clijsters. I admired Justine's game: the big forehand, her speed around the court, her tactical skill as well, but it was the backhand that stood out – the most beautiful one-handed shot, which had become a real rarity by then. I asked her why she used it and she said her coach had tried to make her change to two hands early on in her career but she idolised Steffi Graf as she was growing up and also admired Stefan Edberg so she decided to keep it. As she said, 'It worked okay for them.'

Justine's backhand was sensational and I include her alongside Roger, Stan Wawrinka and Ken Rosewall as my four favourite one-handers. Even in my day, we more petite players had to rely on slice and crafty tactics against taller players such as Margaret Court, Virginia Wade, Betty Stove, Helena Suková and Martina, who were able to generate more power using their longer limbs, and countering their strength caused stress and injury. The majority of Justine's opponents in the early 2000s were the Amazonian aggressive players, but she used her incredible athleticism and tactical savviness to enjoy much success before injuries took over, particularly issues with her right knee and right elbow. She was forced to quit in 2008 because of a chronic knee problem, an announcement that stunned the tennis world as she was ranked No.1 and it was the first time that a top-ranked women's player had retired while at the peak of their game. She said she had been mulling over the decision throughout the previous year because of the fragility of her elbow brought on by struggling against the bigger players. 'I am leaving as World No.1 and that is important as it is always better to go out at the top. I leave without any regrets and I know it is the right decision,' she said at the time. (In 2010, she attempted a comeback but retired again, for good, in January 2011, due to an exacerbation of her elbow injury.)

Ash Barty, another smaller champion (also just under five foot five), had the most beautiful grass-court game in an era when the courts weren't built for her style of play. She loved the Wimbledon grass and she was always a joy to watch as she offered so much more subtlety and nuance than the big-hitting baseliners who were dominating tennis. Variety and flair were the hallmark of her repertoire: she sliced beautifully, she used angles and well-disguised drop shots, she was outstanding at the net and so clever in the way she constructed her points. But, most of all, her weapon was her serve. She had the most amazing kick second-serve that baffled opponents. She really was the complete player. And when she won Wimbledon in 2021, wearing a dress inspired by Evonne Goolagong's famous 1971 scalloped dress in a touching tribute to her Indigenous idol, it was a fairy tale to match that of her mentor's 50 years earlier. After an epic three-set battle with the six-foot-one Karolína Plíšková, Ash seemed a little shell-shocked on court as she hugged the trophy. Of her aim to win Wimbledon she said it had taken her 'a long time to verbalise, to dare to dream it and say it. I didn't sleep a lot last night, I was thinking of the "what ifs".' When I asked if she had a message for Evonne, she choked up and just said, 'I hope I made Evonne proud.'

Watching back home in Australia, Evonne was in floods of tears, saying she was more emotional about Ash's win than she had been about her own first triumph half a century earlier! And, yes, she was immensely proud of her. I was sorry that Evonne wasn't there in the Royal Box to witness the occasion in person at the tournament she loved so much too, but then six months later it was my turn to be in floods of tears on the other side of the world when I watched Ash on television win the Australian Open in front of her adoring fans. How well she handled the immense pressure of a home Slam and then, the icing on the cake, to have Evonne present her with the trophy. To see these two super-nice, fun-loving, inspirational athletes sharing the stage was so moving. Moments in sport don't get much better than that.

It was such a huge disappointment to me when Ash walked away from the game at the age of 25, as the reigning Wimbledon and Australian Open champion. She made the announcement in an Instagram video with her friend and fellow Aussie player Casey Dellacqua. 'I'm so happy and I'm so ready and I just know at the moment in my heart for me as a person, this is right,' she said, revealing that her Wimbledon win – the first time an Australian had claimed a singles title at The Championships in nearly 20 years – was the culmination of her life's goals. Having worked so hard her whole life to be able to compete and win at Wimbledon had changed her outlook as a person and as an athlete, she said. 'To be able to win Wimbledon, which was my dream, my one true dream that I wanted in tennis, that really changed my perspective.' She always talked about the distance she had to travel from Australia to other parts of the world to compete. She could have been a superstar. I guess the money the current generation of players makes from the game early on gives them the opportunity to walk away at a younger age. (In a career that included the highlights of three Grand Slams – and an 18-month break, during which she played semi-professional cricket – Ash earned more than £17.4 million in prize money.) This must make us appreciate the players like Roger, Rafa, Novak, Andy, Venus and Serena, who carry on for so long.

16

ROGER FEDERER

I've mentioned Roger Federer a lot in the course of this book. How could I not? He is the undisputed king of Wimbledon and one of the most gracious champions, both on and off the court. Every match he played, from first round to final, has given such pleasure to fans. Has there ever been a player who made brilliance look so effortless? As Martina once said, 'Federer plays tennis like Michelangelo painted: every stroke is perfection, the end result a masterpiece.'

On one level, it is about the numbers. Roger has claimed a record eight Wimbledon singles titles, equalling Borg's extraordinary feat of winning in five consecutive years along the way. He is the only player in history to reach the final twelve times – and the players who denied him on those four tightly contested occasions were his incomparable peers Rafa Nadal (in that epic five-set battle in 2008) and Novak Djokovic (twice losing in five sets, once in four). I love Jimmy Connors' description of Roger's mastery: 'In an era of specialists, you're either a clay-court specialist, a grass-court specialist, a hard-court specialist … or you're Roger Federer.'

But it's not just about the statistics and records, or even sportsmanship. Novak and Rafa have more Grand Slam titles to their names (24 and 22 respectively, at the time of writing), but Federer's legacy amounts to more than that. The GOAT debate will rage on: is it about statistics or the personal qualities a champion brings to the game and their ability to transcend the sport? Rafa has announced 2024 will be his retirement year, but Novak is on 24 Grand Slams and counting. Without question, though, Roger is the most popular and universally known player, having been voted the ATP fans' favourite from 2003 to 2021 – that's 19 years in a row, an entire generation of tennis followers. Everybody admires his style, his genius, his interaction with the crowds. Roger's appeal is more than his vast array of titles. Even before he announced his retirement in September 2022 at the age of 41, he was hailed as the GOAT by champions from Rod Laver to Lleyton Hewitt, who grew up with him in juniors, and from Borg and Billie Jean to Sampras and Serena. In 2021 BBC Sport viewers voted him the greatest male player of all time. Ditto the Tennis Channel and tennis.com. As for his fellow players, there's no competitive envy, just respect. 'I don't just see the Grand Slam winner, I look at the aesthetics, what you give off on the court,' said Richard Gasquet, a rival known for his equally stunning one-handed backhand. 'For me, Roger is irreplaceable, he's the greatest player of all time when I see the grace he has on the court.'

Great champions become part of Wimbledon lore as a matter of course, but what has been different with Roger is that he embraced history as he was making it, year on year. He played with elegance and a steely desire to win, but also with a sense that the All England Club's Centre Court was his natural domain. He even arrived with a sense of anticipation that his prime playing years would be an era of greatness. I remember in 2002 how much the British press corps yearned for Tim Henman to beat Lleyton Hewitt in the semi-final and have a chance of winning the title, seeing it as a last opportunity … 'because next year Federer will be ready'. Tim sadly didn't win, and Roger was more than ready the following summer to unleash his formidable matured game, mesmerising us all between 2003 and 2019 with his excellence.

Roger brought a lot of emotion to Wimbledon, but, by his own admission, he's not a romantic. 'No, I'm not the kind of guy who sits and looks at Centre Court and tries to visualise what could happen in the next few weeks – or look back for that matter,' he told me. As a junior, his first impression of the All England Club was that 'everything was so new it was like living in a dream world', but even then his curiosity was practical.

> It was a great moment walking through the gates and asking, where is the locker room and where can we eat? Where can we warm up and what are we allowed to do? When do we play and what's the routine?

The first of two matches that stand out most for him as precious memories was his 1998 boys' singles victory. Being presented with the trophy on Centre Court in the Royal Box was 'very special', he recalled, and being allowed into the locker room that Björn Borg and John McEnroe once used was 'very cool'. The most special match he played at Wimbledon? When I spoke to him, he nominated the first time he was scheduled to meet Pete Sampras on Centre Court, in the fourth round in 2001.

> To play five sets against your hero on Centre Court at Wimbledon made all the hard work worthwhile. And then I realised how much fun tennis can actually be ... And of course winning my first title was special, and every other win after that was just absolutely incredible.

And the tears! That was another thing Roger brought to Centre Court. 'My first win was the most emotional; the most surreal. It all came down on me when we spoke on Centre Court,' he said, recalling the post-final interview, but that wasn't the first time he had welled up in front of the cameras.

> The first time I ever cried on court was winning the Davis Cup [tie, against the USA] in Basel, my home town, in 2001 shortly after I'd beaten Pete. Wimbledon, I cried again, then I guess I cried one more time when I entered the Top 10 and when I won Hamburg in 2002. In 2003, after a tough spell on the clay-court season, there was a lot of pressure on me having to do something at Wimbledon. When I got there, I had just won [the warm-up grass-court tournament at] Halle the

previous week and I had this great run at Wimbledon and ended up winning the whole thing. I think I was standing there at 6–2 in the breaker going 'Oh my God – I'm going to be a Wimbledon Champion' and when it all happened I was so, so happy that I couldn't believe it. I kept myself together, received the trophy – which feels like magic in itself – and then you have to speak to the crowd. It wasn't like back in the day when you received the trophy, showed it to the fans, and that was it. The speech to the crowd, to the people in the stadium and the people back at home, was always very emotional for me, explaining my feelings in the moment …

All I feel is relief, happiness. I can barely speak, I can barely stand up. And it all came crashing down on me that day and, in a way, I am happy it was like this, that I lived it fully and I look back at it now and I think, I can feel every sequence that I went through, even though it was years ago now. It was absolutely the most magical moment in my life. If my career had stopped right then, I would have been complete as a tennis player and as a human being.

So many of Roger's Wimbledon finals represent emotional milestones for him personally as well as professionally. Fans might remember the 2009 final against Andy Roddick when there were big statistical records at stake: if Roger won, he would pass Björn's Open Era record of five Wimbledon titles *and* Pete's tally of 14 Grand Slam wins, *and* reclaim the world No.1 crown from

Rafa. The match played out over four hours and 17 minutes, watched by both Borg and Sampras in the front row of the Royal Box. Privately, the match represented another emotional dimension. Also watching was Mirka, Roger's wife, who unbeknown to the public was pregnant with twins. Could Roger achieve these all-time tennis goals when on the cusp of fatherhood? The match was going to turn on a few points here or there, and Roger could not find a way to break the Roddick serve. He lost the first set, 5–7; the next two sets went to tie-breaks, which went Roger's way; he lost the fourth set, 3–6.

Imagine poor Mirka sitting through the final set! Roger still couldn't crack the A-Rod serve ... until the last game. The only break of serve he made got him the win. 'It was totally crazy,' he later recalled, 'but it shows that sometimes you just have to mentally push and stay around and believe that you can manage the situation, and it paid off.' With that, he reached into his racket bag and pulled out a monogrammed zip-up jacket emblazoned with a '15' to commemorate his new Grand Slam men's victory record.

Once a Wimbledon champion, the way Roger dressed for the fortnight, courtesy of his kit sponsors Nike and then Uniqlo, underlined his relationship with the place and its heritage. Back in 2006, he arrived with a regal gold-monogrammed crest on his warm-up jacket, and year by year, his crest or stylised initials moved to his shoes, his racket bag, a blazer, a cable-knit cardigan, even his belt tab. In 2009 he also wore a white suit inspired by a British army uniform. With the glamorous editor-in-chief of *Vogue*, Anna Wintour, often in his corner, Roger personified style as well as supreme skill. Despite the restrictions of the Wimbledon 'almost entirely white' competitors' clothing regulations, he managed to come up with something special each year. 'I see it as a celebration of The Championships,' he told me before his retirement.

> Players used to wear cardigans, long pants, even vests. I just really try to come up with some way to celebrate the history of the game and doing it on the biggest stage, at Wimbledon, is fun. We always try to come up with some personal side stories.

With his easy friendship with the Princess of Wales, the patron of the All England Club, and her family (he and Mirka were guests at Pippa Middleton's wedding), Roger's 'reign' – there is no other word for it! – ran in parallel to the modernising of the royal presence at Wimbledon. In the years of his first visits, players coming onto Centre Court still had to bow or curtsy to the Royal Box. That tradition was discontinued in the year Roger lifted the Wimbledon trophy for the first time, after the Duke of Kent, then president of the All England Club, expressed the wish for it to be abandoned, deeming it an anachronism in modern society. Roger and Mirka also had lunch with Queen Elizabeth II when she visited Wimbledon in 2010: 'That was a wonderful experience, getting to spend some time with her,' he told me. 'Tim Henman was there, Venus was there ... it was an amazing experience for me as a person.' Roll on 20 years and a newly retired Roger picked up a racket to hit balls with the princess to highlight the well-drilled ball boys' and girls' involvement in The Championships. 'I just think the royal presence adds even more prestige to the tournament,' he told me. 'And it's great that we're seeing more and more members of the royal family coming to watch.'

Whether he won them, or watched the rare ones slip from his grasp, Roger's finals were always spectacles fit for royalty. To beat him on Centre Court, other players had to be at their absolute best – as Rafa was in 2008 and Novak in 2014, 2015 and 2019. To be defeated by him, painful as it was – especially for Andy and the home crowds in 2012 – came with the consolation of having lost to a maestro of the game. When I asked Roger what motivated him throughout his long career, he effectively made a declaration of love for the game.

> I love winning … at all costs, you don't want to lose. You give it all you have but for me it's also just a sheer love of the game. I love the geometry of the court. I love every centre court I play on. I love every opponent I can play against. Every crowd is different, so I really try to see the positives in it. Not caring about winning or losing is the worst feeling a tennis player can experience because you want to walk out there for a purpose.

While Federer danced and glided his way into the record books, a new kid on the block bounced into the game: a teenage lefty (though, amazingly, he is actually right handed) with huge biceps and a forcefield of intensity. In 2005 Rafa Nadal arrived at Wimbledon two weeks after winning his first French Open title – the first male teenager to win a Grand Slam singles title since Sampras won the US Open in 1990 – and had a similar impact to Agassi as no one had seen his chosen attire on court before. His distinctive look was the swashbuckling opposite to Roger's old-school elegance, all sleeveless shirts, capri-style shorts and big bandanas. Eyebrows were raised at his unorthodox pirate look. Even though he was knocked out in the second round, he had made a big enough splash for Honor Godfrey, the then curator of the Wimbledon Museum, to issue an appeal to Rafa via the ATP to donate a trademark sleeveless shirt and mid-calf shorts to the collection. 'It's an absolutely fabulous kit and unique, firstly, because he's the first person to wear a sleeveless shirt on Centre Court, and, secondly, because he's wearing pirata,' said Honor. 'We've had tight, short, baggy … but I see his shorts in terms of going back to knickerbockers. The last person to wear those was Sidney Wood in 1931.'

Everyone fell in love with Rafa's 'never say die' attitude. He brought an energy to the court and the crowd lapped it up. He also had more than his fair share of tics and superstitions – 19, according to *USA Today* – from organising his water bottles to rearranging his underwear, touching his nose and tucking his hair behind his ear before every serve. It was fascinating to watch, and to hear about from him. On arranging his water bottles, he explained,

> I put two bottles down at my feet, in front of my chair to
> my left, one neatly behind the other, diagonally aimed

at the court. Some call it superstition, but it's not. If it were superstition, why would I keep doing the same thing over and over whether I win or lose? It's a way of placing myself in a match, ordering my surroundings to match the order I seek in my head.

Another of his rituals was a freezing-cold shower before a match, which he described in his 2011 autobiography as

> the point before the point of no return. Under the cold shower I enter a new space in which I feel my power and resilience grow. I'm a different man when I emerge. I'm activated. I'm in 'the flow', as sports psychologists describe a state of alert concentration in which the body moves by pure instinct, like a fish in a current. Nothing else exists but the battle ahead.

Rafa's intensity has always been his greatest asset along with his ability to battle through adversity and pain, which he has done time and time again. His forehand is outstanding. With its big wind-up and follow-through it is a joy to watch in slow motion, but the strain on the arm and body is immense. He is also so quick about the court. When I close my eyes and visualise him on court at Wimbledon, I see him running; he never stopped chasing every ball down. He plays every point as if it's his last and doesn't dwell on a missed shot, a lost game or even an injury. I loved the way he would come from an exhausting triumph on the clay at Roland-Garros to the grass courts of Wimbledon but never complained about the short break between the two majors, the different bounce and the different movement and shoes required. He just got on with the game in hand and never made excuses. He is loved for his sportsmanship and his humility.

It's also a joy to me that Rafa and Roger have become good friends. Like the best of rivals they are in many ways polar opposites, but they've always had immense respect for each other. Now it's much more than that and their sense of kinship was evident at the Laver Cup at the O2 Arena in 2022 when Roger announced his retirement from the game. Rafa was as emotional as Roger, both in floods of tears, giving the world an insight into their competitive mindset. It was clear that the challenge of facing each other would be much missed and we realised that the strides that these two great athletes made had pushed them to be better players, to push the boundaries and take the game into a stratosphere we never thought could be achieved. Now add a certain tenacious Novak Djokovic into the mix … What an era of tennis. For me, it's been the greatest, most tantalising era of men's tennis.

17

ANDY MURRAY

The highlight of my career at the BBC was, without doubt, watching Andy Murray win Wimbledon in 2013 on that very auspicious seventh day of the seventh month 77 years after Fred Perry was the last Brit to do so. That joyful moment seemed to be the culmination of events that began the previous year, when we were all moved by Andy's emotional runner-up speech. With the weight of the nation on his shoulders – and with the ultimate heavyweight live preview line-up of Borg, Connors and McEnroe debating his chances – he lost out to the mighty Roger Federer. I've never felt worse holding a microphone in front of someone in such emotional distress and yet I knew it was important for the crowd and viewers at home to see how much Wimbledon meant to him. 'I'm going to try this and it's not going to be easy,' he said in a quavering voice.

Everybody talks about the pressure of playing at Wimbledon, how tough it is, but it's not the people watching [who cause the pressure]. They make it so much easier to play. The support has been incredible. Thank you.

The Great British public choked up in sympathy with him. Andy later said that was a turning point. He realised he may never win a Grand Slam title, let alone Wimbledon, and he would have to come to terms with that, but the warmth of the Centre Court's response to his distress was the first time he felt a full force of affection from the public.

The silver lining in that cloud was that less than four weeks later, Andy returned to Centre Court at the London 2012 Games and won the Olympic gold medal for Team GB by beating Roger with the emphatic scoreline of 6–2, 6–1, 6–4. With that extra confidence, he went on to claim his first Grand Slam title at the US Open a few weeks later. He had won a major, and the monkey was off his back. In the meantime, the BBC approached Andy's agent with a request to make a documentary about his life and career in the build-up to Wimbledon 2013 – and luckily they agreed. As Pete Sampras noted when I spoke to him, Andy was someone who, like himself, preferred to keep things simple and make sure distractions were minimal in order to keep focused. Before he played his first match on Centre Court at the age of 18, he'd been playing in front of about 20 people. To cope with the spotlight, he shut himself off from the media as a coping mechanism. But if people don't get to know you and just see you with your guard up, they might think you're grumpy or boring, and you don't get the full warmth of support. I felt strongly that once people could see the real Andy, they'd see the funny, charming and thoughtful side of his personality, and understand what he has put himself through in order to compete with the very best of the world.

I flew over to Miami in December to watch him during his off-season training camp. What an eye-opener. It was fascinating to see the vigorous training he did in the gym and the out-of-the-box approach to keeping him strong, fit and supple. Andy's team in Florida included a Russian ex-ballerina who put him in the most extraordinary positions in Pilates to complement his intensive on-court training. Later in the season, we filmed him in ice baths in Monaco and undergoing rehabilitation for an injury closer to home in Surrey. It was relentless and I admired him immensely. We also caught glimpses of his off-court charity commitments and the commercial demands on his time, often for sponsors.

A few months later, prior to Wimbledon 2013, I went to interview him at his home in Surrey and recorded footage of his happy domestic life with his artist wife Kim Sears. We chatted about various facets of his life, about moving to Spain at 15 years old to train on the clay courts of the Sánchez-Casal Academy in Barcelona ('a big sacrifice', as his parents had to raise £40,000 in fees for his 18 months there). He really opened up about the tragedy of Dunblane in 1996, breaking down in tears as he relived the horrific shootings that took place at the primary school in his home town in Perthshire and the tragedy's long-lasting effect on him. Andy was a nine-year-old pupil when Thomas Hamilton, a local youth club leader, shot dead 16 pupils and one teacher, and injured countless more before turning the gun on himself. The Murray family knew Hamilton. Andy and Jamie had attended his kids' club, and he'd even been given lifts in the Murray family car. Andy and his classmates were on the way to the gym where the shootings took place when they heard the noise of gunfire and someone went ahead to investigate. All the kids were then rushed to safety. Today, residents of Dunblane are grateful that the town's name has gradually become better and more happily known for the Murray connection than for the tragedy.

After filming in their beautiful house, which had Kim's impressive animal portraits on the walls, we decided to accompany them to nearby woodlands for a walk with our camera crew. Andy and Kim loved their two Border terriers, Maggie May and Rusty, and I felt that capturing this would allow viewers to see another dimension to Andy's personality. It wasn't the nicest weather (despite being early June) so Andy wore his wellies. As we were strolling along the heathland path, chatting about how Andy and Kim first met and their life together, Maggie May decided to shoot off in pursuit of some wildlife. I knew the woods well as I had walked my dogs there too and I was aware there was a busy road not far away. Having heard that, Andy took off at speed in his wellies after his beloved dog. Andy had been wearing ankle supports on both legs for two years and all I could think as he rushed off, full pelt, was what would happen if Andy twisted an ankle (or worse) on a rabbit burrow and was forced out of Wimbledon ... I would never be forgiven by the British public. Indeed, I wouldn't be able to forgive myself. Thankfully Andy retrieved Maggie May and after a break for pooch and owner to recover we resumed filming.

I was pleased that the documentary had a great reception. People seemed to feel they'd seen the real Andy Murray for the first time. As Billie Jean said to me, 'Everyone had an opinion on him, he's this, he's that. I'd go, wait a minute, we don't know the guy. So the doc was fabulous.' I'm immensely proud of the team that put that documentary together. I've loved expanding on the coverage of the sport with the documentaries I have done with great champions for the BBC. All of them have been master-minded by an amazing couple, Josephine McCusker and Peter Small. I must also thank Carl Doran, the boss of the documen-tary department, who allowed me to travel around the world chatting to my heroes. He was also a rock during our time on *A Question of Sport* and always a good source of advice.

To then watch Andy claim that title in 2013, in a year when Djokovic was so dominant, was even more special, as I had seen first hand the time and effort he had put in, and how much he deserved to take his place in Wimbledon history. Not least because the pressure of being a British player competing in the world's biggest tournament in front of a home crowd is a chal-lenge that few players can take on.

Every British entry in the draw feels it. Whether you're a junior or a wildcard or a player ranked below the top 50 in the world, the fans are there, backing you fervently, hoping for a fairy tale – because they do happen. But the pressure on Andy, when he was up there battling with Roger, Rafa, Novak and others, was even more immense because it came with realistic expectations. He wasn't someone to back just because he came with 'GB' next to his name. As John McEnroe said to me,

The pressure was way worse for him than any other people I've ever seen, because he's so good that people actually realised that he could win it. But he was also playing against some of the greats of all time, so it wasn't going to be easy. Every year from the beginning of Queen's, it used to be two weeks ... now it's three weeks ... that that was all the media would talk about. If you look at Andy's results, he's handled it unbelievably well. It's amazing how consistent he's been over ten years and to be able to have two Wimbledon titles under his belt is an amazing effort.

Pete Sampras is another champion with an interesting insight into the particular spotlight that Andy had to perform under.

Murray, to have won here a couple times, to deal with that pressure for the two weeks – it's pretty incredible what he's been able to do. The pressure that he was under in 2012 and 2013 particularly. I don't know how he did it, quite honestly. He's dealing with the weight of the country on his shoulders. When I did my thing, I didn't feel any of that. I just had to play and deal with the pressure of competition. He's dealing with the pressure of beating guys, and the media, and the weight of everyone waiting for that first British Wimbledon win. He did it. More power to him.

Pete then wondered what the most pressurised situation for an athlete across all sports could be. 'In my opinion, it's an individual athlete, like Andy, dealing with an event that is probably the biggest event in his home country of Great Britain. He's dealt with this incredibly well. Great effort.'

One of the challenges of hosting the BBC Wimbledon coverage was watching the British players. As someone who loved playing for my country – and when I look back on my career it is our GB Wightman Cup triumphs that mean more to me than winning a Grand Slam and reaching No.3 in the world rankings – I was often a wreck. I used to make sure I was scrupulously impartial on air but of course I always wanted the home players to succeed because I know how special it is to play well at Wimbledon and please an appreciative crowd. As a player whose successes came mostly on hard courts, I also understand the flip side of that and the emotions you go through when you have to acknowledge that you've let not just yourself down but also the incredible supporters who've cheered you through thick and thin.

The most nerve-shredding match was Andy's quarter-final against the Spaniard Fernando Verdasco in that 2013 campaign. He was two sets down and I was living every point with him in the studio, so tense and emotional as he looked like he was down and out. Jo, the sound lady, filmed me screaming and fist pumping and sent the clip to Judy Murray, who later passed it on to Andy and Kim. So embarrassing! Then, incredibly, he battled through the Verdasco challenge and went on to win Wimbledon. I got an email from Judy after his eventual victory saying that I was getting more wound up than she ever would! I don't know how she manages to sit and look so composed in the players' box with the cameras on her as Andy plays with his heart on his sleeve. Jane Henman, Tim's mother, always used to say she lost five pounds through tension every Wimbledon. Without doubt, walking on to Centre Court to announce Andy as that year's winner was the best day of my television career. The journey to that final was immense and then for him to beat Djokovic and emerge victorious after such a seemingly endless, terrifying last game, which really did put us all through the wringer, was incredible.

I was so pleased when he won it again in 2016 – this time for himself. The dream 2013 triumph felt like an achievement for the country more than for him as an individual; he had finally ensured the nation's interminable wait for a men's singles champion was over after nearly eight decades of nail-biting hoping and praying each summer. At the time of that historic win, I know he felt he didn't celebrate enough and he promised his team that if he ever won it again, he would do it on his terms. He would have the celebration he wanted. With the anguish and emotion of securing his status as a Wimbledon champion long gone, a masterclass defeat of the Czech Tomáš Berdych in the semi-final – who had beaten Roger Federer en route to the 2010 final – and Milos Raonic in the final was cue for that big party. Determined to embrace the moment, he hired a club, he drank, he danced. 'I made sure that I really, really enjoyed it this time. It was a big celebration,' he said when I spoke to him afterwards. 'I'd said to my team, this time I'm doing what I want to do. I'm having my friends around me. I don't drink, but I did drink a lot that night, and it wasn't pretty, but we had a good time.'

Did he throw off his ankle supports and hit the dance floor? 'Yeah. I think so. I don't remember too much about it, but I'm pretty sure I was dancing!'

18

EMMA RADUCANU

At Wimbledon 2021 we were all so thrilled to be back enjoying tennis once again, even though the crowds were restricted along with our freedom around the grounds. But that didn't matter because after the pandemic and all the sadness it caused, we were just happy that life was beginning to get back to some normality. What we needed was an uplifting story, one that would make us smile again. Enter Emma Raducanu, an 18-year-old who had a talent for tennis as big as her smile. She arrived at Wimbledon straight after the stress of her A-level exams with a spring in her step and over the course of the first few days captured the hearts of the nation. What a breath of fresh air! Ranked 338th in the world, Emma was given a wild card into the main singles draw and got a favourable opener as she faced Russian qualifier Vitalia Diatchenko. Emma admitted prior to the match that she was nervous and the more experienced Russian took advantage of that and stretched to a 4–1 lead before Emma became accustomed to her surroundings, embraced the crowd support and the fairy tale was under way! Emma has a beautiful all-court game. She moves around the court effortlessly, her return is outstanding, and what has been most impressive is her court awareness and her ability to play the big points well. Even back in the summer of 2021, she seemed the total package!

There was a buzz among seasoned tennis observers, with people saying 'she's the real deal'. Emma looked surprised when the winners whizzed off her racquet. In her press conferences, she was fun, witty, a headline-writer's dream, and of course the nation embraced her. No one could have written a better introduction to tennis.

She seemed shocked by the big names she had brushed aside – Markéta Vondroušová (who would two years later be crowned Wimbledon champion) in the second round and Sorana Cîrstea, the experienced Romanian, in the third round. For her fourth-round match against the Aussie Ajla Tomljanović on No.1 Court, television screens were set up at her school, Newstead Wood School in Orpington, so that staff and pupils could watch her. Prime Minister Boris Johnson congratulated her on Twitter, wishing her luck, saying, 'The country is behind you.' And then it all caught up with her. In a rain-delayed late-evening match on so-called Magic Monday – when all the singles quarter-finals were played before they introduced play on Sunday to decongest the schedule – Emma was forced to retire with breathing problems, having lost the first set and trailing 0–3 in the second. Stage one of the fairy tale was over, with speculation about her suffering a 'panic attack', but a blockbuster was just around the corner.

I admit I was as shocked as anyone after Wimbledon when I heard she had left her coach, the very experienced and respected Nigel Sears (Andy Murray's father-in-law), the man who had steered her through her astonishing Grand Slam breakthrough, but that isn't close to how astounded I was when she sacked Andrew Richardson, a former player turned coach who had helped Raducanu in her younger years and was brought in to guide her through her American tour culminating in her extraordinary US Open victory. How any player who goes through three qualifying rounds and seven main-draw matches without dropping a set to take the title in only their second Grand Slam can then sack their coach is beyond me. What more could he have possibly done? Andrew should have received a huge bonus not a P45! I wish she had added to her team, and not dismantled it, and remained loyal to a coach who made her dream come true.

Before we talk more tennis, let's deal with 'ballgate'. The US Open is the only Slam where the men and women use a different ball. In 2021 the men used an 'extra duty' ball, which means the felt is woven slightly more loosely than the 'regular duty' one used by the women. Craig Tyzzer, Ash Barty's coach at the time, said that Ash could never win the US Open while this ball was used as it diluted her weapons. The regular duty balls favour the flat hitters rather than those who like to use spin. Ahead of the tournament, the then world No.1 Iga Świątek said the balls used at the US Open were 'horrible'. After much debate, it was decided that in 2023 the same ball would be used by both the men and women, thereby stopping any more criticism. Having said all that, there is always a style of play that Slams will favour.

I remember there was much discussion around Wimbledon changing the grass, and also the Australian Open moving to a surface called Rebound Ace in 1988 before it changed again to Plexicushion in 2008. However, in 2021 the US Open women's draw saw two outstanding clean-hitting young talents mesmerise the more fancied regular tour players as they caused upset after upset to reach the final. No one would have predicted at the start of the tournament that Emma Raducanu, ranked 150, and 19-year-old Leylah Fernandez of Canada, ranked 73, would face off for the title.

Emma's fairy tale in New York, and Leylah's too, took the tennis world by storm. It was so exciting and we felt we had been given a glimpse into the future of women's tennis. Sadly, as we have seen many times before, the demands of trying to cope with all the pressures and distractions that come with success are hard to deal with and both players have struggled to recreate that form. Hopefully now their rankings have dropped and expectations aren't as high, both players can rebuild their careers and fulfil the promise that they showed in 2021. Personally, I'd love to see Emma enjoy her tennis in the same way we saw when she first came on to the tour. Most players thrive in the climb up the ladder to the top of the game, experiencing and learning from the highs and lows that they encounter along the way. For Emma, though, there was no journey: she was catapulted into superstardom and all that comes with it and, although financially rewarding, I'm not sure that it's been a happy experience.

2024 is a great opportunity for her. Back after operations on both wrists and her left ankle, she has reset and started again with a lowly ranking (301 as of 1 January 2024) and few of the expectations that amount to paralysing pressure. After all, when Coco Gauff won the US Open in 2023, and finally stopped being paralysed by the big occasion of the majors, she was the 19th different winner of the women's singles in the last 32 Grand Slams. So many winners of women's Grand Slam singles titles could walk through Wimbledon village without being pestered by fans. So Emma joins a large gang of women aiming to build on a single Grand Slam victory, led by Coco, and including Elena Rybakina, Markéta Vondroušová, Sofia Kenin, Barbora Krejčíková, Jeļena Ostapenko, Sloane Stephens and Bianca Andreescu, with Caroline Wozniacki on the comeback trail, not to mention four-times Grand Slam winner Naomi Osaka back on tour after having a baby, the two-times Australian Open Champion Aryna Sabalenka and a young Mirra Andreeva waiting in the wings. My one hope is that when Emma does eventually hang up her rackets she looks back on the game and her playing years with the same affection that so many of us do.

19

WIMBLEDON 2024 AND ONWARDS

Fifty Years of Magic and Counting

In compiling this book, I've realised how lucky I've been to experience this wonderful annual event at the All England Club from both sides of the fence, as a player and as a broadcaster, and how important it has been to me and will continue to be in my new role as a fan. I've realised how much The Championships have evolved since I first stood nervously outside those imposing gates as a youngster. The grounds have changed dramatically, and yet when I walk around them, the place doesn't feel that different. The grass has changed to produce a higher, more reliable bounce. There are retractable roofs on Centre and No.1 Court. The Aorangi practice facilities mean competitors warm up on site (in my day, we had our daily practice sessions at Queen's) so fans have the thrill of seeing more of the players milling around the place. The site has expanded and has so many great features for competitors and spectators alike, but it still retains a feeling of an English country garden with the imposing ivy-clad Centre Court as the centrepiece. The ever-evolving innovations have transformed the Club, but they haven't changed its soul.

The Wimbledon I fell in love with as a kid has grown but it is still just as magical and is still the greatest tournament in the world. As I look towards future Championships, the most significant change of all is the personnel at the helm. The first female chair, Debbie Jevans, took up the post after the 2023 Championships. The tournament referee from 2024 is Denise Parnell, the first ever female referee at a Grand Slam event. They are both former players, both great friends of mine and trailblazers within their field. And then there is Catherine, the Princess of Wales, presenting the trophies … I am sure Billie Jean and I will be discussing their success over a cup of tea and a bowl of strawberries and cream this summer. I can't wait.

ACKNOWLEDGEMENTS

A huge thank you to Sarah Edworthy for all your hard work and for the relentless hours you spent on this book. I could not have done this without you. You are a superstar.

Thank you to Lorna Russell at Ebury for encouraging me to follow up on *Calling the Shots* with a second memoir. It's been a pleasure working with your team again.

To Lizzie Stafford and Emily Rees Jones at M&C Saatchi Merlin, thank you for your hard work, support and friendship.

To David Luxton, thank you for always being there in my corner.

Thank you to BBC Sport for allowing me to use quotes from the many interviews I've conducted over the years. Also a huge thank you for the privilege of fronting Wimbledon for 30 fun-filled years.

I'd like to thank the great champions and legends of the game for giving up their time to talk to me about the Championships we love.

To Carl Doran, Jo McCusker and Peter Small. I'm so proud of the many documentaries we created over the years. You are extremely talented and the nicest people to work with.

A special mention for Tim Henman for making sure there was always a glass of chilled champagne ready for me when I came off air. So thoughtful...

• • •

In addition, Sarah Edworthy would like to thank the following people: Robert McNicol, Club Historian at the All England Lawn Tennis Club, who welcomed us to the Wimbledon Library, opening up a treasure-trove of resources and cuttings books, and also for reading the draft for factual accuracy.

Frederick Waterman, author and former international sports writer, for sharing a salient anecdote; Margaret and Fred Lyle, for their enthusiasm in finding Sue Barker connections stateside; and Alix Ramsay, for answering random queries with her unparalleled knowledge of the tennis circuit.

Particular thanks go to Liz and Paddy Edworthy for providing a weekend writing haven with full butler service; and to Rory, Isabella, Alexander and Emily Ross for their tremendous support.

And big thanks, as ever, to my agent David Luxton for taking the project from proposal to final proof.

Finally, I am hugely grateful to Lorna Russell and Michelle Warner at Ebury for their expertise, patience and unflagging enthusiasm.

IMAGE CREDITS

PLATE SECTION 1

Hulton Archive / Stringer (Image 1)
Central Press / Stringer (Image 2, 9)
Paul Popper/Popperphoto / Contributor (Image 4)
Trinity Mirror / Mirrorpix / Alamy Stock Photo (Image 5)
Evening Standard / Stringer (Image 6)
Bettmann / Contributor (Image 7)
Fox Photos / Stringer (Image 8)
Rob Taggart / Stringer (Image 10, 15)
Bob Thomas / Contributor (Image 11)
Steve Powell / Staff (Image 12)
Eamonn McCabe/Popperphoto / Contributor (Image 13, 14)
Bob Martin / Staff (Image 16)
Professional Sport / Contributor (Image 17)
Eileen Langsley/Popperphoto / Contributor (Image 18, 19)

PLATE SECTION 2

Eamonn McCabe/Popperphoto / Contributor (Image 1)
Bob Martin / Staff (Image 2)
Henning Bangen / Staff (Image 3)
Jacques DeMarthon / Staff (Image 4)
Simon M Bruty / Contributor (Image 5, 7, 8)
Popperphoto / Contributor (Image 6)
Clive Brunskill / Staff (Image 9, 14)
Gary M. Prior / Staff (Image 10)
Mike Hewitt / Staff (Image 11)
Getty Images / Staff (Image 12)
Rebecca Naden/PA Archive/PA Images (Image 13)
Professional Sport / Contributor (Image 15)
Pool / Pool (Image 16)
Justin Tallis / Stringer (Image 17)
Adam Stoltman / Alamy Stock Photo (Image 18)
Robert Prange / Contributor (Image 19)
Ben Queenborough / Alamy Stock Photo (Image 20)

INDEX

Morecambe, Eric 76
Morozova, Olga 30, 164
Mortimer, Angela 40, 60–1, 62–3, 153
Morton, Miss A.M. 179
Mottram, Buster 71, 82
Mottram, Linda 82
Mottram family 82
Mouratoglou, Patrick 266
Moyá, Carlos 244
Muguruza, Garbiñe 129, 268
Mulligan, Martin 62
Murray, Andy 165, 180, 247–8, 252, 284–91, 294
  career longevity 271
  and Djokovic 129, 189, 288, 291
  and Federer 7, 280, 284–5, 288
  psychological resilience 55
  and Sampras 240, 285, 289–90
  and Serena Williams 264–5
  training setup 16
  and the Wheelie Bin challenge 190
  and Wimbledon 2012 141–2
  and Wimbledon 2013 75, 229, 241, 246, 284, 286, 290–1
Murray, Jamie 97, 189, 190, 286
Murray, Judy 229, 290

Nadal, Rafa 10, 45, 69, 112, 165, 225, 251, 273, 278, 280–3, 288
  career longevity 271
  and COVID-19 189
  and Djokovic 7
  and Federer 129, 137–8, 229, 280–1, 283
  Grand Slams 274
  hairstyles 155
  and Kyrgios 250
  possible retirement 13
  psychological resilience 55
  rituals of 281–2
  serve 266
  style 281
Nalbandian, David 165, 240
Năstase, Ilie 71–2, 109–10, 114–15, 138, 251
National Tennis Centre 190

Navrátil, Mirek 173–4, 175
Navratilova, Jana (Martina's mother) 171, 172, 173, 174
Navratilova, Jana (Martina's sister) 171, 172
Navratilova, Martina 34, 40, 54, 97–9, 106, 146–9, 151, 163–4, 168–86, 227, 269
  background 171–6
  and Borg 109
  and Chrissie Evert 7, 128, 159, 166–74, 186, 205, 256
  and COVID-19 189
  and Federer 273
  fitness 183–4
  and junior tennis 169–70
  mental strength 55
  outfits 86–7, 91
  and Steffi Graf 212–14
NBC 222
Netflix 27
New Orleans 125–6
New York Times (newspaper) 10, 117, 173
Ngarigo people 73–4
Nick Bollettieri Tennis Academy 222
Nieminen, Jarkko 180
Nike 278
Norrie, Cameron 26
Novotná, Jana 97, 177
Nyström, Joakim 206

O2 Arena 283
Olmedo, Alex 59
Olympic Games 225, 253
  1988 Summer Olympics, Seoul 212–13, 215
  2012 Summer Olympics, London 285
  2024 Summer Olympics, Paris 212, 215
One Show, The (TV show) 190
O'Neal, Tatum 120
Open Era 6, 47, 68, 70, 104, 112, 134, 156, 213, 277–8
Original Nine 35, 105–6